THE ALLURING TARGET

THE ALLURING TARGET
In Search of the Secrets of Central Asia

by

Kenneth Wimmel

Foreword

by

Ella Maillart

The earth, which once danced and spun
before us as alluringly as a celluloid ball
on top of a fountain in a rifle range,
is now a dull and vulnerable target.

PETER FLEMING

Trackless Sands Press
Washington ♦ Palo Alto

Library of Congress Cataloging-in-Publication Data
Wimmel, Kenneth
The Alluring Target, in search of the secrets of Central Asia /by Kenneth
Wimmel
p.   cm.
Includes bibliographical references (p.   ) and index.
ISBN 1-879434-48-2 (pbk. : alk. paper)
1. Asia, Central —Description and travel.   2. Travelers—Asia, Central.
I. Title
DS327.8.W56   1996   915.804'3'0922—dc20   95-52545

Printed on acid-free paper
Manufactured in the United States of America
Cover design by Anne Masters Design, Inc.
Book design by Florri DeCell
Map by Paulina Kopestynsch

First Edition

This book is for
Christina Krishna
a daughter of East and West

Contents

Illustrations

The author and publisher wish to thank the following for permission to reproduce illustrations appearing on the following pages.

A note about names

Writing about Asia during past years and decades poses two problems: identifying geographical locations, and transliterating into the Roman alphabet names and terms originally written in other writing systems. One very recent example of the former problem is the name of the former capital of Russia. It was recently changed to Saint Petersburg from Leningrad, which in turn had been changed from Petrograd, which had been changed from its original name, Saint Petersburg. If one is writing about the nine-hundred-day siege of the city in World War II, which name does one use? Probably Leningrad, its name at that time. Many examples of the latter problem occur in Indian geography. The name of the city in northern India identified on maps today as Kanpur was commonly written by the British as Cawnpore. Which spelling is used by historians writing about the massacre that occurred there during the Great Mutiny of 1857? They commonly use the old British spelling, the one that appeared on maps at that time.

Many place names in Central Asia have changed during the past century, and the Romanization of many of those that have not changed, notably Chinese names, has been altered by newly adopted systems of Romanization. Thus, the westernmost Chinese province is identified on today's maps as Xinjiang; on maps thirty or forty years old, as Sinkiang or Sin-kiang. When Sven Hedin and Aurel Stein traveled, it was commonly called Chinese Turkestan by writers of English. The name of China's capital, now written as Beijing, until recently was spelled Peking, except during the 1930s and '40s, when it was renamed Peiping by the Kuomintang government. Mongolia's capital is now Ulan Bator, but Roy Chapman Andrews knew it as Urga. And so on.

The geographical terminology and system of Romanization used in this book are those used by the travelers who are the subjects of the book, or those in general usage at the time they traveled. Names therefore sometimes differ from one chapter to another. While this may sometimes cause confusion for a reader who attempts to trace the routes of the journeys on modern maps, it would be even more confusing to adopt modern usage throughout that would be at variance with that used in the accounts the travelers themselves wrote.

Foreword

by
Ella Maillart

Ever since I first ventured out onto Lake Geneva as a child in a small sailboat, I have loved boats and the sea. Lake Geneva is a difficult and unforgiving school for the sailor, because the winds that swirl down from the Alps can be very tricky, so I learned to be a careful sailor. I dreamed of sailing in my own boat to the South Seas, perhaps to find paradise, because I had been deeply shocked by the European war of 1914–18 and all the books that appeared about it. Alas, that remained only a dream, never to be realized. I did fulfill another dream, however, one that began when I first looked down on the Takla Makan Desert from atop a 17,000-foot mountain in Russian Turkestan. I dreamed of traveling through Central Asia and finding people not yet influenced by our civilization.

It may seem strange that someone in love with boats and the sea should love the deserts of Central Asia. The Takla Makan is as far from the sea as you can get. Yet, the sea and the desert are strangely similar. The illimitable expanses of both, stretching away to the horizon on all sides, can inspire exhilarating feelings of freedom, of being master of your own fate. Both the desert and the sea can also be pitiless to the lazy, the unprepared, the unwary traveler who ventures upon them. He may pay with his life for his shortcomings.

My friend Peter Fleming and I traveled from Peking across Central Asia to Kashmir many years ago, in 1935. We were not explorers like Sven Hedin or Aurel Stein. Many others had gone before us, including the people whose stories are told in this book. We were not geographers mapping new ground, or anthropologists studying newly discovered tribes of primitive people, or archeologists uncovering lost civilizations. Peter called our journey an "escapade." Peter was very charming, clever, and witty, and perhaps he regarded it that way. I prefer to think that we were travelers. We were not tourists.

Traveler is really another name for seeker, whether one seeks sunshine, fun, inspiration, or wisdom. I began to travel when I was eighteen. I was instinctively obeying a strong urge when I began, but I came gradually to realize that I traveled to become wiser. Perhaps I succeeded. I learned that "primitive" Central Asian nomads are less tormented than we are in the West. They are more at ease in their world which they understand perhaps better than we understand ours. They understand and accept the natural rhythms of life, like hunger and the contentment that comes with satisfying hunger. Each person is not a lonely individual struggling against the whole world, but a member of a clan or tribe. He is part of an organic whole, part of something bigger than himself. He is not an end in himself. We Westerners suffer, unable to integrate ourselves into a living concept bigger than ourselves.

Four times I started for Central Asia, but at the end of each journey I found that my own discontentment, which had caused me to start the journey in the first place, colored everything I saw. Perhaps understanding that is the beginning of wisdom. I lived for several years in an ashram in southern India. I discovered there that the stability of a traditional society, built upon a metaphysical concept of the universe, provides for the spiritual, mental, and physical needs of man, and each is given the degree of importance it merits. Life is linked to the eternal laws of nature and the heart. In Central Asia and in the ashram in India, I think I found some of the wisdom I was seeking.

From time to time I receive letters from people who say they want to re-create the journey Peter and I made across Asia, and they seek my advice and blessing. I tell them it cannot be done. Too much has changed. Trains and monstrous trucks now churn up storms of dust in the desert where camel caravans used to plod. Busloads of tourists now can reach Kum Bum. My correspondents plan to travel in four-wheel-drive vehicles and they will carry computers and radios linked to satellites that will keep them chained to the world they want to leave behind. If you would re-create my journey, you can do so only through the power of your imagination, using books like this one and the books Peter and I wrote.

Travel if you must to Central Asia to see for yourself the majesty of the mountains, the awesome emptiness of the deserts, the hardy self-reliance of the people. You will be richly rewarded, and perhaps you, too, will gain some wisdom. But your journey will be different from mine.

Preface

The men and women who are the heroes and heroines of these pages are mostly forgotten today, except among small groups of specialists in such fields as geography, archeology, and paleontology. That is both surprising and lamentable. It is surprising, because all these startlingly audacious people were famous in their lifetimes, and many of their books became bestsellers when they were published. Today, the people are largely forgotten, and most of their books are out of print and hard to find. Their obscurity is lamentable, because their experiences are the stuff of adventure, and the accounts they wrote are among the best pieces of travel writing to be found anywhere. As the relentless march of technology continues to shrink the world and squeeze the wonder and adventure from travel, the experiences of these travelers and the accounts they wrote can be savored with even greater relish by the general reader than when they first appeared before the public.

I became acquainted with these people during the course of a career in the Foreign Service spent mostly in Asia. For example, I was first introduced to Sven Hedin in a cluttered room on the top floor of the American Consulate General in Calcutta. All American consulates and embassies have staff libraries. They are usually miscellaneous collections, accumulated in fits and starts over years or decades, intended for the education of the staff about the country and region in which they are serving. The Calcutta staff library was the usual jumble of books in a locked room filled, like an attic, with flotsam and jetsam no one really wanted but no one could muster the will to pitch out. While rummaging through the "library" one dull afternoon, I came across a matched pair of thick books tucked in a corner of a bookshelf and covered with dust. They were Sven Hedin's *Through Asia*. I took them home, and quickly became hooked by the great Swede's tale of adventure and discovery. I met the other traveler authors at various times in various places, often in a similar serendipitous fashion.

They all have been dead a good many years, except one. As I write,

Ella Maillart lives alone in a flat in Geneva near where she was born ninety-one years ago. Stooped, frail, stiffened by painful arthritis, more than a little hard of hearing, she nevertheless still displays the self-reliance, the forthright honesty, the warm humor that has sustained her throughout an extraordinary life. She maintained a close friendship with her traveling companion Peter Fleming until his death. She befriended Alexandra David-Neel whose home at Digne is situated less than two hundred miles south of Geneva, and exchanged correspondence with Sven Hedin and Aurel Stein. She became acquainted with Owen Lattimore, another traveler of Central Asia, and Jawaharlal Nehru. She has a fund of stories about all of them. She is a delightful dinner companion.

I am convinced there are many people, like myself, dissatisfied with the pseudoadventures of contemporary travel literature that clutter the shelves of their local bookstores. It is in the hope of bringing those kindred souls together with these extraordinary, forgotten people that this book is written. These brief sketches should serve only to introduce this cast of amazing characters. Anyone interested enough to read these pages through is urged to seek out the travelers' own original accounts even if they are hard to find, so that he can become acquainted with the authors at firsthand. The effort will, I promise you, be richly rewarded.

KENNETH WIMMEL
Bethesda, Maryland
December 1994

1

The Alluring Target

Does anyone in the last decade of the 20th century call himself an explorer? Almost certainly, no. When people mention exploring today, they almost always associate the idea with outer space, and the person who does the exploring is not called an explorer but an astronaut or a cosmonaut, or perhaps an astronomer who does not leave his planetarium but relies upon remotely controlled spacecraft to do his exploring for him. Today our planet is "spaceship Earth" and we look upon ourselves as passengers on a little blue-and-white globe whirling through unfriendly space. The Earth is no longer a big, hostile place to be explored, subdued, exploited. It is our fragile home that we must protect. Wild animals are no longer dangerous beasts that offer us the stark choice: kill or be killed. They are endangered species that share our spaceship with us. We must consciously protect them if they are to survive. This evolving attitude toward the planet on which we live and toward the other species that share it with us is a characteristic that distinguishes us, who live at the end of the 20th century, from everyone who lived through all the millennia before us.

As recently as one hundred years ago the idea of spaceship Earth was inconceivable. The Earth was still a big, potentially hostile, partially unknown place. By 1890 the most celebrated geographical mystery of the 19th century, the source of the Nile, had, it is true, been solved, and Africa was no longer so dark a continent as it had been fifty years earlier. But there were still large mysterious patches on the map of the world which held no one knew what. Mapmakers no longer wrote "here be dragons" on those blank spaces, as they did in medieval times. But they still did not know exactly what lay at the South Pole or at the North Pole, nor could they be certain whether the highest mountain or the highest waterfall or the lowest point below sea level on Earth had yet been identified. There were still pockets in sub-Saharan Africa and the Amazon rain forest never seen by a European, and there were tracts of mountain and desert in Asia and Africa where no human being had yet set foot. A young man in 1890 could still aspire to become an explorer in the traditional sense of penetrating to places "where no white man had ever been," perhaps to find a mountain higher than Everest or a waterfall greater than Niagara, or a tribe of people hitherto unknown in Europe or America.

If there might still be fascinating things to discover on the face of the planet a century ago, there definitely were—and perhaps still are— equally fascinating things to rediscover. The science—or art—of archeology was in its infancy. The gold of the Egyptian pharaoh Tutankhamen still lay buried under the sands of the Valley of the Kings, not to be uncovered for more than a quarter-century. The very existence of the ancient Indus Valley civilization in the Indian subcontinent was unknown, not to be revealed until the 1920s by British archeologists. Archeology, no less and perhaps more than geography, offered vistas of adventure and possibilities for fame and fortune to the aspiring explorer in 1890.

No area on Earth was a more alluring target to the explorer of a century ago than the great heartland of the Eurasian landmass. Like the polar regions and still hidden pockets of Africa and South America, Central Asia posed a formidable physical challenge. It is the huge area lying, roughly, north of the Himalayas, south of Siberia, east of the Caspian and Aral Seas, and west of the borders of China proper. Geographers already knew before the end of the 19th century that this great swath of the Earth's surface contained the highest mountain ranges and some of the most dreaded deserts in the world. The great Tibetan tableland, with an average altitude of 13,000 feet (as much as 15,000 feet in the north) is on a level with the highest peaks in the Alps and only slightly below the snow line at that latitude. With an area of 770,000 square miles, Tibet alone is two-and-a-half times the size of Scandinavia. Somewhere in it, still unmapped in 1890, lay the sources of the great rivers of Asia—the Yangtze, the Yellow, the Mekong, the Salween, the Indus, the Brahmaputra, the Ganges. Some geographers speculated that it might hold a mountain higher than Everest.

The deserts to the north of Tibet are every bit as formidable as the Sahara, and they lie in the middle of the world's largest continental landmass behind the highest mountain ranges in the world. Sven Hedin, probably Central Asia's greatest explorer who nearly lost his life in the Takla Makan Desert of Chinese Turkestan, called that desert "the worst and most dangerous . . . in the world." Kashgar, on the western edge of the Takla Makan, lies farther from the sea than any other city on Earth. In sum, the great heartland of Eurasia at the end of the 19th century held geographical questions and posed physical challenges for the would-be explorer as great or greater than anywhere else in the world. As Sven Hedin, who was in a position to know, wrote, "travel in Asia is not a dance upon the dropping petals of the rose."

The allure of Central Asia in 1890 carried a dimension other, still largely unexplored, regions did not possess. It was associated with antiquity, with ancient civilization. Across it had wound the Silk Road, the artery that connected East and West before the birth of Christ. It was the meeting ground of three of the great civilizations of antiquity: Rome, India, and China. Marco Polo crossed it, and from within it streamed forth the hordes of Genghis Khan. Who in 1890 knew what treasures and secrets of antiquity might lie forgotten in its fastness?

Stone Age man lived in Central Asia for thousands of years and left behind numerous implements to mark his presence. The oases around the rim of the Takla Makan Desert were probably first settled by people from northern India who pushed north across the mountain barrier of the Himalayas into the Tarim Basin, perhaps as early as the second millennium before Christ. But the earliest travelers to leave records of journeys across the Eurasian heartland were Chinese. In the second century B.C. the Han emperor Wu Ti sent an official of his household, Chang Chien, on an expedition to the west in connection with Chinese efforts to protect themselves from the Huns, the predatory nomads of Central Asia who later became the scourge of Europe. Chang Chien was away thirteen years and penetrated as far west as Samarkand and Bokhara. When he returned to China, his reports revealed to the Chinese for the first time the existence of such lands as Persia and, probably, Rome.

The travels of Chang Chien were the beginnings of the Silk Road, the caravan route—or, more properly, routes—across Central Asia that connected China with the Near East and, ultimately, the Mediterranean. There developed two major arteries of the Silk Road. Both began in China at Sian (or Chang-an, the capital of the Han, Sui, and Tang dynasties) and led northwest to Tun-huang. There the two branches separated to follow either the northern edge of the Takla Makan Desert in the middle of Chinese Turkestan along the base of the Tien Shan Mountains; or the southern edge of that dreaded desert along the base of the Kunlun Mountains that shielded the high table-land of Tibet. They came together again at Kashgar in the extreme west of Chinese Turkestan and continued on through such fabled cities as Tashkent, Bokhara, and Samarkand to Persia, Iraq, and the Mediterranean coast. Just short of Kashgar, a branch went off to the south to Afghanistan and India. The Silk Road carried much more than silk. Traffic in a variety of goods flowed between China, India, and the Near East. But it was silk that was the most sought-after of its goods. The term itself seems to be of relatively recent origin, having apparently been coined in the 19th century by a German geographer, Ferdinand von Richthofen.

But even before Chang Chien made his epochal journey, before there was a Silk Road, Buddhism began to make its way in the opposite direction from India across the Himalayas and through the oases of Central Asia to China and beyond. War and politics were the reasons for Chang Chien's travel; religion was the even more powerful motivating force behind the travel of the two greatest of early Central Asian travelers, Fa-hsien and Hsüan-tsang. They were Buddhist monks who traveled from China to obtain the pure, original texts of the Buddhist scriptures from the Buddhist holy land, India, the land of the Buddha's birth.

Fa-hsien left China in A.D. 399 and traveled the southern branch of the Silk Road from Tun-huang through Khotan and across the Pamirs to India. His impression of the deserts of Central Asia has been echoed by many another traveler since:

> In the desert were numerous evil spirits and scorching winds, causing death to anyone who would meet them. Above, there were no birds, while on the ground there were no animals. One

looked as far as one could see in all directions for a path to cross, but there was none to choose. Only the dry bones of the dead served as indications.

He remained in India for ten years, then traveled south to Ceylon and, probably, Java, before returning to China by sea in the year 412. He wrote an account of his journey and translated many Buddhist texts he brought back from India.

Hsüan-tsang was a leading cleric of the early Tang dynasty who traveled about two centuries after Fa-hsien. Born in A.D. 602, he was the fourth and youngest son of his family. At the age of twelve he was admitted to study as a novice at a Buddhist monastery in Loyang. A precocious student whose abilities were early recognized, he was elected by his peers as a priest when only fourteen years old. Eventually he made his way to Chang-an, where he lived in a community of monks at the Temple of Great Learning. He became disturbed by the constant disputes that erupted among his fellow monks over matters of religious dogma, and he conceived the idea of traveling to India to obtain the pure Buddhist texts and to "question the wise men on the points that were troubling his mind." He applied to Emperor Kao-tsu for permission to leave China, but was refused. He ignored the imperial decision and set out on his journey in A.D. 627.

One of the most difficult portions of an exceedingly difficult journey was getting out of China into the desert to the west. Hsüan-tsang had to elude border guards, although the captain of one border post, a devout Buddhist, was friendly and supplied him with provisions. He urged the pilgrim not to enter the desert, but the monk was adamant: "If you insist on detaining me, I will allow you to take my life, but Hsüan-tsang will not take a single step backward in the direction of China." He became lost in an area that had "neither bird, nor four-legged beast, neither water, nor pasturage." But he retraced his steps and found his way finally through the oases of Hami and Turfan along the northern branch of the Silk Road as far as Tashkent and Samarkand, then south across the Pamirs to India.

He remained in India for fifteen years. He visited all the Buddhist holy places and collected a library of religious texts. He returned across the northern mountain barrier to the southern Silk Road and the kingdom of Khotan. At Tun-huang he sent another petition to the Chinese emperor, this one asking permission to return to China. This time the answer was favorable and the emperor even received the pilgrim personally. When they met, the emperor inquired about the monk's earlier disobedience in leaving China. Hsüan-tsang's reply revealed the diplomatic finesse that must have often served him during his travels. "I did indeed request your gracious permit three times over," he said. "But, receiving no favorable answer and knowing myself to be so insignificant a subject, I could not suppose that you even knew of my request."

Hsüan-tsang returned to China with some 657 Buddhist books, together with 150 religious objects. These were to be the foundation for the teaching of Buddhism in China. He spent the rest of his life in monastic seclusion, studying and translating into Chinese the texts he had brought back. He wrote an account of his journey that is probably the major source of information we possess about India and Central Asia in the 7th century, a period when both areas enjoyed a respite from warfare and reached high degrees of artistic and cultural attainment. Sir Aurel Stein, the great 20th-century archeologist of Central Asia, called him "my patron saint."

Even as early as the time of Hsüan-tsang's travel, some of the great oases of the Silk Road had been, or were being, abandoned. The flow of the glacier-fed rivers that arise in the Kunlun Mountains and eventually disappear in the Takla Makan Desert was dwindling, forcing the settlements to be abandoned and moved to the south, farther up the rivers. Later, Chinese control of the remote western marches of the Celestial Empire weakened as the power of the Tang dynasty declined. Fierce Tibetans invaded some of the oases. The greatest oases depended upon great irrigation systems, which in turn depended upon intensive maintenance made possible by peaceful and orderly government. As the Tang dynasty declined and Chinese authority weakened, the irrigation systems deteriorated and the cities succumbed to the desert sands. With the subsequent passage of centuries, their locations and even their existence were forgotten, except to a few nomadic desert dwellers.

In the first half of the 13th century, Genghis Khan, who ranks with Julius Caesar and Napoleon among the greatest military geniuses of all time, led the Mongols out of Central Asia to conquer the greatest empire ever known. Mongol armies were victorious from the South China Sea to the gates of Vienna. Mongol depredations in Poland and Hungary prompted fearful Christian rulers in Europe to send envoys to negotiate with the apparently invincible Great Khan in Central Asia. Two of those intrepid travelers, John of Plano Carpini (Giovanni da Pian del Carpini) and William of Rubrouck (Willem van Ruysbroeck), left accounts of their journeys that contain invaluable portraits of the society of the terrible Tartars at the height of their conquests. Both travelers recorded seeing evidence of the ferocity of the Mongol armies in the lands they crossed to reach the Mongol capital. Devastated, plundered cities and the bones of slaughtered populations lay strewn along their paths.

Carpini was a Franciscan monk from northern Italy, sent by Pope Innocent IV in 1245 to carry a letter to the Emperor of the Mongols. A corpulent churchman over sixty years old, he made a grueling and amazing journey on relays of Mongol horses across Poland, Russia, and Mongolia to the camp of the Great Khan near the Mongol capital, Karakorum. He was present at the great assembly of Mongol nobles for the enthronement of Güyük, a grandson of Genghis Khan, as emperor in July 1246. Brother John traveled when the Mongol conquest was at its flood; he explains that, as he writes, a Mongol army is occupying Aleppo in northern Syria, and no one can say where or when their march of conquest will end. His *History of the Mongols* includes a chapter on "How to Wage War Against the Tartars," a surprising subject for a follower of Saint Francis. But it addressed the panic that the bloodthirsty and hitherto unbeatable invaders from the East had aroused throughout Europe.

Brother John found little to admire among the Mongols. Their homeland was unpleasant:

> It is large, but otherwise—as we saw with our own eyes, for during five and a half months we traveled about it—it is more wretched than I can possibly say.

The Mongols themselves he found to be arrogant, cruel, dirty, and untruthful. He reviewed both their good and bad traits, but found the latter to outnumber the former:

It is impossible to put down in writing all their evil characteristics on account of the very great number of them.

Carpini's narrative is the oldest surviving European account of travel in Central Asia. It also contains the first reference in European writing to the Chinese.

William of Rubrouck, like Carpini, was a Franciscan but from Flanders in northern Europe. In 1253 he was sent by King Louis IX of France (Saint Louis) on a more purely religious mission to the Mongols. His account of his journey is addressed to the king.

William's narrative is much longer, more detailed, and contains fewer judgements than John's, although he, too, found the terrible Tartars to be very different from his own people: " . . . and when I came among them, it seemed to me, indeed, as if I were entering another world." By the time he arrived at the Mongol capital in the middle of Mongolia, he had come to dislike his hosts as much as Carpini had. His feelings had become as uncharacteristically truculent as his brother Franciscan's:

[The Mongols] are now so much puffed up with pride that they believe the whole world is anxious to make peace with them. But indeed, if I were given leave, I would preach war against them throughout the world with all my strength.

He met the Great Khan, Mangu, another grandson of Genghis, who had succeeded Güyük as emperor in 1251. Brother William's account is considered by scholars to be the most complete and authentic portrait we possess of the Mongols at the height of their conquests, before they became sinicized and embraced Buddhism.

A third narrative of travel in Central Asia in the 13th century is among the most famous pieces of travel literature ever produced. Marco Polo crossed the heartland in 1274 to reach the China of Kublai Khan, another grandson of Genghis Khan who founded the Yüan dynasty in China and established his capital at Peking. Carpini and William of Rubrouck had traveled across Russia and Mongolia. Marco Polo traveled the Silk Road, much to the south of the routes of the other two, and his famous narrative is a snapshot of the great link between East and West just before it became severed. The conquests of Tamerlane, another descendant of Genghis Khan, in the 14th century, and the successful efforts of European mariners to find sea routes connecting East and West effectively put an end to use of the land route across the heartland. Traffic along the Silk Road between China and the Near East dwindled after the 14th century, and Inner Asia, the vital link between East and West in the ancient world, became a terra incognita in the West.

The European explorers in the great Age of Discovery after the 14th century were sailors. The empires they created—the Portuguese, the Dutch, the Spanish, the British—were maritime empires created and maintained by sea power. Only after they had ranged over all the oceans of the world did European attention turn to the more arduous challenge of land exploration.

In the 17th century religion again was the impetus that pushed travelers into the Eurasian heartland, this time Christian missionaries from Europe. Jesuit priests, who became established in Peking during the 16th century, accompanied the emperor Kang-hsi on his campaigns in Mongolia and helped him map the country. Jesuits and Capuchins from Portuguese outposts in India lived in Tibet for years. Two Jesuits, Grueber and d'Orville, traveled from Peking to India through Tibet and its capital, Lhasa, in 1661.

But few Western travelers were willing to follow them and face the difficulties inherent in reaching that isolated land. By the early 19th century the Tibetan priests, who were both temporal and spiritual leaders, closed the country's borders to foreigners, probably fearing that foreign influence would undermine their authority. The last Europeans in the 19th century to succeed in reaching Lhasa were two French priests, Régis-Evariste Huc and Joseph Gabet, who did so in 1846. Thereafter, for more than half a century, no European was able to reach the Tibetan capital, although several tried. To the north of Tibet, in the deserts of Chinese Turkestan, only a few nomads and shepherds roamed where the great oases along the Silk Road had flourished almost two millennia earlier. Still further north, in the grasslands of Mongolia, the ferocious Tartars, tamed by Tibetan Buddhism, docilely tended their flocks, their immense conquests six centuries earlier only a dim memory to be wondered at.

But a new force was thrusting into the heartland. The march of

Tsarist Russia across the steppes into the deserts and mountains of Central Asia is a major theme of 19th-century Asian history. It aroused increasing apprehension in British India and prompted the "Great Game," a complicated chess game of espionage, exploration, diplomacy, and, on occasion, sabre-rattling by Britain and Russia, as the British sought to forestall the Russian advance, and the Russians sought to avoid or overcome British resistance. The great plateaus, mountain ranges, and deserts of the heartland were their chessboard.

The Great Game prompted both sides to send agents into Central Asia to spy out the land and find out what the other side was up to. These intrepid travelers, some of them virtually forgotten today despite the incredible adventures they experienced, became the early explorers of the modern era in the great heartland. The British in India sent several agents, both British and Indian, across the Himalayas and the Karakorums during the middle decades of the 19th century. Several Indians, who were known only by numbers for reasons of security, traveled as Buddhist pilgrims across Tibet and Chinese Turkestan, surreptitiously measuring the land for mapmaking. It was their measurements, brought back to India at great risk to their lives, that enabled an Indian cartographer in 1852 in Calcutta to announce excitedly to his British supervisor, the Surveyor General of India, that he had identified the highest mountain in the world. The Surveyor General named it after his predecessor, one of the great Surveyors General of India, Sir George Everest.

The Russian advance toward the east brought with it one of the great explorers of Asia. Nikolai Mikhailovich Przhevalsky was a Russian Army officer who made four lengthy expeditions into Central Asia and Tibet between 1870 and 1885. In 1879, on his third expedition, he tried, unsuccessfully, to reach Lhasa. Przhevalsky brought to light a great deal of information about many aspects of the entire region, and his detailed writings stimulated interest in the region among European geographers, not least among them Sven Hedin.

By 1890 the great age of worldwide European exploration that had been in progress for more than four hundred years was drawing to a close. Only a few geographic mysteries to compare with the source of the Nile remained unsolved. Within twenty-five years, man would reach both poles. The airplane was not yet invented, but before forty years passed, man would even fly over both poles. But in 1890 there still remained geographical, archeological, and other secrets waiting to be revealed in Central Asia. The narratives that follow describe how some of the most intriguing of those secrets were uncovered.

The people who are the heroes and heroines of these accounts were not the only Western travelers in Central Asia between 1890 and 1935. Nor were they, necessarily, the most important, although at least one of them, Sven Hedin, must rank high on anyone's list of the greatest explorers of this century, and Sir Aurel Stein continues to stand as a giant figure in the world of archeology. What makes all of them worth reading about is that they were unusual, fascinating people who wrote exciting accounts of their journeys. The journeys themselves are, without exception, breathtaking in their audacity and replete with both adventure and humor.

Taken together, these travelers and the accounts they wrote reflect the era they span: the end of the great age of exploration. They range from the trail-blazing explorations of Sven Hedin to the "forbidden journey" of Ella Maillart and Peter Fleming who offered no justification for it, except that they wanted to make it. The age of exploration was giving way to the age of travel; the journey itself was becoming its own justification.

2
Sven Hedin

Buried Cities Along the Ancient Silk Road

When I am dead, I hope it may be said:
"His sins were scarlet, but his books were read."
HILAIRE BELLOC

The three shepherds tending their sheep beside the dry river bed did not expect any visitors. They were, after all, on the bank of the Khotan River in the Takla Makan Desert of western Chinese Turkestan. In early May the river bed was dry, except for a few pools here and there where troughs that had been scooped out of the sand when the river flowed still held water. It was those random pools that enabled their herds and flocks to live along the river when its flow stopped. The moisture retained by the sandy banks kept alive the vegetation on which the animals fed. In late June the river bed would fill up again and become a shallow torrent when the snow melted in the Kunlun Mountains to the south, where the source of the river lay. Occasionally, a caravan of mules or camels passed, following the river bed from Khotan in the south to Aksu in the north. But hardly anyone else would venture into the dreaded Takla Makan with the hot weather already well along, and members of a caravan did not stop to pass the time of day with shepherds. So when the youngest shepherd, while rounding up some stray sheep, was suddenly confronted by a

13

haggard-looking stranger, he stood for a moment petrified by surprise.

"Salaam Aleikum [peace be with you]," said the stranger in a weak voice, but the startled young man turned and disappeared into the trees. He returned with an older man. The stranger was obviously from somewhere far away but, to the shepherds' surprise, he spoke their language.

> "I am a European. I entered the desert from the Yarkand River. My men and camels died of thirst, and I have lost everything. For 10 days I have had nothing to eat. Give me a piece of bread and bowl of milk, and let me rest near you, for I am tired to death."

They took him to their hut, gave him some bread and a bowl of milk, and invited him to rest.

He had entered the desert almost a month earlier with a small caravan of four men and eight camels. But, following his guide's erroneous information, he had misjudged the distance across the wasteland to the Khotan River, and the group had run out of water well short of their goal. One by one, the camels dropped. In their last camp all their baggage was abandoned. Two of the men were driven to drink camel's urine, mixed with sugar and vinegar, which left them overcome with violent cramps and vomiting, writhing in agony on the sand. They slaughtered a sheep they had brought with them and drank its coagulated blood.

One by one the men collapsed. The leader and one other man drove themselves forward, walking across the enormous sand dunes at night, and burying themselves in the sand during the burning daylight hours. After several days only the leader was still on his feet but at the point of collapse when he came upon one of the pools of the Khotan River. Soon afterward he happened upon the shepherds.

He subsequently learned that two of his men had survived. But two others, all his camels, and his pet fox terrier were dead. Most of his equipment was lost or damaged beyond repair. His expedition was irretrievably smashed, and he was forced to return to his base at Kashgar.

The leader was Sven Anders Hedin, and his brush with death in the dreaded Takla Makan did not deflect him from his goal—to explore the vast unknown of Central Asia.

Hedin's explorations and travels constitute a remarkable record of courage, endurance, and accomplishment. Beginning in 1885, when

Sven Hedin dressed in his traveling clothes in 1897, shortly after his initial Asian expedition when he first discovered forgotten cities buried in the desert sands.

he was twenty years old, he spent much of his life crisscrossing Central Asia and Tibet until he became as familiar with that mysterious and inhospitable region as any Western traveler in the 20th century. Geographers, geologists, archeologists, paleontologists, anthropologists, and scientists in other fields have followed in Hedin's footsteps, studying the sites and peoples that he first revealed to the Western world. They have often acknowledged their debt to his pioneering explorations. But Hedin was no mean scientist himself, and he amassed an amazing quantity of data that have helped to guide the way for those who have come after him.

One of Hedin's greatest assets as an explorer was his extraordinary ability to learn languages. He was fluent in English, French, German, and Russian. Early in his career he mastered Persian and Turkish and later also Mongolian and Tibetan. This is why in his early explorations he could travel with only locally recruited porters and, from time to time, guides. During one expedition he did not see another European for two years.

Exceptionally courageous and tireless, in 1893–97 Hedin traveled 6,520 miles in the unknown regions of Central Asia, in addition to more than 8,000 miles by rail or carriage to his jumping-off point in Kashgar in western Chinese Turkestan and back to Sweden from Peking, the terminus of his first journey. Of those 6,520 miles, no fewer than 2,000 were through regions no European had ever visited before. As for the other portions of the journey, no more than three travelers had preceded him over any of them. In a few places he was told by the local inhabitants that he was moving into areas never before visited by a human being. His two subsequent journeys of exploration were no less impressive in scope and daring.

Hedin was born in Stockholm on February 19, 1865. His imagination was fired early by the accounts widely circulated in Sweden of the exploits of the 19th-century Scandinavian explorers trying to reach the poles; he resolved to become an arctic explorer and the first person to reach the North Pole. But fate pointed him in another direction.

At age twenty, as he was finishing school, he was asked to travel to the Russian Caucasus as the tutor to the son of a Swedish engineer working with an oil-exploration team in what was then the world's largest oil field. He soon found himself in Balakani, a town near Baku on the shores of the Caspian Sea. Upon completion of his assignment there, he took the opportunity to travel through Persia and Mesopotamia. As a result of this journey he decided to abandon his dream of reaching the North Pole and become an explorer of the deserts and mountains of Asia.

*Hedin (center) with Russian officers at Pamirsky Post. The Russian presence
"proclaimed the sovereignty of the Czar over the Roof of the World," Hedin wrote.*

After graduation from the University of Uppsala with a degree in
geology, he went to Berlin to study geography under Ferdinand von
Richthofen whom he considered "the greatest authority of his day on
the geography of Asia." Before completing his studies, however, in 1890
he was invited to join, as an interpreter, a Swedish-Norwegian diplomatic mission to Naser od-Din, Shah of Persia. He happily accepted
and soon returned to Teheran. After the mission completed its task, he
left it to journey through northern Persia and Russian Turkestan as far
as the ancient city of Kashgar in Chinese Turkestan. The trip was intended as a reconnaissance for a more ambitious journey he planned to
make into the territory east of Kashgar.

In Kashgar he stayed ten days with Nikolai Petrovsky, the Russian
Consul General, whom he found to be very helpful and very well informed about Central Asia. Petrovsky owned a library of "the best books
that have been written on subjects connected with Central Asia." Hedin
considered him to be "a thorough man of science." He also met Francis
Younghusband and George Macartney who had been sent into Central
Asia by the British authorities in India to investigate Russian activities in

the region (although they said nothing to Hedin about their reasons for being in the city). Younghusband soon returned to India, but Macartney stayed in Kashgar as an agent of the British government.

But Hedin had to return to Sweden to complete his studies and prepare for his great exploration. He departed Kashgar on December 24, 1891, on a "jolly journey" that was "a wild and whizzing expedition on horseback, by sleigh, and by carriage through all of Western Asia."

Back in Europe, Hedin completed his studies as well as his preparations for future endeavors. In a long memorandum seeking support from the King of Sweden, he explained his reasons for wanting to make such a dangerous trip. "Immense areas of the almost inaccessible Desert of Gobi, and endless wastes in the highlands of Tibet, are to this day as little known as the Polar regions," he explained to the king. The principal object of the journey was

> to disperse the clouds which still rest over a great part of Central Asia. An expedition to that part of the world which was the cradle of the Aryan race, and from whose dim interior the Mongols streamed out over the whole of Asia and part of Europe, and where there is such a host of geographical questions still awaiting solution, is one of the most important undertakings within the domain of geographical discovery. The object of my prospective journey is to traverse Asia from west to east, from the Caspian Sea to Peking, and in particular to explore the intermediate regions which are least known.

Hedin left Sweden in October 1893. After crossing Russia as far as Fergana on the edge of Central Asia, he decided he would go on to Kashgar, the departure point for his explorations, by crossing the great Pamir upland in the dead of winter. He was warned by the staff of the Russian governor of Fergana at Margelan that such a journey would be very dangerous. Winter temperatures in the Pamirs reached -45° F and sudden snowstorms, called burans, could blind a traveler, while sudden avalanches could engulf the unwary in a few seconds. The bones of animals and even of people killed by avalanches along the track Hedin followed through the Pamirs were visible evidence of the truth of this warning. But Hedin was not deterred and on February 23, 1894, he left Fergana in high spirits.

Accompanied by three men recruited in Fergana as guides and baggage handlers, Hedin proceeded toward Pamirsky Post, reputed to be the highest Russian fort anywhere. The trip was 294 miles and every bit as rugged as he had been warned it would be. At one point he recorded the lowest temperature he would ever record on any of his journeys in Asia—36.8° below zero Fahrenheit. Inside his tiny tent, although it was packed with his porters who retreated there to escape the intense cold, the temperature was -12° F.

His route onward from Pamirsky Post to Kashgar led close by Muztagh Ata Mountain, the "Father of Ice Mountains." The highest (25,600 feet) mountain in the Pamir uplands, it had spawned many legends among the local Kirghiz nomads, and it fascinated Hedin. He decided he would try to climb it, although

> every man I talked to, without exception, assured me that it would be utterly impossible to reach the top. The precipices and yawning chasms would prove insuperable obstacles to progress. The flanks of the mountain were sheathed in ice as bright and smooth as glass. On them and on the summit storms roared without cessation; and if I were so venturesome as to defy the giant, he would bid the winds sweep me away like a grain of sand.

Hedin undertook the ascent with six Kirghiz tribesmen and nine yaks, but carried no mountain-climbing equipment (in 1894 there was little special equipment in existence). At an altitude of 17,500 feet his eyes became inflamed. This caused him "excruciating agony," and he had to abandon the climb, but vowed to try again as soon as he could. With a bandage covering one eye and a dark lens protecting the other, he continued on to Kashgar and arrived there on May 1.

Hedin remained two months in Kashgar to allow his eyes to heal. His next goal was Lop Nor, the great lake on the other side of the Tarim Basin. He wanted to solve the "Lop Nor question," a major mystery of 19th-century Asian geography. The great lake, mentioned in ancient Chinese annals, had been found in the 1880s by a Russian explorer, Nikolai Mikhailovich Przhevalsky, much further south than early Chinese maps had shown it to be. Przhevalsky had reported it was fresh-water rather than the salt lake that had been earlier reported. Hedin had learned about these questions from Von Richthofen, and he made their solution one of his principal concerns. But he decided to spend the summer months in the cooler regions of the eastern Pamirs and attempt to cross the formidable Takla Makan Desert in the Tarim Basin later in the year.

He returned to Muztagh Ata to map the glaciers around the base of the mountain and to make another attempt to reach the summit. With five Kirghiz and six yaks, he again ascended the mountain and reached 20,160 feet. But he realized he could not reach the summit in one day, and had to descend. He tried another route a few days later, but was stopped by a tremendous crevasse. The next day he made a fourth try, prepared to camp at the 20,000-foot level and then attempt the summit the next day. Again, they reached 20,160 feet. Two of the Kirghiz became sick from the altitude during the climb and returned down the mountain. Hedin and the two remaining men camped.

> We all showed symptoms of mountain sickness—singing in the ears, deafness, a quick pulse, a temperature below normal, and insomnia.

Even so, Hedin was able to admire the spectacular vista spread before him in the moonlight. But the next morning a lashing gale enveloped their camp in whirling snow. It was obviously impossible to continue, and Hedin had to retreat down the mountain:

> I rode a big black yak, strong as an elephant. I left him to his own devices, for it was useless to guide him. I could not see my hand before my face, on account of the whirling, whipping snow. The yak waded, plunged, jumped, and slid downward through the snow, diving like a dolphin in the drifts. I had to press my knees hard, or I would have been thrown from the saddle by the yak's sudden and spasmodic jerks. At times, I lay back to back with the yak, only to feel, a moment later, the tips of his horns in my stomach.

He gave up; the mountain had won. He continued for several months mapping in the Pamirs, and by November was back in Kashgar.

On February 17, 1895, Hedin embarked on "a journey which proved to be one of the most difficult I ever undertook in Asia." He entered the desert in April, traveling from the Yarkand River across the totally waterless sand dunes of the Takla Makan toward the Khotan

Hedin (center), aboard a yak and accompanied by Kirghiz tribesmen, about to begin his ascent of Muztagh Ata, "the Father of Ice Mountains."

River. Too late he found his men had failed to bring along enough water. The journey nearly cost him his life. Two of his companions died, and all of his camels succumbed. Hedin only narrowly escaped dying of thirst himself. Finally, with the expedition irreparably crippled and many of the instruments damaged or destroyed, he was forced to return to Kashgar, arriving there in June 1895, almost a year to the day after his departure from that city.

He remained in Kashgar only a few weeks, long enough to refit and reform his expedition and to order new equipment and supplies from Europe. He would spend the summer months in the southern Pamirs and again attempt the desert crossing when the weather cooled. On July 12 he again set out from Kashgar with Islam Bai, the most reliable and trustworthy among his assistants, and with two servants and six horses for a summer with the Kirghiz in the Pamirs.

On October 3 he was back in Kashgar to collect the large quantity of scientific equipment and supplies he had ordered the previous summer from Europe to replace what he had lost in the desert. On December 14 he again set off into the desert accompanied by Bai, five servants, and nine horses. His immediate destination was Khotan, an ancient city southeast of Kashgar which had once been an important oasis along the

Silk Road. It was already famous in China in the eighth century, and Marco Polo noted its importance when he visited it in 1274.

In Khotan, Hedin heard stories of ancient cities buried in the sands of the Takla Makan Desert to the north of Khotan, and he resolved to find them. On January 14, 1896, he left Khotan with four men and headed northeast toward the Keriya River near which the cities were reported to lie. As the small party penetrated further into the desert, the sand dunes grew ever higher until they topped fifty feet. Finally, in a depression between the giant dunes, they came across a kottek, or dead forest, of sun-bleached, wind-scoured tree stumps protruding through the sand. It was obviously the remnants of a once-verdant forest destroyed by the devouring desert sands. Nearby, Hedin's guides led him to the ruins of a city they called Takla Makan.

Hedin had already come upon the ruins of settlements in the desert, but Takla Makan was different. What survived of other ancient dwellings was of sun-dried clay. The houses of Takla Makan had been built of poplar. There was no trace of clay or stone dwellings. The upper portions of the houses, which numbered in the hundreds, had long ago disappeared; what remained above ground were posts six to ten feet high. The lower portions had been covered by sand, and a bit of excavation revealed portions of walls made of bundles of reed stalks fastened to stakes and coated with clay mixed with chaff which produced a tough, durable material.

The walls were decorated with paintings, some showing female figures clad in airy garments, kneeling in prayer. There were paintings of men with black beards and mustaches—clearly not Chinese—and of dogs and horses and boats rocking on waves—scenes decidedly strange in the midst of the sere desert. Hedin and his companions also unearthed a quantity of gypsum figures of Buddha in relief, four to eight inches high. A life-sized human foot modeled in gypsum was found, clearly all that remained of a large image of Buddha. Hedin's companions speculated that they had hit upon the ruins of a Buddhist temple or monastery. In other houses they uncovered more paintings, as well as a silkworm chrysalis, the axle of a wheel (probably part of a spinning wheel), and fragments of earthenware pitchers.

Hedin was not an archeologist, and he had neither the time nor the resources to do extensive excavations. He had clearly come across

Sven Hedin measuring the height of sand dunes in the Takla Makan desert.
His meticulously drawn maps proved invaluable to later travelers.

the site of a major Buddhist city of great antiquity, but he had no way of learning when the city had flourished or when it had been abandoned. There was evidence of an extensive irrigation system. Silk had obviously been cultivated and industries had flourished.

The houses had been large and beautifully decorated. The city clearly dated back at least to the early years of the Christian era, and it must have been abandoned because of the encroachment of the desert sands. But it remained for later archeologists with plenty of time and well-equipped expeditions to uncover its secrets.

Hedin had to move on. He collected as many samples of Takla Makan's artifacts as he could carry and took careful sightings to establish the precise location of the buried ruins. He later wrote that finding the lost city

> was one of the most unexpected discoveries that I made throughout the whole of my travels in Asia. . . . Who could have imagined that in the interior of the dreaded Desert of Gobi, and precisely in that part of it which in dreariness and desolation exceeds all other deserts on the face of the Earth, actual cities slumbered under the sand, cities wind-driven for thousands of years, the ruined survivals

of a once flourishing civilization? And yet there stood I amid the wreck and devastation of an ancient people, having awakened to new life the city which had slumbered for a thousand years.

Continuing north down the Keriya River where no European had ever traveled before, Hedin within a few days came upon a community of shepherds who had never before seen a European. Indeed, they lived such isolated lives that they had never seen another human being except their closest neighbors. They were shy and obviously lived on the most primitive level. Hedin met a thiry-five-year-old man who had never visited a town or city and could not conceive what a town or bazaar was like.

Two of the shepherds told Hedin about another ancient city buried in the sand to the north along the Keriya River which they called Kara Dung (the Black Hill), and they guided him to it. It turned out to be on a smaller scale than Takla Makan but apparently of the same period. One building measuring 249 by 279 feet was built around a courtyard in which stood a smaller structure, probably a caravansary. Some of the houses contained well-preserved wooden beams and many shards of earthenware. But once again, Hedin could not tarry long and pushed on northward along the Keriya River through the desert.

He traveled for more than a year, looping, crisscrossing, and doubling back through Central Asia and northern Tibet. He reached Lop Nor and found it to be a "wandering" lake that is constantly changing its position due to sandstorms and shifting river beds. The Lop Nor of his day was, he found, actually two sets of lakes, both to the south of the position of the lake given on ancient Chinese maps. He spent months passing through enormous tracts of apparently totally uninhabited desert and mountain. A constant danger was the kara buran, or black desert blizzard, which could strike with virtually no warning and sweep everything before it:

My tent-poles were snapped in two, and only the half-poles could now be used. With great difficulty my men had managed to pitch the tent in the shadow of a clay hillock. It was guyed with ropes and heavy boxes piled on its edges. The camels, freed of their loads, lay stretched out in the direction of the wind, their necks and heads flat on the ground. The men wrapped themselves up in their cloaks

A delicate drawing of a young Kirghiz woman by Hedin. The intrepid explorer was also an accomplished artist and writer.

and huddled under their tent cloth, which could not be pitched. The drift-sand beat against the tent cloth, and the particles filtered through and covered everything within. The storm lasted all day, all night, and part of the next day, and when at last it had shot past, hurrying westward, and calm was again restored, we felt queerly, as after a long illness.

He pitched his tent at altitudes above 16,000 feet in below-zero weather. As had been the case throughout most of his journey, he was totally out of communication with the outside world for the entire time. In March 1897 he arrived at his final destination, Peking, but remained there only twelve days before starting on his journey home to Stockholm. Three routes back to Europe were open to him: across the Pacific via the United States; by mail boat via India and the Suez

Canal; or overland via Mongolia and Siberia. Not surprisingly, he chose the last, the most physically demanding but perhaps the most interesting of the three. On May 10, 1897, he arrived back in Sweden, having spent three years and seven months exploring the heartland of Asia.

Hedin had numerous adventures and made many noteworthy geographical and scientific observations after he departed Kala Dung, but he came across no more buried cities. There were still vast reaches of desert and mountain in the Asian heartland he had yet to traverse, however, and another buried city, even bigger and more significant than Takla Makan, lay sleeping in the sands of the Gobi, awaiting discovery.

A detailed account of that first journey, entitled *Through Asia*, was published in 1898. Hedin was a facile writer who could make his experiences come alive for the reader. These two early examples of his skill—one taken from a letter to his family, the other from *Through Asia*—describe meeting a desert caravan at night; and the scene he saw as he stepped from his tent on that moonlit night at 20,000 feet on Muztagh Ata:

> Of a sudden one hears the muted sound of bells far away. It is a strange music, it creates an impression that is magical. It makes one sleepy. The sound gets more and more precise, finally it is very close. Like huge black ghosts, the camels appear out of the darkness; slowly, majestically, with dignity they move across the desert sands.

> The outermost parts of the glacier were bathed in moonlight. . . . Light clouds, dancing before the gentle southern breeze, formed in rapid succession concentric rings, halos, and the like in all the colors of the rainbow. . . . A dead silence everywhere—not an echo from the opposite wall of rock. . . . The breathing of the yaks was visible, but not audible. The animals stood silent and motionless. . . . The clouds flitted noiselessly by. . . . A curious feeling of being at a vast distance from the Earth took possession of me. It was difficult to realize that the four continents lay actually below my feet; and that a girdle drawn around the Earth at the level where I stood would cut off only the tops of a very few mountains in Asia and South America. . . . I seemed to be standing on the confines of space—cold, silent, boundless.

In later years Hedin's talent for evocative description made him a popular lecturer in Europe and America. At the end of his recital of the first disastrous foray into the Takla Makan Desert audiences reportedly scurried for the water fountains.

Only a little more than two years had passed after Hedin's return to Sweden when he set out on his second great journey of exploration. Kashgar was again his jumping-off point, but this time he proceeded along the northern edge of the Takla Makan Desert just south of the towering Celestial Mountains, and the first portion of this journey was accomplished on water. He brought with him from Europe a collapsible boat in which he and his party made their way north down the Yarkand river to where its junction with the Aksu river marks the beginning of the Tarim, the mightiest river of Central Asia. They continued down the Tarim for several months until, in early December, it became solid with ice. They then struck off into the desert north of Lop Nor—the utterly waterless waste called by Marco Polo the "Desert of Lop."

Hedin ran the same risks as during the initial foray into the Takla Makan in 1895, and he and his party again came close to succumbing to thirst. But once again he survived.

In the desert wastes, where "no trace of life in any form was to be seen," the explorer came again upon the remains of a dead forest, much like the one he had come upon just before discovering Takla Makan. In some furrows in the sand the wind had uncovered sea shells "which crackled under our feet like dry autumn leaves." They were obviously in the dry bed of an ancient sea or lake. A little later they came upon the remains of wooden houses on a small hill. In the houses, they found some Chinese coins and wooden carvings representing a man holding a trident and others with wreaths and lotuses. Next, they came upon a clay tower which they climbed. From the top they could see three other towers in the distance. Another buried city! But Hedin decided with regret to depart the next day—the hot season was fast approaching, and their water supply was running low.

The following day, when they decided to try to dig for water, they discovered that their only spade had been left behind at the ruins. The man sent back to fetch it got lost in a blinding storm. When he caught up with the party several days later, he brought with him not only the spade, but some beautifully carved wooden boards he had found in some house ruins near another clay tower some distance from where the party had first stopped. Hedin immediately realized that the site was even more extensive—and potentially more important—than he had at first thought:

> I grew dizzy, on seeing these artistically carved scrolls and leaves; and having learned from Orbek that there were more of them, though he had been able to bring only two samples, I wanted to go back. But what folly! We had water for only two days. All my travel plans were upset. I must return to the desert next winter!

As his next objective Hedin had had Lhasa, the "forbidden" capital of the "forbidden land" of Tibet. A government of Buddhist priests (lamas), headed by the Dalai Lama, had for years kept Tibet's borders closed to all foreigners. Its remoteness and geographic inaccessibility combined to make it easy to keep it a hermit kingdom. No European traveler had been able to reach Lhasa in more than half a century. Hedin had planned to make an attempt to penetrate the forbidden kingdom all the way to its capital. But now he decided to postpone the trip:

> A hazardous journey to Lhasa, in disguise, was rather a whim, a sporting feat; whereas a systematic examination of the desert city might be of incalculable importance to science. I therefore devoted the winter to the desert and its mysteries.

A year passed, however, before they were able to return to the site of the city. They retreated from the desert's increasing heat to explore further around Lop Nor, then moved south to spend several months in the totally unexplored wilderness of the high plateau of eastern Tibet, often at altitudes exceeding 16,000 feet. In late winter Hedin again turned north toward Lop Nor and the buried city. On March 3, 1901, they reached the site and camped at the foot of a twenty-nine-foot-high clay tower. The men began digging in the ruins of wooden houses nearby. Hedin felt exhilarated:

> We were now cut off from the world. I felt like a king in his own country, in his own capital. No one else on Earth knew of the existence of this place.

But as he looked over the lifeless, desolate waste that surrounded him, he also felt a mixture of doubt, anxiety, and hope:

Would this niggardly soil, which, beyond doubt, contained many secrets hidden in its bosom—would it reveal to me something that was known to no other human being in the world? Would it yield up to me some of its treasures? Would it grant me an answer to the host of questions that thronged in upon my brain? . . . I had changed my original plan simply and solely that I might come back here. Surely it was not to be a mere waste of time! Surely my pains were not to be thrown away!

They found scraps of blankets, bits of human hair, pieces of rope, Chinese coins, and other odds and ends. Their findings resembled, Hedin decided, a rubbish heap, but one rich in potential for archeologists. They also found wooden friezes of images of Buddha and of flowers and ornaments. In three places entire door frames remained upright. One door actually stood ajar, as if it had just been left open by the last inhabitant to leave the ancient city, although Hedin speculated that that must have happened some fifteen hundred years before.

He offered a prize to the first man to find human writing in any form. After a few days, one of the men came upon a wooden board with inscriptions written in India ink that were still sharp and clear after lying buried for centuries. But Hedin could not identify the mysterious markings. He knew they were neither Arabic, Chinese, Mongolian, nor Tibetan (scholars in Europe later established that they were in Kharosti, a syllabic writing system used in northwestern India before about A.D. 500). A while later, a strip of paper with Chinese ideographs was found in the same location under two feet of sand and dust. Altogether, some 200 such strips were uncovered, along with forty-two inscribed wooden tablets. Two writing brushes, of the kind the Chinese use to this day, were also found.

Hedin realized the importance of these discoveries, even if he was unable to decipher their content, and he felt a sense of triumph:

> These fragmentary documents would now put the crown upon my toilsome investigations, the object of my study and attention for so many years. . . . I held in my hands the story of a bygone age. I hoped to re-awaken it to life. . . . I would not have exchanged these scraps of torn and dirty letters for untold gold.

The group remained only six days in the deserted city. As had happened the year before, the hot weather loomed and they had to escape from the absolutely waterless desert before it was too late. They labored from first light to the fall of darkness, excavating sites and uncovering documents on wood and paper, coins, jewelry, and other artifacts. They were able, however, to explore only a small number of the half-buried buildings. On March 9 they retreated south to Charkhlik, an oasis on the southern branch of the Silk Road, with their precious load of artifacts. There Hedin packed all the specimens, totaling eight camel loads. These were sent off in a caravan to Kashgar and from there back to Stockholm.

Hedin reorganized his remaining men and animals and laid in stores enough to last ten months, preparing to begin his long-postponed "sporting feat:" a visit to Lhasa. He sent two of his men to locate a lama who could speak Tibetan. They returned with a holy man, Shereb Lama, from Urga, the capital of Mongolia. He had studied in Lhasa and wanted to return there. He agreed to accompany Hedin and his group. They turned south and climbed through the Kunlun Mountains to the Tibetan plateau and passed through country they had visited the year before.

After several weeks Hedin decided that the large caravan had approached as close to the capital as they dared, and only a small party could safely continue on. He donned his disguise:

> Seated outdoors before the fire, I underwent treatment by Shagdur and Shereb Lama. The former shaved my head, and even my moustache, till I was as smooth as a billiard-ball; the latter rubbed a mixture of fat, soot, and brown pigment into me. I became almost frightened at the sight of myself in my polished watch case, my only mirror. We were in high spirits, laughing and chatting like schoolboys.

Accompanied only by Shereb Lama and two of the Mongols, he embarked on his "wild ride" to the Tibetan capital.

> Off to Lhasa! Whether we succeeded or not, the experience would be something extraordinary. If successful, we would see the Holy City, unvisited by Europeans since [Régis-Evariste] Huc and [Jo-

seph] Gabet in 1846, or 54 years before. And if we failed, we should be entirely at the mercy of the Tibetans, becoming their prisoners, with no inkling of how that captivity might end.

They traveled in incessant rain at altitudes above 16,000 feet. Having encountered groups of Tibetans, they began to suspect that their approach toward Lhasa had been reported to the Tibetan authorities in Lhasa. A cat-and-mouse game ensued with groups of Tibetans who tried to persuade them, or frighten them, into turning back. Finally, they met a large group of armed men who were accompanying the governor of the province they were passing through, an official called the Kamba Bombo, who told Hedin he must turn back. When Hedin protested, the Kamba Bombo politely but firmly insisted: "No; not one step further toward Lhasa. That would cost your heads—and mine, too. I do my duty. I get orders from the Dalai Lama."

Hedin was impressed by the Tibetan's firm but polite manner. His experience was in sharp contrast to the encounter Arnold Henry Savage Landor had written he had with the Tibetans a few years earlier. Hedin wrote about the Tibetans in a manner very different from Landor.

> In those days it was impossible for a European to travel to Lhasa. Przhevalsky, Bonvalot, De Rhins, Rockhill, Littledale, all had met with the same insurmountable resistance. Two years later, Lord Curzon sent his Anglo-Indian army to Lhasa. It opened the southern road to the Holy City by force, and 4,000 Tibetans were killed. That was called war. But the Tibetans had asked for nothing but to be left in peace. When the Tibetans under the Kamba Bombo outwitted me, they too used peremptory means, but no violence, and they made their will effective without staining their hands with blood. On the contrary, they treated me with the utmost consideration. As for myself, I had the satisfaction of going to the limit of the adventure without capitulating until the opposition proved absolutely unconquerable.

Thwarted, however politely, in his attempt to reach Lhasa, Hedin decided to travel across Tibet to the west, then south to India. He spent three months traveling, escorted by large contingents of Tibetan soldiers. His hosts were friendly, even hospitable, but uniformly firm

A typical Hedin encampment in Tibet during his third Asian expedition.
Hedin departed Leh with fifty-eight horses and thirty-six mules and arrived in
Shigatse six months later with six horses and one mule. The rest had died of
exhaustion and exposure.

in preventing him from approaching Lhasa. He reached India in time
for Christmas, and spent three months in that country as a guest of
the Viceroy, Lord Curzon, who became a friend and admirer. On June
27, 1902, he arrived back in Stockholm. During three years in Europe, he sorted out all the material collected in Asia and produced a
six-volume scholarly compilation of his discoveries and observations as
well as a two-volume popular account entitled *Central Asia and Tibet*.

On October 16, 1905, Hedin again set out for Asia on his third,
and last, great journey of exploration. This time the objective was
Tibet, the area of Central Asia that offered the greatest opportunities
for geographical exploration. He traveled overland through the Russian Caucasus and Teheran to India from where he proposed to launch
his expedition. But this undertaking was opposed by the Tibetans
and the Chinese. As for the British, he had been able to win the support
of Lord Minto, the Viceroy who had just replaced Curzon, but John
Morley, the Secretary of State for India, was against his entering Tibet.

Sven Hedin striking a rather heroic-looking pose with his staff on his third Asian expedition. He spent two years exploring Tibet to fill in the "white spaces" on maps of the region.

Hedin obtained a passport for Chinese Turkestan and announced he was traveling from India north to Kashgar in Chinese Turkestan, but then turned abruptly east through Ladakh and entered Tibet. He traveled with his caravan across the Chang Tang, the great Tibetan Sea of Grass, on the northern Tibetan tableland. He made for Shigatse, the town near the monastery of the Panchen Lama who ranked second in the Tibetan hierarchy to the Dalai Lama. The trip from Leh in Ladakh to Shigatse took six months and was the brutal physical ordeal that characterized Hedin's explorations. For the first eighty-one days they encountered not one human being. Temperatures often reached -25° F. Having departed Leh with a caravan of fifty-eight horses and thirty-six mules, he arrived in Shigatse with six horses and one mule; all the rest had succumbed to exhaustion and exposure. The remaining horses would also soon die of exhaustion.

To Hedin's surprise, in Shigatse he was received cordially by the Panchen Lama who gave him the run of the area. The Dalai Lama had fled Tibet when the Younghusband mission entered the country three years earlier, and was still away. The Panchen Lama was therefore the supreme ruler in the country. Hedin stayed in Shigatse several months. He was able to observe the spring festival activities (the same festivities that Alexandra David-Neel would observe in Lhasa several years later).

Despite the head lama's cordial patronage, the presence of a foreigner for so long in the second city of the hermit kingdom aroused resentment among the Tibetans, and Hedin decided to move on. He was escorted by Tibetans and warned he could not go to Lhasa, but otherwise could travel pretty much as he pleased. But now, several years after his aborted "wild ride" to the Tibetan capital, his intentions had changed:

> The longing I had, in 1901, to penetrate the Holy City in disguise, was completely gone. The charm of the unknown had passed. A whole corps of officers, and thousands of Tommy Atkinses, had been there with the Younghusband and [Major] General [James] Macdonald expedition only three years before.

But he did spend two years traveling around Tibet, exploring the "white spaces" on his maps that were always objects of fascination to him. This journey was perhaps the most fruitful of the three in terms of geographic exploration. He explored and mapped in detail the great area he called the Trans-Himalaya. He reached the sources of the Indus, the Sutlej, and the Brahmaputra rivers—three of the great rivers of South Asia—and pinpointed with precision their location. But he found no more forgotten ancient cities. A three-volume account of this journey is entitled *Trans-Himalaya*.

After his return from his third journey of exploration, Hedin spent the next several years preparing, with the help of specialists, detailed and lengthy scientific reports of his discoveries and observations. In 1916 he spent seven months traveling through the Middle East, but it was not until in 1926 that he returned to Asia. Lufthansa, the German airline, wanted to survey a possible air route from Berlin to Peking through western China and asked Hedin to lead a group of scientists to explore the various possibilities. The air connection was never established, but Hedin obtained funds to continue scientific explorations in western China with a large group of distinguished Chinese and European specialists. Between 1926 and 1935 the group spent eight years in the field; their reports have totaled more than fifty published volumes.

Hedin's later life was marked by political controversy. He held strong political views which he formed early in life and never changed. He greatly admired Germany, perhaps as a result of his early years of study in Berlin. He supported Germany in World War I and became an early supporter of the Nazi regime in the 1930s, although his ancestry, as he proclaimed with pride, was one-sixteenth Jewish. He was suspicious of Russia and its designs on Scandinavia, although he had sought and received the Tsar's support for his explorations. After a visit to the Soviet Union in 1923, he wrote sympathetically of the Soviet regime and urged that Sweden extend diplomatic recognition. He considered Britain a symbol of rapacious imperialism, which he considered evil, yet he became very friendly with Lord Curzon, the most imperialistic of all British viceroys in India. He supported the Kuomintang regime of Chiang Kai-shek in China and wrote a laudatory biography of the Generalissimo.

An unflattering portrait of Hedin is drawn by Charles Allen in *A Mountain in Tibet*, an account of European attempts to explore Tibet during the 300 years between the early 1600s to the early 1900s. Allen's focus therefore is on Hedin's Tibetan explorations rather than his discoveries in the Tarim Basin. In Allen's account, the explorer's tenacity and singleness of purpose become an almost pathological fixation, driven in part by a consuming desire for public adulation. He is described as ruthless and often brutal in pursuing his objectives and unwilling to acknowledge the accomplishments of other explorers. Some of his claims of geographic discoveries in Tibet are challenged. Allen focuses particularly on the third journey of exploration in Tibet, and he provides an excellent account of Hedin's disputes with the Royal Geographical Society in Britain over some of his claims of discovery.

Unfortunately, only two chapters of an entire book are devoted to Hedin, more space than to any of the other explorers, but not enough

The ruins of a house at Lou-Lan surrounded by absolutely lifeless desert. Once a thriving Silk Road oasis, Lou-Lan was abandoned in the 4th century A.D. and its location subsequently forgotten until discovered by Sven Hedin.

to present his achievements in full. Allen's interpretation of Hedin's personality and character may be open to question, but his book is obviously well researched. His brief treatment only underscores the need for a complete and balanced biography of Hedin in English.

Hedin never married. During remarks he made at a banquet given in his honor in Moscow in 1923, and later published in his book *Peking to Moscow*, he explained:

> It might interest the ladies present why I am not married. I have been in love many times, but Asia remained my bride. She has held me captive in her cold embrace, and out of jealousy would never let me love any other. And I have been faithful to her, that is certain.

Sven Hedin left Asia for the last time in 1935. He died in Stockholm in 1952.

The buried cities along the Silk Road were not the most significant of Hedin's many discoveries during his years of exploration in Central Asia, but they were the most dramatic. They were also significant enough to attract, within a few years of their discovery, several well-equipped archeological expeditions. It remained for these expeditions, notably those by Sir Aurel Stein, to reveal the story behind these mysterious ruins. Hedin's city of Takla Makan became known to Stein as Dandan Oilik, or "place of the houses of ivory," a name given it by local tribesmen who visited the place in the hope of finding buried treasure (a hope never realized). Stein found that the ruins had unfortunately been damaged by the treasure seekers, but his systematic excavations nevertheless revealed much about the history of Dandan Oilik. It had flourished for centuries with a mixed population drawn from China, South Asia, and the Middle East as a way-stop on the southern branch of the Silk Road.

Stein found ruins of Buddhist temples with frescoes dating from the centuries preceding the invasion of Central Asia by the Muslims in the eighth century A.D. The frescoes and paintings he uncovered were of the Greco-Buddhist style that flourished in northwestern India in the early years of the Christian era—the Gandhara style that incorporated Greek influences dating back to the invasion of Alexander the Great. Stein uncovered packages of paper manuscripts written in an early Indian Brahmi script. Chinese coins found at the site and other evidence indicated clearly that it had been abandoned late in the eighth century A.D. A rich, flourishing city with orchards watered by extensive irrigation systems, had gradually succumbed to the encroaching desert. For more than a millennium it had been forgotten, except for a few local treasure hunters.

The strips of paper Hedin found among the ruins he discovered in the "Desert of Lop" date from the third century A.D. and are the oldest paper ever discovered. Interestingly, they do not contain accounts of great historical events but, rather, mundane recordings of routine commercial transactions. They were found in what apparently was the stable of the house of a wealthy Chinese merchant who carried on trade along the Silk Road. Along with the inscriptions on the wooden tablets Hedin's men had found at the same location, they were sufficient to reveal what Hedin had discovered.

He had come upon the ancient, semi-legendary kingdom of Lou-Lan that had flourished during the centuries just before and after the birth of Christ. It lay between China of the Han dynasty and the feared Huns to the northwest. China began to have contact with Lou-Lan during the second century B.C., and the city became a frontier settlement on the Silk Road. Around A.D. 70 the kingdom was absorbed by China under the Han dynasty.

Lou-Lan stood beside the ancient lake of Lop Nor. When Hedin came upon its ruins, they lay in a desert utterly devoid of life of any kind. But at the time of the birth of Christ, Lou-Lan had apparently supported a large population. The records Hedin found mention "seed-corn banks," "armies," and "numerous farms." During the second and third centuries A.D. the Chinese maintained a large garrison, because Lou-Lan was a frontier post guarding the Celestial Empire against the predatory nomadic tribes to the west. There had been extensive agriculture supported by a sophisticated irrigation system. Travelers along the Silk Road stopped in its inns, peasants brought their goods to be sold in its markets, soldiers of the garrison thronged its streets and spent their pay in its shops. At times the city must have been crowded with a polyglot population from far and near.

When Hedin stood in the partially excavated ruins of a temple and looked at the other ruins around him, he imagined to himself how the scene must have looked nearly two thousand years earlier:

> This little temple, with its tasteful and minute ornamentation, must have been a perfect gem of artistic construction. I can imagine how beautiful a spot it was—the temple, with its elegant facade, which was probably painted as well as adorned with wood carvings, embowered amid shady poplar groves, with an arm of the lake touching it, and the green or yellow reed-beds spread all round it, except where they were interrupted by patches of cultivated ground irrigated by the water of the winding canals! Round about it were the scattered villages, their clay towers peeping over the tops of the woods. . . . Southward stretched far and wide the bluish-green waters of Lop Nor, set about with forest groves, and bordered by immense expanses of reeds and sedge, swarming with fish, wild duck, and wild geese. . . . At the present day, one could nowhere find in that part of Asia houses decorated with such tasteful and artistic feeling as these were.

The scene had changed, and now "the country resembled a cemetery." As the Han dynasty declined and fell, Chinese control of the western desert lands weakened. The besieging barbarians drew an ever-tightening ring around the city. Some of Hedin's recovered documents spoke of the "hooting of the owls," the clamor of combat against the nomads who were drawing nearer and nearer. The Chinese finally withdrew altogether early in the fourth century, and the nomads moved in. The canals of the irrigation system silted up, and the lush fields grew sere. Later, the Tarim River shifted its course to empty into new lakes further south. The ancient lake dried up, the forest and reed beds died, and Lou-Lan was abandoned to the desert. Although its existence continued to be known from Chinese annals, its location became lost in the mists of time until Hedin's discovery of the mysterious ruins in the dry desert lake bed.

Hedin was a geographer, not an archeologist, but he felt a special pride in his discovery of the long-lost Lou-Lan. Writing in the 1920s, he summed up his feelings:

> To this day I like to dream of its past greatness and its glamour. . . . not a single one of our ancient Swedish rune-stones is older than the fragile wooden staffs and paper fragments I found in Lou-Lan. When Marco Polo made his famous journey through Asia in 1274, the sleeping city had already lain a thousand years unknown and forgotten in the desert. And after the great Venetian's journey, it was to slumber 650 years more before the ghosts of its past were roused to life, and their ancient documents and letters made to shed new light on bygone days and mysterious human fates.

Sven Hedin was a complex personality whose remarkable accomplishments are overshadowed by his vigorous espousal of extreme political views. When he died, he was almost totally forgotten, and he is little known today except among a handful of scholars and specialists. He was, nevertheless, one of the great explorers of modern times and perhaps the greatest explorer of Central Asia and Tibet. His extensive, detailed scientific writings became a key source for the study of the historical and cultural geography of Central Asia and Tibet.

Bibliography

Sven Hedin was a prolific author, and his collected writings based upon his explorations and travels are voluminous. They can be divided into two categories: the scientific treatises, and the more popular accounts intended for general audiences. The following list includes just a few titles from the latter category that recount his early journeys of exploration. Only one biography of Hedin has been published in English.

Allen, Charles. *A Mountain in Tibet.* London: Andre Deutsch, 1982. An entertaining account of British exploration of the Himalayas in the 19th century by the author of *Plain Tales of the Raj.* The focus is on the search for the holy Hindu mountain, Mount Kailas.

Hedin, Sven. *A Conquest of Tibet.* London: Macmillan, 1935. A popularly written account of the author's expedition into Tibet.

   Central Asia and Tibet. 2 vols. New York: Charles Scribners Sons, 1903. The account for general readers of Hedin's second expedition.

   My Life as an Explorer. Garden City, N.Y.: Garden City Publishing Co., 1925. A brief account for general readers of the author's first three Asian expeditions.

   Through Asia. 2 vols. London: Methuen, 1898. A general interest account of the first Asian expedition.

   Trans-Himalaya. 3 vols. London: Macmillan, 1909. An account for general readers of the third Asian expedition.

Hopkirk, Peter. *Foreign Devils on the Silk Road.* London: John Murray, 1980. An entertaining account, by the author of *The Great Game,* of early discoveries in Central Asia. Includes chapters on Sven Hedin and Aurel Stein.

Kish, George. *To the Heart of Asia.* Ann Arbor: University of Michigan Press, 1984. A disappointing biography of Hedin, written in a pedantic and pedestrian style, which focuses on his work as a geographer.

Kohlenberg, Karl. *Sven Hedin: Vorstoss nach Innerasia.* Balve/Sauerland: Engelbert, 1976.

Selander, Sten. *Sven Hedin. En Aventyrsberattelse.* Stockholm: Bonnier, 1957.

Wennerholm, Eric. *Sven Hedin. En Biografi.* Stockholm: Bonnier, 1978.

3

Arnold Henry Savage Landor

Latter-day Munchausen?

A. Henry Savage Landor,
Nothing lacked except for candour.

Hilaire Belloc

In 1898, when Sven Hedin's two-volume account of his first Asian
journey of exploration, entitled *Through Asia*, appeared in print, another book, also in two volumes, describing another Asian journey of
exploration, was also published. It carried a title much longer and more
provocative than Hedin's: *In the Forbidden Land: An Account of a Journey in Tibet, Capture by the Tibetan Authorities, Imprisonment, Torture,
and Ultimate Release.* The author was Arnold Henry Savage Landor.

Landor wanted to be known, first and foremost, as an explorer,
although he sometimes described himself as "an artist and traveler."
His autobiography, which was published just three months before he
died in 1924, was entitled *Everywhere: The Memoirs of an Explorer.* It
was perhaps a more appropriate title than he realized.

During the course of a remarkable life, Landor had certainly traveled to many places, and it is possible that some of them had never
before been visited by a European, as he wanted people to believe. But
he certainly had not been everywhere, and it is open to question whether
he could legitimately lay claim to being an explorer. So the title he

*Henry Savage Landor in his traveling attire,
including his trademark straw boater.*

chose for his life story appropriately reflects the nature of the man himself in that it was transparently an exaggeration of the truth. Moreover, some of the contents obviously must be discounted as exaggerations, if not outright untruths, as was suggested in some of the reviews. But the intriguing and difficult question about the autobiography—and all other writings by Landor—is "how much exaggeration and where?"

Landor wrote more than a dozen books, each a long and detailed account of a journey he had made to some remote corner of the world. When he died, lengthy obituaries appeared in the London *Times* and the *New York Times*. A long entry was included in *Who Was Who*. All suggested a life of astonishing derring-do and accomplishment (although the London *Times* was careful to say that Landor "claimed" to have done this and that).

Landor comes through in all this as a kind of real-life Indiana Jones, embarking on ostensibly scientific expeditions to little-known parts of the world and thereby plunging into incredible adventures. But even during his lifetime many doubts were expressed, by reviewers of his books and others, about the veracity of some of his claims of what he saw and did on his travels. Since he always traveled alone, except for locally recruited porters and guides, there are no other accounts of his journeys against which his claims could be checked.

Born on June 2, 1865, in Florence, Italy, he was the grandson of Walter Savage Landor (1775–1864), the English poet and writer who spent his last years in Italy. Henry's mother, whom he deeply loved, was Italian, and both English and Italian were spoken at home (he later wrote that he did not learn to speak English until he was six or seven years old). Although he spent much of his life traveling, he always had a home in or near Florence. For a time, he studied engineering and mathematics at a technical institute in Florence. But because he displayed some artistic talent, he was permitted to put aside his technical studies, which he hated, in order to study painting with an Irish artist resident in Florence. At about the same time, he became "deeply entranced" by a book about Samuel Baker's explorations on the Nile:

> Oh, how I was longing to be a man and do like Sir Samuel, and go
> and see new countries and meet savages and wild beasts. Little did
> I know at that time that in the way of adventure, I should have in
> later years enough to fill the lives of twenty men.

When he was fifteen, Landor began the travels that were to take him around the world several times. He went first to England to visit relatives. Although he was a British subject, he had never visited England. But he soon grew restless and moved to Paris to study art. He wandered on to Spain, Tangier, Malta, and Egypt (where he was disappointed in the Sphinx) before returning to Britain briefly. Then, off to the United States and Canada where, he later wrote, he was disappointed with the Statue of Liberty but impressed by Niagara Falls. As was his habit throughout his life, he claimed that in America he met a crowd of celebrities. He supposedly had a "private audience" with President Benjamin Harrison and mingled with such personalities as actress Lillie Langtry (whom he found "a trifle plump"), the granddaughter of Abraham Lincoln, and a very young William Randolph Hearst.

Still restless, he crossed the continent to Vancouver and took ship to Japan where he stayed for more than a year, notably exploring the northern island of Hokkaido. He moved on to Korea, China, and Australia, and by 1892 was back in Europe. He quickly produced two books about his Asian travels which, he said, caused "a sensation." At Balmoral Castle Queen Victoria listened "entranced" to his account of his travels on Hokkaido. The Royal Geographical Society invited him to give a lecture to its members about his travels. Later, Landor's relations with the Society would become strained when the Society questioned some of the claims made in his later books, but he remained a Fellow until he died in 1924.

In 1897 Landor embarked on the journey that would make him famous. He had decided to visit Tibet and, more specifically, Lhasa, the capital of the "forbidden land." His account of this journey, however, would raise doubts about his truthfulness that would plague him for the rest of his life.

Tibet was not a surprising choice for someone who had dreamed since childhood of being an explorer. In the latter half of the last decade of the 19th century it was one of the last places in the world, aside from the two uninhabited polar regions, that still held the lure of the remote, the unexplored, the unknown. Though the first Western contact with Tibet had occurred as early as 1627, subsequent contacts were few and far between. The last Europeans to succeed in reaching Lhasa had been two French priests in 1846. The last known visit by an Englishman had occurred in 1811. But despite this absence of contact, Tibet was very much a topic of discussion in Britain in the 1890s because of the "Great Game" being played between Russia and Britain in Central Asia (see Chapter 4). Landor undoubtedly heard and read about it and, if he wanted to become known as an explorer, there was no better spot on Earth with which to have his name associated than the "forbidden land."

Landor left three published accounts of his journey to Tibet. The longest and most detailed appeared in the two-volume work published in 1898 soon after his return. An abridged one-volume version of that book appeared in 1904, probably prompted by the attention being given to the Younghusband mission to Tibet, then in progress (it was reissued, with some slight additional text, as *An Explorer's Adventures in Tibet* in 1910, the same year Younghusband brought out his own account). Finally, an even briefer description appeared in Landor's autobiography.

The first two do not always agree with the autobiography. For example, in the 1898 account Landor says he originally planned to travel through Russia and enter Tibet from the north, but his plans ran into difficulties: he had to change them and travel via India, thus entering from the south. In the autobiography, however, he does not mention any plans to travel through Russia and gives the impression that he had always planned to travel via India. "It was, in my days, deemed impossible to penetrate into Tibet from the south through India," he wrote with obviously more than a touch of pride in his ability to do the impossible.

The proposed journey was looked upon with favor by practically no one except Landor himself. The Tibetans for decades had made known their policy of keeping their borders closed to foreigners. China was the ostensible suzerain of Tibet, but the increasingly feeble Ching dynasty of the Manchus was unable to exercise any real control. Nevertheless, China cooperated with the Tibetans who used the fiction of Chinese control to fend off unwanted incursions by foreigners by saying Chinese permission was needed to enter the country.

The British authorities in India, mindful that the complicated relationship that had been carried on with Russia in Central Asia for decades now focused increasingly on Tibet, did not want a rambunctious private traveler barging into such a delicate situation. However, they did not actually prevent him from proceeding across the border, and Landor claimed that Lord Salisbury, the Prime Minister, "was interested in the venture."

Landor entered India at Bombay and traveled north by rail to the Kumaon area in the foothills of the Himalayas southwest of Nepal. He spent some weeks in Naini Tal and Almora, two British hill stations, preparing for his journey. In Almora he hired a former Indian policeman named Chanden Sing to serve as his personal valet. Sing turned

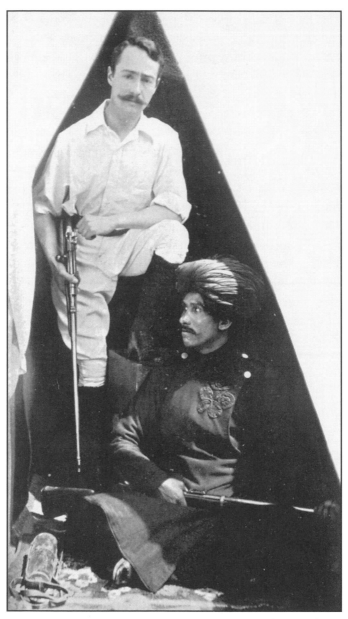

*Landor "in camp" with his faithful servant Chanden Singh.
The spotless condition of their clothes and tent suggests that the picture
was snapped in a photographer's studio rather than a remote
mountain or jungle camp.*

out to be one of the two most faithful of Landor's locally hired men who stayed with him through thick and thin to the end of the Tibetan adventure.

In Gyarbang Landor recruited thirty porters with the help of Dr. H. Wilson, a Methodist missionary there, who accompanied him during the first stage of his foray into Tibet. In particular, he hired the second of his two most faithful servants, a leper named Mansing who is sometimes described as a "coolie" and sometimes as his bearer's bearer. Despite his affliction, Mansing was "as strong as an ox," the strongest of all Landor's porters. He had at one time been a famous brigand in the area around Lhasa and had reportedly killed many people. Landor only later came to realize what a stalwart follower he had hired in Mansing.

While still in India, Landor learned that his proposed journey, which he had tried to keep secret, had been divulged to the Tibetan authorities. Thereafter, the story of his Tibetan adventure is an account of the Tibetans' efforts to capture him or frighten him enough to cause him to turn back, and his attempts to avoid capture and keep going:

> The Jong Pen of Taklakot [the local Tibetan governor just over the border], on hearing of my proposed visit, sent threats that he would cut off my head and confiscate the land of any man who came in my employ, besides menaces of "flogging" and "beheading" anyone caught with me. Personally, I paid little attention to these intimidations.

Ascending at one point to an altitude of 22,000 feet as they crossed the border, Landor and his party entered Tibet sometime in late June. They soon encountered groups of Tibetans, some of them brigands and in particular one group of thirty mounted armed men. Landor's companions became frightened and refused to go any further, so in the face of constant threats from the armed Tibetans, the group turned and headed back towards India. But Landor was determined to reach Lhasa, and he told Dr. Wilson that he was doubling back into Tibet and proposed to do so alone.

> "No, no, it is impossible, Mr. Landor," cried the doctor with tears in his eyes. "That must mean death to any one attempting it."
> I told him I was quite determined.

The poor doctor was dumbfounded. He knew that it was useless to try to dissuade me. I went into the tent to rearrange and reduce my baggage, making a load small enough to carry on my back, in addition to the daily kit and instruments.

As it turned out, Landor went back accompanied by five of his porters who forgot their fear of the Tibetans, as well as Chanden Sing and Mansing. Dr. Wilson and the others took what baggage could not be carried back to Gyarbang. Landor and his small party departed in the middle of the night during a storm to elude detection by any Tibetans who might be watching:

> We put out our hurricane lantern, and at 2 A.M., when the gale was raging at its height, driving the grit and snow like spikes into our faces; when the wind and cold seemed to penetrate with biting force into the marrow of our bones, when, as it seemed, all the gods were giving vent to their anger by putting every obstacle in our way, a handful of silent men, half frozen and staggering, left the camp to face the blizzard.

The parting was dramatically moving:

> "The dangers of your journey," whispered Dr. Wilson, "are so great and so numerous that God alone can guide you through. When I think of the cold, hunger and hardships you will have to endure, I can but tremble for you."
> "Good-bye, doctor," said I, deeply moved.
> "Good-bye," he repeated, "good—" and his voice failed him.

Their immediate goal was a sacred lake called Manasarowar just across the border in western Tibet. The small group again encountered hostile Tibetans, and they began to travel at night and hide by day:

> During our night marches, up and down mountain ranges of considerable height, we naturally had adventures and escapes far too numerous to relate here in detail and I shall not give a full description of each march on account of the unavoidable monotony such a narrative would entail. In constant storms of grit and snow, we crossed range after range, traveling by night and hiding by day, camping at very great altitudes and undergoing considerable privations.

Out of food and subsisting for a considerable time on stew made of nettles, they succeeded in reaching Lake Manasarowar where supplies could be purchased. Having reached the lake, Landor was about one hundred miles, as the crow flies, from Almora in British India whence he had departed some weeks before. He was about six times that distance from Lhasa, much of it every bit as difficult as the territory he had already covered.

Landor deceived the Tibetans in the towns around the lake into thinking he was a "Hindoo doctor" on a pilgrimage to holy places. Lake Manasarowar and a mountain to its immediate northwest, Mount Kailas, are the holiest places of pilgrimage for Hindus in India. The lake, with a circumference of forty-five miles, is large enough to appear to be an inland sea. Pious pilgrims bathe in its waters to wash away their sins. It lies in the Tibetan chang-tang, or sea of grass, the heart of pastoral life in Tibet. The area is green and temperate during the summer months with plenty of animal and bird life. Around the lake shore lie several villages and towns. The lake region is therefore a place to replenish supplies after the mountain crossing from India.

Mount Kailas, at 21,850 feet, is not one of the giant peaks of the Himalayas. Its importance lies in its being regarded in Hindu mythology as the Shivalaya, or Abode of Shiva, the Destroyer who is one of the Hindu trinity of gods, along with Brahma, the Creator, and Vishnu, the Preserver. Shiva is thought to live on Mount Kailas with his consort, Parvati, spending his time in meditation, singing hymns, and performing his cosmic dance. Pilgrims spend several days making a complete circuit of the mountain. The lake and the mountain have been the goals of devout pilgrims from India for millennia since before the dawn of history in the subcontinent. For Landor to assume the guise of a "Hindoo doctor" on a pilgrimage—if he could successfully pull it off—therefore was a logical stratagem. Although he had been in India only a short time, he claimed that by the time of his arrival at the lake, he could speak Hindustani, the lingua franca of northern India, with fluency and that he conversed with his Indian porters in that language.

After resting and laying in much-needed supplies, Landor and his party pushed on, meeting groups of Tibetans from time to time. Those who appeared threatening, Landor faced down by the sheer force of his overpowering personality or, at times, by wreaking terrible havoc with his rifle-butt.

Along the way, they happened upon the source of the Brahmaputra River which Landor apparently immediately recognized as the source of the mighty river, although it was "a little rivulet, hardly six inches wide." He wrote,

> I must confess that I felt somewhat proud to be the first European who had ever reached these sources, and there was a certain child-ish delight in standing over this sacred stream, which, of such im-mense width lower down, could here be spanned by a man stand-ing with legs slightly apart.

The remaining five porters again became frightened and refused to go further. Landor decided there was no use trying to keep them by force and discharged them by giving them their pay. They returned to India, carrying with them much of his baggage. His party, now re-duced to three, himself and his two "faithfuls," went on.

Landor's supplies were now carried on two yaks he had purchased. While crossing a river, one of the animals lost its pack saddle with most of the food supplies, including all of the tinned provisions. This was a major setback, but Landor resolutely went on, despite his now-bleak prospects:

> Our situation can be summed up in a few words. We were now in the center of Tibet, with no food of any kind, no clothes to speak of, no boots or shoes, except those we wore, which were falling to pieces. What little ammunition I had left could not be relied upon, owing to its having been in the water on several occasions; and round us we had nothing but enemies.

But they were finally nearing the Sacred City and Landor began to think about what he would do when he reached his goal:

> I intended proceeding, dressed as a European, until within a few miles of Lhassa. Then I would leave my two men concealed in some secluded spot, and assuming a disguise, I would penetrate alone during the night into the city. . . . To avoid betraying myself by my inability to speak Tibetan fluently, I thought of pretending to be deaf and dumb.

They went on "hungry, worn out, with our feet lacerated." They ate absolutely nothing for several days. Landor felt sorry for his two companions who were "in a dreadful condition." But they remained steadfast:

"Never mind if we suffer or even die," said the poor fellows, when I expressed my sympathy for them. "We will follow you as long as we have strength to move, and we will stand by you, no matter what happens."

Something soon did happen. They came upon a group of Tibetans who acted very friendly and sold them a large quantity of provisions. In an unguarded moment, however, Landor was suddenly seized from behind by several Tibetans and thrown face down on the ground. But the doughty explorer was not to be easily subdued:

I was surrounded by some thirty men, who attacked me from every side, and clinging to me with all their might, succeeded in grabbing again my arms, legs and head. Weak as I was, they knocked me down three more times, but each time I regained my feet. I fought to the bitter end with my fists, feet, head, and teeth each time that I got one hand or leg free from their clutches, hitting right and left at any part where I could to disable my opponents. . . . I was able to hold my own against them for some twenty minutes.

He and his companions were finally taken prisoner, and their ordeal at the hands of the Tibetans began. They were tied with ropes, their pockets and their nearby camp were rifled of everything of value. They were then dragged to the nearby settlement.

The three were thrown into separate tents, but before they parted, Landor admonished his men, "do not let them see that you suffer." He resolved to keep a very stiff upper lip, no matter what: "I had on many previous occasions found that nothing carries one further with Asiatics than to keep calm and cool." After lying alone for awhile, he was taken to a larger tent occupied by a crowd of lamas. He saw Chanden Sing taken into a separate compartment, heard him interrogated, then flogged—Landor counted fifty strokes. Later, he watched Chanden Sing receive more flogging with knotted leather thongs tipped with lead until the bearer was "bleeding all over."

Landor was interrogated by a Grand Lama, called the Pombo, about his maps and notebooks, but he refused to admit any wrong-doing. Suddenly, a rainstorm erupted. It brought the meeting to a sudden end, because, "in Tibet . . . a shower has a great effect upon the people, and even massacres have been known to be put off until the rain should cease."

Taken to another tent, Landor met a Tibetan army officer called the Rupun. It transpired that the Rupun had been sent from Lhasa with a large force of soldiers to arrest Landor. But he had become sympathetic to Landor because of Landor's show of stoic bravery, and they entered into an amazing conversation, considering the circumstances.

The Rupun treated Landor to a long disquisition on the Tibetan army, taking particular pains to teach him the names of the various ranks. Landor responded with a lecture about the British military. Landor does not say what language they used to conduct this exchange, but apparently they were able to converse on a quite sophisticated level without an interpreter.

They hit it off wonderfully, and Landor decided that "the Rupun possessed a good deal of dry humor." So friendly did they become that the Rupun returned surreptitiously in the middle of the night, loos-ened Landor's bonds, and told him to escape. But Landor refused, saying "I must stay with my men." The Rupun seemed "rather vexed," but treated Landor "with increasing respect and deference." So ended the first day of captivity.

The next day, Landor spent the morning "in a lively conversation with the soldiers, partly to divert my thoughts and partly to improve my knowledge of Tibetan." In the afternoon one of his interlocutors informed him with obvious relish that "before the sun goes down, you will be flogged, both your legs will be broken, they will burn out both your eyes, and then they will cut off your head." He was taken outside, his ropes exchanged for a pair of handcuffs, iron fetters were fastened on his ankles, and the two were joined by a heavy chain. He was hoisted onto a pony with a saddle "worthy of description." It had a very high back from which protruded five or six sharp iron spikes which dug into the small of his back. Mansing, still bound, was put bareback on another pony. Chanden Sing remained a prisoner in a small mud hut.

Surrounded by an armed escort, Landor and Mansing thus were galloped off across the country for miles.

> But for those awful spikes in the saddle, the ride would not have been so very bad, for the pony was a fine spirited animal, and the country around was curious and interesting.

It was so interesting that the ever-alert explorer carefully observed the nature of the surrounding topography as he rode. He noted that they were passing sand hills of increasing size.

> The circumstances under which I was now traveling did not permit me to ascertain the quality of the sand, or make any accurate investigations as to where the sand came from, but a glance around the country made me feel sure that it came from the South.

After a ride of several miles—"the spikes in the saddle were lacerating terribly the lower part of my spine"—they came to a hill crowned by a fortress and a large lamasery where the Pombo and his men waited by a tent. On the ground was a prism-shaped log. Landor was "torn roughly off the saddle," and made to stand upon one of the sharp edges of the log. His legs were spread as far apart as they could go, and he was bound to the log. The Pombo flourished a red-hot iron in his face, then held it "about an inch or two from my eyeballs, all but touching my nose." Landor's vision, especially his left eye, was affected by the intense heat. But the explorer did not flinch, and the Pombo finally threw down the iron.

> My position was not enviable as I stood with my legs wide apart, with my back, hands and legs bleeding, and seeing everything of a ghastly red tinge; amidst the deafening, maddening noise of gong, drum, cymbals and horn; insulted, spat upon by the crowd . . . all I was able to do was to remain calm and composed, and to watch with apparent unconcern the preparations for the next sufferings to be inflicted upon me.

The Pombo now took up a double-edged sword, measured one edge against Landor's neck, then twice brought it down with great force "disagreeably close to my neck." During the entire time, the crowd milling around the Pombo shouted, "kill him, kill him." But the Pombo then dropped the sword.

The execution was apparently postponed, and Landor reflected:

> The scene is one that I am not likely to forget, and I must say for the Tibetans that the whole affair was very picturesquely carried out. Even the ghastliest ceremonies may have their artistic side, and this one, performed with extra pomp and flourish, was really impressive.

Mansing was now tied to the log, and Landor's arms were pulled upward behind his body by a rope which was tied to a high post, leaving him half-suspended and "feeling as if . . . my limbs were getting pulled from their sockets." Mansing was also suspended by his arms from behind.

> The pain was at first intense, the tendons of the legs and arms being dreadfully strained, and the spinal column bent so as nearly to be broken in two. The shoulder blades forced into close contact, pressed the vertebrae inward, and caused excruciating pains along the lumbar vertebrae where the strain was greatest.

Again, rain began to fall, and the ceremony ended. The two prisoners were left outdoors tied to the log in the darkening downpour, and the second day of captivity ended.

The following morning the Pombo returned with his bloodthirsty entourage who were still shouting, "kill him, kill him." While Landor remained tied straddled to the log, his arms still suspended behind him, the Pombo spent several hours going through Landor's belongings—his sextant, photographic equipment, paint box, and so forth—and asking Landor about each item. The two engaged in a verbal fencing match about the items.

Among the articles was Landor's bath sponge which was dry and flattened. The Tibetans had never before seen a sponge.

> When their curiosity was appeased, they took it and threw it away. It fell near me in a small pool of water. This was a golden opportunity to frighten my jailers, and I addressed the sponge in English, and with any word that came into my mouth, pretending to utter

incantations. The attention of the Lamas and soldiers was naturally quickly drawn to this unusual behavior on my part; and they could not conceal their terror when, as I spoke louder and louder to the sponge, it gradually swelled to its normal size with the moisture it absorbed. The Tibetans, who at first could hardly believe their eyes at this incomprehensible occurrence, became so panic-stricken at what they believed to be an exhibition of my occult powers, that there was a general stampede in every direction.

For Landor, "in a way, all this was entertaining and, anyhow, it served to pass away the time."

In the afternoon one of the lamas tried to fire Landor's rifle, but he failed to shove home the bolt, and the rifle misfired, exploding in his face, which amused Landor. In late afternoon, the Pombo decided to release him from the log, "thus ending the most terrible twenty-four hours I have ever passed in my lifetime."

Now seated next to the Pombo in front of the tent, Landor watched a lengthy exhibition of horsemanship by the Tibetans. The Pombo then led Landor into the tent where he went into a hypnotic trance in which his head made "wild circular movements" and his body was contorted by "eccentric movements of his limbs." When he finally was brought out of it, he was pale and exhausted. Landor "told him that the dance was beautiful, but that I was very hungry." The prisoner was fed a delicious yak stew, and as night came on, the Pombo retired. Later, some lamas tried to force Landor to drink poisoned tea. He suspected foul play and spat it out. But he had swallowed a little, and he suffered excruciating pains in his stomach. Thus ended the third day.

The next day the Pombo resorted to "incantations and reference to occult science" to decide whether to cut off Landor's head. Three times his incantations, which employed parings from Landor's finger- and toenails, advised decapitation. But the Pombo noticed that Landor's hands were webbed between the fingers higher than usual. Since possessors of such fingers, according to the Tibetans (according to Landor), are impervious to harm, the Pombo decided Landor's life should be spared and he should be returned to India.

Landor and Mansing, neither one now forced to ride on a spiked saddle, were returned to where Chanden Sing was imprisoned. Landor and Chanden Sing, both still manacled, were put on ponies, while Mansing was made to walk, or rather dragged by a rope tied around his neck and pulled by a mounted Tibetan. In this fashion, accompanied by a numerous mounted guard, they spent the next five days traveling 178 miles. Along the way, Landor tried to disconcert his captors.

> At one point, having exhausted every means I could think of to inspire these ruffians with respect, I resorted to the performance of some ventriloquial feats, pretending to speak and to receive the answers from the summit of the cliff. The Tibetans were terror-stricken.

He also kept a journal of the journey back to India

> on a small piece of paper that had remained in my pocket when I had been searched by the Tibetans. My hands being rather supple, I was enabled to draw my right hand from out of its cuff, and, with a small piece of bone I had picked up as my pen, and my blood as ink, I drew brief cipher notes and a map of the whole route back. . . . I had to content myself with taking my bearings by the sun, the position of which I got fairly accurately by constantly watching the shadow projected by my body on the ground.

The three captives were in the last extremes of exhaustion and deprivation:

> All our property had been taken from us, and our clothes, in rags, were swarming with vermin. We were barefooted and almost naked.

The group traveled west, and they arrived finally at Lake Manasarowar. The three captives were unbound. Landor bathed in the lake and discovered a man whom he recognized as being from Gyarbang, the town across the border in India where Dr. Wilson lived. The man told him that Wilson had crossed into Tibet and was then in Taklakot. Landor, overjoyed, persuaded the man to return to Taklakot to tell Wilson that he was still alive.

The three prisoners were taken in hand again by their guards and marched off toward the Indian border. It became apparent to Landor that they were heading toward the Lumpiya Pass, one of the higher passes in the region and difficult to traverse even in mid-summer.

We were informed that we should be left at the point where the snows began, that the Tibetans would give us no food, no clothes, and no blankets, and that we should be abandoned to our own devices. This, needless to say, meant certain death.

Realizing that they could not hope to cross the pass in their condition, the three prisoners turned on their captors:

We three semi-corpses collected what little strength remained in us, and suddenly made an attack on the soldiers with stones; whereupon, incredible as it may seem, our cowardly guard turned tail and bolted!

Landor and his companions turned back towards Taklakot. After another brush with some cohorts of their old enemy the Jong Pen, they arrived at Taklakot where they were overjoyed to find Dr. Wilson. The missionary had heard reports that Landor and his party had been captured and beheaded, and he had crossed into Tibet to learn the truth of what had happened. He was accompanied by the Political Agent in Gyarbang, a man named Karak Singh. Upon learning that Landor was still alive and, moreover, near Taklakot, they persuaded the Jong Pen to allow Landor to come to the town by threatening that an army would be sent from India if he did not. The Jong Pen thereupon called off his men and permitted Landor and his companions to reach Taklakot.

Under Dr. Wilson's care, Landor and his companions recovered their strength. The group then crossed back into India to Gyarbang. Landor's condition was much improved, but he had by no means recovered from his ordeal:

The injuries to my spine were severe, and gave me much trouble. At times, the whole of my left side became as if paralysed. Besides, I invariably experienced the greatest difficulty in sitting down when I had been standing, and in getting up when I had been sitting down. Through the great strain they had undergone, my joints continued stiff and swollen, and remained so for months. I could see comparatively well with my right eye, but was unable to use the left at all.

"Our cowardly guard turned tail and bolted!"
One of several drawings done by Landor to illustrate In the Forbidden Land.

At Gyarbang, where he had recruited his porters, he recognized "several of the men who had betrayed me." He became incensed when he was told that they would not be punished and, despite his debilitated condition, took vigorous action:

> I took justice into my own hands, proceeding with a stout stick to teach some idea of faithfulness, whereupon the entire population of the village ran up to get the fellows out of my clutches . . . the fight became general until, ill as I was, and alone against some 150 men, I succeeded in routing them!

Landor also encountered Mr. Larkin, the Political Agent in Almora, who had been sent by the Government of India to conduct an inquiry. Larkin was headed for Tibet, and Landor accompanied him. They climbed through snow twelve feet deep to the crest of the Lippu Pass where they were to meet the Jong Pen of Taklakot, to whom Larkin had sent a letter about his inquiry. But the Jong Pen failed to show up, and the two Englishmen finally retreated back into India to Almora. Larkin filed a report, and Landor went by train to Bombay and from there by ship home to

Italy. He had been in Tibet a little over four months.

In October 1898, almost exactly a year after Landor's escape from Tibet, *In the Forbidden Land* was published, and it was a sensational success. The first printing was immediately succeeded by a second in November, and a new edition appeared the following May. Reviewers hailed the plucky explorer's bravery and fortitude in the face of such dangers. For example, *The Spectator*, a highly regarded British periodical, said in a long review:

> If we may regard this narrative as absolutely accurate—and Mr. Landor gives the most circumstantial details of place, name, altitude, physical conditions, state of commissariat, and so forth—then the record is one of the most remarkable statements of endurance and adventure recorded by any traveler in modern times.

A review in the *New York Times* said, "no one presumes to question the truthfulness of Mr. Landor's terrible story."

In 1899 Landor returned to the Himalayas for "a punitive expedition," presumably directed against all the Tibetans who had so mistreated him. He carried "weapons, ammunitions and explosives" and recruited a small army of hillmen on the India-Nepal border. But he was opposed by both the British and Nepalese governments, in addition to the Tibetans, and he was able to slip over the border into Tibet only briefly. Even so, he was able to give "a sound whipping to some of those who had previously behaved so infamously." Having thrashed them, he treated them to dinner, because "I ever made it a point to reward people after I had punished them as I did not want them to bear ill-feeling." He also claimed to have set a mountaineering record by reaching an altitude of 23,490 feet on Mount Lumpiya in Nepal. His account of this expedition, entitled *Tibet and Nepal*, was published in 1905.

Reviews of *Tibet and Nepal* were more divided than those for the previous book. *The Athenaeum* said, "it is difficult to take Mr. Landor seriously, and we find it impossible to follow his tour geographically." But another reviewer writing for *The Academy and Literature* magazine disagreed:

> Is he speaking the truth or lying? The present writer can only say that, for his part, he believes this author to be sincere and correct,

and one of the pluckiest, truest-hearted and most enterprising men in the world, to boot.

One cannot help wondering about the identity of the author of that unsigned review.

From 1899 until the eve of World War I, Landor dashed around the world without letup and wrote long books about each trip. He spent months at a time in Persia, the Philippines, China during the Boxer Rebellion, Equatorial Africa, the Matto Grosso, and the Andes Mountains.

During World War I he visited the Western Front, as well as Italy, the Balkans, and Greece. But after 1913 he did no more exploring and produced only one more book, his autobiography. He died at his home near Florence on December 26, 1924.

Sven Hedin somewhere in his writings on Tibet makes passing mention of Landor and calls *In the Forbidden Land* "an extraordinary Munchausen romance." A British official, serving in northern India when Landor entered Tibet, later said of Landor, "Oh! He is the common or garden variety of liar." Sir Francis Younghusband in a newspaper interview scoffed at Landor's "tales of cannibals in Tibet." Is *In the Forbidden Land* really just a product of a latter-day Baron von Munchausen, the notorious 18th-century German teller of tall tales?

Reaching an altitude of 22,000 feet in 1897, as Landor claimed to have done crossing into Tibet, would have been close to a mountaineering record at that time. It was an especially astonishing feat, because Landor carried no mountaineering equipment. His claimed record of 23,490 feet in 1899 is even more incredible. In his account of it, he says that on the day of the ascent he started at 5 A.M. from his camp somewhere below 15,000 feet, reached the summit, and returned to his camp by 6 P.M. An authenticated record of 23,360 feet was set in 1906 on Mount Trisul by Dr. Tom Longstaff, a record that stood for many years. Longstaff started at 4 A.M., climbed a total of 6,000 feet, as opposed to Landor's claim of more than 8,500 feet, and returned by 7 P.M. But perhaps most eye-popping in Landor's account is his description of the clothes he wore:

> Comparatively light boots of medium weight, such as I would wear in London on a wet day. In the way of clothing, I wore what I would wear on a stroll down Piccadilly—garments of the thinnest

tropical material, no underclothing, a straw hat, and a small bamboo stick in my hand.

Histories of mountaineering published in recent years do not dispute Landor's claim; they simply omit any mention of him.

In his autobiography, Landor defended himself against critics of his Tibetan journey and claimed his trip had been made for scientific purposes:

> My exploration was not intended to be a mere stunt. . . . if my scheme could be realized, I might solve many geographical problems of great importance—and all of which I eventually did solve.

Despite his claim of constantly making all sorts of scientific observations with sophisticated equipment as he traveled, Landor had absolutely no scientific training of any kind. He had never set foot in a university. His map of southern Tibet included in *In the Forbidden Land*, which he pointed to with great pride as revealing new-found geographical data, was, his critics scoffed, just an artistic copy of maps available from the Indian Geographical Survey.

But an appendix to *In the Forbidden Land* contains sworn statements made by seven people in India, as well as Landor himself, immediately after his return from Tibet. Dr. Wilson, Chanden Sing, Mansing, the political agent in Gyarbang, and others supported Landor's story to the extent that each had personal knowledge of it. Chanden Sing and Mansing both confirmed that they and Landor had been captured by the Tibetans and tortured. Dr. Wilson confirmed that he, Landor, and the others had reached 22,000 feet while crossing into Tibet and, moreover, that Landor was carrying a pack weighing sixty pounds at the time. There are several letters from some of these people written to Landor over subsequent months further confirming his story. The appendix also contains closeup photographs of Landor taken soon after his arrival back in India. They show a gaunt, sunken-eyed man who has from all appearances undergone a harrowing physical trial. The photographs are printed alongside similar photographs of Landor taken just prior to his departure on the trip, and the contrast, as obviously intended, is striking. There are sworn statements from attendants at the missionary hospital in

*Before-and-after photographs showing the effects of Landor's ordeal in Tibet.
The photographs on the left was taken in February 1897, and those
on the right the following October.*

India where Landor and his companions were first treated, attesting to the
severity of their injuries and wounds.

Landor apparently suspected his story would not be believed and
went to the trouble, immediately upon his return when he was still

Landor around 1912 when his exploring days were over.

suffering physically, of obtaining the affidavits and the photographs. Unless all these statements are bogus and the photographs doctored, one must conclude that Landor was in Tibet and that he did undergo a terrible physical ordeal there.

As the flood of Landor's subsequent books about his travels poured forth between 1900 and 1913, reviewers expressed increasing skepticism about his claims of what he had seen and done. Even so, *National Geographic* magazine in 1904 described *Gems of the East*, Landor's account of his journey through the Philippines, as "the most complete and accurate description of [the Philippines], their climate, people, and customs which has yet been published in popular form." In 1908 the same magazine published a forty-one-page "brief summary" of *Across Widest Africa*, his account of his solo journey from Djibouti to Dakar, illustrated with many photographs Landor had taken. In an introduction, the editor called it "a remarkable trip," and described the book as "a very noteworthy contribution to geography." His last travel book, *Across Unknown South America*, was included by the *New York Times* among its "Best Hundred Books of the Year" for 1913.

Sometimes, when a critic thought he had nailed Landor in an exaggeration or inconsistency, further investigation suggests that the critic may have spoken too hastily. One reviewer of Landor's autobiography singled out an anecdote recounting how he was routed from his bed in a London hotel by a fire and had to stand outside on the sidewalk in a flimsy kimono for hours until daylight. The temperature, he said, was twelve degrees below zero. The reviewer pounced on the story:

> To a New Yorker, the statement is apparently innocuous. But zero weather is unknown in the south of England. Should this be called poetic license?

But Landor gives the precise date: January 5, 1893. The London *Times* of that date reported that the weather that day was "bitterly cold." The minimum temperature was fourteen degrees. Fourteen degrees Fahrenheit, which the *Times* presumably meant, converts to about eleven degrees below zero Celsius. Landor does not specify whether he meant Fahrenheit or Celsius, but he should be given the benefit of the doubt. The temperature that night was, after all, unusually low, as he claimed.

There is no mention in any of Landor's writings that he was ever tempted to marry or even that he was ever in love. Except for his mother and sister (*Everywhere* is dedicated to his sister), he seems to have formed no emotional attachment to any woman. Women appear in his life story only as figures in the seemingly endless parade of celebrities he claimed he had known.

Landor's obituaries tended to focus on *In the Forbidden Land*, his first great success. The *New York Times*'s three-column headline said, "Landor Lived to Tell of Tortures in Tibet" and called his account "a book that thrilled the world." The long valediction included recollections of the man himself:

> He attributed his excellent health to his simple regimen, especially his fondness for fresh air. In the late winter of 1910, he was seen on

Broadway in a thin muslin suit without an overcoat when everyone else was bundled up. He was then about forty-five, straight and vigorous, hard as nails.

Other obituary writers were less admiring. The *Nation*'s writer compared him with "flashing meteors and gorgeous comets," but added,

> I conclude with profound regret . . . that his records are permeated with egoism, with carelessness, with straining for effect. . . . . They do, however, present a picture of extraordinary accomplishment by a gifted man, untrained, and without stable character.

The *New York Herald Tribune* said:

> The elder [Walter Savage] Landor wrote *Imaginary Conversations*, the younger wrote of travels that may have been embroidered here and there by imagination; but, for that matter, did not Herodotus and Marco Polo draw the long bow?

When Landor's critics were done with pointing out his shortcomings as an explorer, as a scientist, as a writer, as an artist; when they had finished ridiculing his egotism and penchant for self-promotion; when they had exhausted their efforts to shoot holes in his accounts of his travels; they all came finally to agree with Landor himself that he had "adventures enough to fill the lives of twenty men."

Bibliography

Henry Savage Landor wrote more than a dozen books, each, except his autobiography, about a journey he had made to some part of the world. The following include only those titles relating to his two trips to Tibet. Landor's books have all been long out of print, and copies are not easy to find. No biography of Landor has ever been published.

Hopkirk, Peter. "The Bizarre Adventure of Henry Savage Landor" in *Trespassers on the Roof of the World.* Los Angeles: Jeremy Tarcher, 1982. A brief, amusingly written account of Landor's 1897 expedition.

Keay, John. "Everyone Tried to Be My Friend" in *Explorers Extraordinary.* London: John Murray, 1986. Brief, amusing biographical sketch drawn obviously from *Everywhere,* with fairly detailed description of South American trip.

Landor, A.H.S. *An Explorer's Adventures in Tibet.* New York: Harper Bros., 1910. A reissue of the 1904 one-volume abridgment of *In the Forbidden Land.*

Everywhere: The Memoirs of an Explorer. New York: Frederick A. Stokes, 1924. The bulk consists of one-chapter summaries of Landor's previous books. He settles old scores, but says very little about his personal life.

In the Forbidden Land. 2 vols. London: William Heinemann, 1898. The account of the first Tibetan journey. His best known book.

"The Highest Altitude Ever Reached By Man." *Harper's Weekly* (March 25, 1905), 430-31. His account of his climb in September 1899 that he claimed set a mountaineering world record.

Tibet and Nepal. London: William Heinemann, 1905. The account of the second Tibetan journey.

4

Sir Francis Younghusband

Matchlocks and Maxims at 15,000 Feet

Whatever happens, we have got
The Maxim gun, and they have not.

HILAIRE BELLOC

At the turn of the century it was a multifaceted fascination that
Tibet exerted on imaginations in Europe, especially in Britain.
There was, first of all, the inevitable fascination with a huge, remote,
and virtually inaccessible plateau, higher than the highest in the Alps
and shielded by the most stupendous mountain ranges in the world.
Exactly what lay on this vast "roof of the world?"

No one was quite sure, and geographers wanted to know. Some thought
that a mountain range even higher than the Himalayas might lie to the
north of that great barrier between India and Tibet. Then, too, the Tibetans had created a strange society totally alien to Europeans. It was a theocracy, a country ruled by a government of priests presided over by the Dalai
Lama who claimed to be an incarnation of one of his early predecessors.

The priests belonged to a strange, exotic branch of Buddhism
known as "lamaism." They were rumored to engage in eerie, sometimes horrible rites. They drank from cups made from human skulls—
human blood, some stories said—and used rattles made from human
arm and thigh bones.

The Potala, the Dalai Lama's combination palace, fort, and lamasery in the capital, Lhasa, was a huge, even monstrous structure that one early European traveler likened to a Rhenish castle. Who knew what treasures or marvels or horrors might lie within its massive walls? Moreover, Tibet was the "forbidden land." The Dalai Lama, abetted by his impotent but cooperative suzerain power, China, had kept the country's borders closed to foreigners for decades. The Tibetans threatened torture and even death to any foreigner who violated their borders, as Arnold Henry Savage Landor's account of his Tibetan adventure in 1897 had graphically demonstrated. Neither Landor nor anyone else—not even such intrepid explorers as Nikolai Przhevalsky or Sven Hedin—had succeeded in penetrating the formidable geographical and man-made barriers shielding Lhasa.

By the turn of the century British fascination with Tibet had developed still another facet and had expanded beyond the confines of the universities, of the Royal Geographical Society, and of the pages of lurid pulp fiction to reach all the way into the corridors of power in the Foreign Office, 10 Downing Street, and Buckingham Palace. Tibet had become an object of interest to those people concerned with what today would be called geopolitics. They feared it was becoming part of the playing field for the "Great Game."

The term "Great Game" was used perhaps as early as the 1840s to describe the complicated relationship that evolved during the 19th century between Britain and Russia in Central Asia. A "semi-clandestine duel" is how one writer described it. It was the background for Rudyard Kipling's novel *Kim*. Under four Tsars, Russia had pushed steadily east and southeast to annex huge swaths of territory in the Caucasus and Central Asia. The tottering khanates that were the remnants of the conquests of Genghis Khan and Tamerlane fell one by one to a conquest that reversed the tide that had swept west repeatedly for centuries out of the steppes and deserts of the East. By the 1890s, the Russian drive eastward seemed a force that would only be stopped by the sea to the east and south. According to one calculation, the Russian Empire had been expanding towards the east at the rate of 20,000 square miles a year for four hundred years.

British governments in Calcutta and London became increasingly alarmed as Russian frontiers were pushed eastward and southward until they were all but contiguous with Britain's Indian Empire in South Asia. It was widely believed in London that a major reason for the expansion was the consuming Russian desire for a warm-water port that was ice free the year round. An Indian port on the Arabian Sea or the Bay of Bengal seemed a likely target of Russian ambitions. But the threat the British saw and feared was not only to India. "The stronger Russia is in Central Asia, the weaker England is in India and the more conciliatory she will be in Europe," one Russian statesman was reported to say.

Britain sent spies—some British, some Indian—north of the Himalayas, the Karakorams, and the Pamirs to find out what the Russians were up to. A British consul general in Kashgar in far western Chinese Turkestan kept watch on Russian activities. But, as Hedin noted during his many visits to the city, he enjoyed much less prestige than his Russian counterpart. Britain fought two wars in Afghanistan, in 1841 and again in 1879, as part of the Great Game to keep the Russian menace at bay.

As the 19th century drew to a close, reports were received in Calcutta and London of Russian intrigue in Tibet. They seemed to indicate a logical continuation of the Russian expansion that had been going on for most of the century. In particular, the reported activities of one mysterious man convinced the British that the Russians were insinuating themselves into the little-known land that sat on the very northern doorstep of Britain's Indian Empire. This conviction—by no means shared by everyone in London or Calcutta—finally gave birth to the Tibet Frontier Commission which turned out to be the last inning of the long-running Great Game.

In the unfolding drama of the Tibet Frontier Commission, the two men most responsible for its creation are mostly off-stage presences. One of them remains throughout it a mysterious unseen figure whose presence is nevertheless decisive, while the other who actually set it in motion appears only briefly. They never met, and they make an odd pair: Aharamba Agyan Dorjieff and George Nathaniel Curzon.

A Buryat Mongol and a Buddhist who spent several years in a Tibetan monastery, Dorjieff became a friend of the Dalai Lama. He came to the attention of the British in 1900 when he was reported to be in Saint Petersburg carrying a confidential message from the Dalai

Lama to the Tsar. The following year he returned to the Russian capital with a Tibetan delegation. The British became convinced that Dorjieff was a Russian agent sent to cement relations with Tibet.

Dorjieff's shadowy off-stage presence ended after December 1901, when he was reported to have had a private audience with the Russian Empress, but his influence continued to affect the situation. In August 1902, the British Minister in Peking reported hearing of a secret agreement concluded between Russia and China about Tibet, presumably as a result of Dorjieff's intrigues.

George Nathaniel Curzon became Viceroy of India in 1898, at the age of thirty-eight the youngest man ever appointed to that position. Since his university days he had been regarded as someone destined for great things, and the Viceroyalty was regarded as just one more step toward the premiership.

A man with presence and influence in British corridors of power, Curzon came to the Viceroyalty armed with probably greater knowledge and understanding of Asia than any Viceroy before or after him. He had already served as Under Secretary for Foreign Affairs and Under Secretary for India. He had traveled in India and Central Asia, and his book, *Russia in Central Asia*, had been published in 1889. He believed that Russia's eastward thrust posed a threat to British interests in South Asia, and he was a strong advocate of a "forward policy" that pushed British influence northward from India to counter the Russian thrust. Reports of Dorjieff's mysterious comings and goings and other Russian machinations in Tibet convinced Curzon that Britain must break through the barrier erected by the Tibetans to counter the growing Russian influence there. He was able to persuade a lukewarm British government in London to approve his proposal that a mission be sent to negotiate with the Tibetans.

The matter to be negotiated was not a Russian presence in Lhasa. In 1890 Britain had concluded an agreement with China, Tibet's ostensible suzerain, to fix the undefined border between India and Tibet, to open trade between the two countries, and to place a British trade representative in Tibet. But the Tibetans had consistently ignored the agreement, saying they were not bound by an agreement to which they had not been a party. They had violated the border the British considered established, they had torn down border markers, imprisoned British subjects who dared enter Tibetan territory, confiscated the property of British subjects (yaks and other animals belonging to Indians and Sikkimese who wandered back and forth across the border) and, most importantly, they had not permitted a British representative to reside on their territory. It was to bring an end to these Tibetan provocations and negotiate enforcement of the terms of the 1890 agreement (which, incidentally, would establish a British presence in Lhasa to keep an eye on the Russians) that the Tibet Frontier Commission was created. The man Curzon chose to lead it was Francis Younghusband.

Born on May 31, 1863, practically in the shadow of the Himalayas in India, Younghusband was the son of an Indian Army officer. All his life he was a lover of mountains, remote places, and solitude. He was also strongly attracted to mysticism and the study of religion, an aspect of his personality intensified by the awe and wonder he felt when surrounded by the massive grandeur of the high Himalayas. He also came to believe, in common with many well-meaning 19th-century Europeans, that the civilized nations of Europe had an obligation to educate and aid the more backward peoples of the world—and the moral right to rule them while doing so. After graduation from Sandhurst, the British military academy, he returned to India to serve with an Indian Army cavalry regiment.

In 1886 Younghusband spent six months in China traveling through—and to some extent exploring—Manchuria. For his return to India, his military superior suggested that he travel overland from Peking through Central Asia and across the Himalayas to Kashmir. It was an intimidating but stimulating idea:

> I nearly burst with excitement at the prospect. Since the time of Marco Polo, six centuries before, no European had traveled from China to Central Asia.

On the eve of departure from Peking the full impact of the impending journey sunk in:

> Nowhere in Peking had we been able to obtain information about the road across the desert. I had never been in a desert and here were a thousand miles or so of one to be crossed. Nor had we any information about the state of the country on the other side of the

Lord Curzon dressed in the robes of the Viceroy of India in a photograph taken in Calcutta in 1903. He advocated a "forward policy" to block Russian advances in Central Asia.

desert. . . . Lastly, at the back of all, looming darkly in the extremist distance were the Himalayas, to cross which had previously been considered a journey in itself.

He was twenty-three years old. He left Peking on April 4, 1887, with two Chinese servants, and crossed the Zangaria Desert (the northern Gobi) to Hami; then proceeded across the northern edge of the Tarim Basin along the southern slopes of the Celestial Mountains to

Kashgar and Yarkand and, finally, south to Kashmir across the Himalayas. It was a minor epic of adventure—seven months without a European companion through largely unmapped terrain.

In the middle of the Gobi Younghusband traversed the feared Turfan Depression, well below sea level and oppressively hot:

> I had read in some book that at Turfan it was so hot that people lived in holes underground. I never quite believed it, but today I found it was a real fact.

In western Chinese Turkestan he camped among hostile Kirghiz tribesmen:

> As I mounted to ride away, crowds of these rough Kirghiz collected round me, gesticulating wildly. I asked Rahmat-ula-Khan what was the matter, and he said they had determined not to let me through their country. They argued that no European had been let through before . . . and they did not see any reason why I should be allowed to. Some of the more excited were for resorting to violent measures.

But his faithful Pathan guide, who demonstrated an unsuspected talent for diplomacy, was able to extricate them peacefully from the danger.

The last stage of the journey, from Yarkand to Leh and Srinagar across the Karakorams, aroused Younghusband's sublime love of high mountain fastnesses. Rounding the bend of the trail at one point, he suddenly found himself at the base of Godwin Austen (now more generally known as K2 or Dapsang), the second highest mountain in the world:

> It made me literally gasp. My whole being seemed to come to a standstill, and then to go rushing out in a kind of joyous wonder. The sight of that tremendous mountain, so massive, firm, and strong, so lofty and so dazzlingly pure, left an impression which has lasted through life. For some time, I stood apart, absorbed in contemplation of this wonder.

He was the first European to view K2 from the north, from the perspective of Central Asia.

The small party also faced danger and physical hardship in the extreme. Younghusband slept with his revolver in hand fearing sudden attack by Kanjuti tribesmen who were known to sortie out from their remote valleys in Hunza to murder travelers and plunder caravans. After months of hardship endured while crossing the burning desert, they faced the bitter cold and dangers of a Himalayan crossing with their clothes in tatters.

When he set out from Peking, one of Younghusband's principal goals was to cross the 19,000-foot Muztagh Pass, never before crossed by a European, to ascertain whether it could, indeed, be crossed and used as a route for invasion of India. He and his party had no mountaineering equipment, and their soft leather boots, designed for travel in the sandy desert, were particularly unsuited for clamoring over rocks and glaciers. Nevertheless, they began the climb with the utmost confidence.

As they toiled upward across a tremendous glacier toward the summit, they suddenly were brought up short at the edge of an almost sheer precipice of ice:

> Had the decision rested with me alone, the probability is we should never have got over the pass at all. What, however, saved our party was my holding my tongue. I kept quite silent as I looked over the pass, and waited to hear what the men had to say about it. They, meanwhile, were looking at me and, imagining that an Englishman never went back from an enterprise he had once started on, took it as a matter of course that, as I gave no order to go back, I meant to go on.

They were able to complete the crossing without a major mishap, but Younghusband reported that the pass was "fit only for acrobats."

He arrived in Srinagar, the capital of Kashmir, dressed in a sweeping Yarkand sheepskin coat, wearing long leather boots, terribly worn, his face roughly bearded and black from exposure to the sun. People on the street addressed him as a Yarkandi. His account of the journey, based upon the diary he kept, was published more than a decade later in *The Heart of a Continent*.

Younghusband's remarkable exploit drew him to the attention of the highest British authorities in India. Sir Frederick Roberts, the Commander in Chief of all British forces in India, paid a visit to the headquarters of the young captain's regiment and singled out the returned explorer for fulsome praise. Younghusband was summoned to Calcutta to give a report personally to the Viceroy.

He decided that a military career in India, in view of the settled and peaceful condition of the country in the 1890s, offered the prospect of nothing but boring garrison duty, and he obtained a transfer to the Political Department as a political-military officer. Service with the "politicals" offered an opportunity for further exploration and adventure in the Himalayas and Central Asia—a chance to take part in the Great Game.

In 1891 he was asked by the Viceroy to go north to Chinese Turkestan to investigate Russian activity in Central Asia. He spent the winter in Kashgar where he met Sven Hedin who, on his first visit, was preparing for his initial journey of exploration:

> [Hedin] impressed me as being of the true stamp for exploration—physically robust, genial, even-tempered, cool and persevering . . . I envied him his linguistic abilities, his knowledge of scientific subjects, and his artistic accomplishments; he seemed to possess every qualification for a scientific traveler.

He also became acquainted with the Russian Consul, Petrovsky, who made a very favorable impression on Sven Hedin. Younghusband's opinion of the Russian was very different:

> He was agreeable enough company, but a man with whom friendship was impossible. He had no sense of honor, and did not pretend to have any. He said frankly that he lied on principle, and thought we were hypocritical in pretending to be better than we really were. He acknowledged that we were straight and did not deliberately tell lies, but thought us fools not to.

On leave in England following the Kashgar journey, Younghusband was introduced to the Under Secretary of State for India who was eager to hear about the Russians in Central Asia:

> He knew the whole subject well, and was keenly interested in it. No one else I had met—not even in India—was so well informed and so enthusiastic. And he was young and fresh and very alert and able. His name was George Curzon, and this was his first appoint-

Francis Younghusband in 1903.

ment. My meeting with him then was the beginning of a friendship that lasted for thirty-four years, until his death.

In 1894, during a tour of India that extended into Central Asia,
Curzon visited Younghusband in Chitral, a small tribal kingdom in the
Himalayas, where Younghusband was serving as Political Resident.

By the turn of the century, Younghusband had become something
of a legend in British India, and his friend Curzon was serving as
Viceroy. So when Curzon in 1903 looked around for someone to
command the Tibet Frontier Commission, the experienced
political-military officer he so admired was a logical choice.

In June 1903 Curzon summoned Younghusband to Simla, the
summer capital of British India in the foothills of the Himalayas, to

offer him the post of Commissioner and explain the expedition's purposes. Younghusband shared Curzon's suspicions of Russian intentions in Tibet. He had no firsthand knowledge of the country, despite having on several occasions sought permission from his superiors in India to travel there, but his experiences in the mountains and deserts to the west convinced him that Russia harbored designs against India and therefore could logically be expected to establish a base in Tibet. During his travels in Central Asia Younghusband had encountered several Russian military expeditions probing to the very frontiers of British India. Several Russian officers had told him pointblank that Russian army officers "thought of nothing else" but invading India. On one occasion he had been detained briefly by a Russian military expedition in what was indisputably Chinese territory, and accused of violating Russian territory. Curzon's proposal also fired his imagination with its prospect of a visit to the "forbidden land" where no Englishman had set foot for nearly a century. He accepted the Viceroy's offer with enthusiasm.

Curzon explained that he had wanted to send the expedition to Lhasa, but the government in Britain balked at the idea of forcing entry into Tibet all the way to the capital. The authorities in London agreed only to negotiations with the Tibetans in a suitable place inside Tibet as close to the border as possible. The Chinese and the Tibetans had agreed to send representatives to the spot the British had chosen for the meeting. It was called Khamba Jong.

Viewed from one perspective, the story of the Tibet Frontier Commission is a story of bureaucratic muddle, indecision, and vindictiveness. It is a tale of men in London charged with making decisions about a problem and a place far away about which they had little knowledge and less understanding. It tells of men on the spot always urging more aggressive action—once the initial decision to take action was made in the first place—while their distant superiors, racked by indecision, were willing to approve only half-measures which solved nothing. Finally, it tells, in part, how the careers of two capable, dynamic men were blighted.

Younghusband traveled east from Simla to Gangtok, capital of Sikkim, then north to rendezvous with his three hundred-man military escort, then across the border to Khamba Jong. There he met the Chinese delegate and the Tibetan chief secretary and his entourage. The Tibetans listened to Younghusband's recital of the British position, then objected to the meeting being held in Tibetan territory. They withdrew, and the first attempt at negotiation ended.

Although Younghusband remained in Khamba Jong three months, sometimes receiving delegations of Tibetans, he made no progress in getting negotiations started. His advisors emphasized that fruitful negotiations could only be held with Chinese and Tibetans of the highest rank, and therefore must be held in Lhasa. The mission heard reports that the Tibetans had gathered more than two thousand men on the heights above the British camp and were determined to force an incident when winter came. All this Younghusband reported to Simla.

In Khamba Jong he met the abbot of a monastery at Shigatse who represented the Panchen Lama whose authority was second only to the Dalai Lama. He thought for a while that this "charming old gentleman" might be able to break the impasse. It turned out he was wrong, but he did learn from his conversations with the abbot the nature of the people with whom he had been sent to negotiate:

> Whatever intellectual capacity [the abbot] may have had was not very apparent to the casual observer. He corrected me when I inadvertently let slip some observation implying that the Earth was round, and assured me that when I had lived longer in Tibet, and had time to study, I should find that it was not round, but flat, and not circular, but triangular, like the bone of a shoulder of mutton.

The impasse continued and, on October 10, Younghusband was summoned back to Simla for a conference with Curzon. The Viceroy rehearsed with him all the objections to remaining in Khamba Jong and all the reasons for moving further into Tibet, with or without the consent of the Tibetans. Curzon then sent to London a telegram with his recommendations.

He urged that the commission, with a greatly strengthened military escort, occupy the Chumbi Valley inside Tibet through which lay the easiest and most direct route to Lhasa. It should advance as far as Gyantse, a major settlement halfway to Lhasa.

The reply from London, which finally arrived on November 6, was to be quoted time and again in the months that followed as the definitive statement of British policy and intentions:

In view of the recent conduct of the Tibetans, His Majesty's Government feel that it would be impossible not to take action, and they accordingly sanction the advance of the mission to Gyantse. They are, however, clearly of opinion that this step should not be allowed to lead to occupation or to permanent intervention in Tibetan affairs in any form. The advance should be made for the sole purpose of obtaining satisfaction, and as soon as reparation is obtained, a withdrawal should be effected. While His Majesty's Government consider the proposed action to be necessary, they are not prepared to establish a permanent mission in Tibet and the question of enforcing trade facilities in that country must be considered in the light of the decision conveyed in this telegram.

It was, as Younghusband later wrote, a "curious telegram." Curzon replied on November 24:

The view that we are going to Gyantse simply in order to secure from the Tibetans legal reparation or satisfaction is not quite understood by me.

Younghusband later wrote:

It is remarkable that a document which was so often quoted to the Russian Government, to the Indian Government, to the Chinese Government, and which the Indian Government on one occasion quoted to me in terms of admonition, should have described with so little precision the real purpose of the advance.

London never clearly explained what was meant by "obtaining satisfaction" or "reparation," nor was it clear what answer was intended to "the question of enforcing trade facilities." The telegram had been drafted by St. John Brodrick, who had just replaced Lord George Hamilton as Secretary of State for India. In that position, he would inevitably play a key role in the life of the Tibet Frontier Commission. Brodrick was a friend of Curzon, but that relationship would change in the next months because of disagreements about the expedition.

So, without any clear agreement among the British leadership as to the goal to be achieved by the advance to Gyantse, and in the absence of any clear understanding on the part of the Viceroy or the mission's commander as to what their superiors in London wanted it to accomplish, Younghusband arranged to advance his expedition further into Tibet. He proceeded to the railhead at Siliguri, then north into the Chumbi Valley to join the mission's greatly enlarged military escort. It totaled about 1,150 British and Indian fighting men supported by four pieces of mountain artillery and four Maxim machine guns.

The Chumbi Valley lies on the Tibetan side of the international border established by the 1890 Sino-British agreement, but it is more Indian than Tibetan in character. It is one of the principal routes by which to enter Tibet from the south. The British trade representative, who was to have been established by the 1890 agreement, would have been placed in Yatung at the south end of the valley, just inside the border. The British had agreed to that placement reluctantly; they would have preferred in 1890 to have their representative closer to Lhasa. A group of British mountaineers, who in 1921 undertook a reconnaissance in preparation for the first major mountaineering assault on Mount Everest in 1922, assembled at Darjeeling and proceeded north through the Chumbi Valley toward their objective. Charles Kenneth Howard-Bury, one of the leaders of that reconnaissance expedition, described the valley as attractive and inviting:

> The Chumbi Valley is one of the most fertile and prosperous valleys in all Tibet; the houses are large and well built, reminding one very much of Tirolese villages. The rainfall here is but a quarter of that which falls on the other side of the Jelap La; potatoes, barley, wheat, apples and pears all grow well here. The air everywhere at this time of year [May] was scented by the wild roses. From Yatung to Phari was twenty-eight miles, two days' easy march up the Chumbi Valley.

Younghusband and his expedition were entering the valley just at the onset of winter, and its aspect was not nearly so welcoming for them as for the Everest mountaineers. With his years of experience in the Himalayas and the mountains of Central Asia, he was under no illusions as to the difficulties his enlarged mission faced in overcoming the physical and human obstacles they faced.

The escort was commanded by Brigadier J.R.L. Macdonald of the Royal Engineers (Lord Kitchener, the Commander in Chief in

India, was also of the Engineer Corps and had personally selected Macdonald for the assignment). Like Younghusband, Macdonald had extensive experience in the Himalayas. However, his presence did nothing to lighten Younghusband's burdens. He was not in good health, and it deteriorated as the expedition proceeded north. He proved to be ineffectual both as a commander and as a fighting man, always counseling withdrawal. Perhaps worst of all, he outranked Younghusband, although Younghusband was in charge of the mission. Their relationship, and the question of who was really in command, were never sorted out.

It should be noted that Younghusband, in his account of the Lhasa expedition, let pass any opportunity to criticize his escort commander, although at least some criticism would have been justified. His forbearance was seen by his admirers—and he had many, both in India and in Britain—as characteristic of the gentlemanly Indian army colonel.

Appointing an officer from the engineers as escort commander was probably calculated. The engineering and logistical problems an advance into Tibet posed were as great, if not greater, than the military and diplomatic challenges. Everyone expected strong armed resistance sooner or later from the Tibetans, so a strong military force was needed.

Such a force needed transport and supplies—hundreds of tons per day. They had to build their own road as they went along, and everything had to be transported from the railhead at Siliguri by beasts of burden or on men's backs. They were venturing into largely unknown country at extreme altitudes in the dead of winter. The Jelap Pass, the entryway into the Chumbi Valley, lies at an altitude of 14,400 feet, while Siliguri is about four hundred feet above sea level. During one fifteen-mile stretch, the expedition climbed more than 10,000 feet. The group totaled about ten thousand men, including seven thousand "followers"—porters, animal herders, and other support people. The column was more than four miles long, winding snakelike up a zigzag track.

Younghusband expected opposition at the Jelap Pass, but none occurred. They descended into the Chumbi Valley and moved north through Yatung, where they met a delegation of Tibetans and Chinese who urged them to go back. Younghusband politely refused.

They moved on to the head of the valley at Phari, where they occupied a massive fort that had been evacuated by the Tibetans. It was January 6, and the weather was what one might expect at such a time in such a place. Younghusband, who was not given to exaggeration about cold weather or physical hardship, later wrote:

> The cold was now terrible. Piercing winds swept down the valley, and discomfort was extreme. Near our camp was a big waterfall frozen solid.

Ahead was the Tang-la Pass at 15,200 feet. The commissioner decided to pause on the other side at a tiny village called Tuna until the weather moderated.

They arrived in Tuna, "the filthiest place I have ever seen," the next day in a temperature of -18° F. On January 12 several hundred Tibetans appeared in the plain below to request a discussion. Younghusband sent an aide to whom the Tibetans gave a demand that the expedition return to Yatung. If it did not, they said, it could expect resistance, and the Tibetans threatened to call in aid from "another power." Told the British would continue forward, they withdrew. Reports soon reached the British camp that they had begun to build a wall across the line of march a few miles ahead.

A few days later, Younghusband, accompanied by two young officers, on an impulse rode over to the Tibetan camp "just to have a talk with their leaders and to explain our views to them in a friendly way." The Tibetans listened to what he had to say, but he found them not only uncooperative, but actively hostile. They demanded that he withdraw and detained him until he agreed to wire their demands to the Viceroy. They also told him there definitely were no Russians in Lhasa. They disliked the Russians, they claimed, just as much as they hated the British.

Younghusband's impulsive though well-intentioned act put the lives of himself and his two companions, as well as the success of his mission, in grave danger. He later acknowledged that he was fortunate to be able to leave the Tibetan camp unhurt. The three British officers could have been killed or held hostage by the Tibetans who might have demanded the mission's withdrawal in exchange for its commander's life.

The British wintered for three frigid months in Tuna. At night the temperature reached -25° F. The wind blew incessantly. Officers later said that a cup of tea, if not drunk immediately after being poured from a kettle hot off the fire, became a block of brown ice. They received almost weekly visits by groups of Tibetans whose messages were always the same: withdraw. In the middle of March, Younghusband wrote to the Chinese Amban, or resident, in Lhasa informing him the mission would soon move forward to Gyantse to begin negotiations.

On March 31 the British force advanced twelve miles to Guru, where the Tibetans waited in defensive positions behind a wall flanked by small forts. The British troops, with weapons at the ready, advanced to the wall. The two forces stood facing each other silently across the barrier. Not a shot had been fired. Younghusband later described the scene:

> Our infantry were in position on the hillside only twenty yards above them on the one side; on the other our Maxims and guns were trained upon them at not two hundred yards' distance. Our mounted infantry were in readiness in the plain only a quarter of a mile away. Our sepoys were actually standing up to the wall, with their rifles pointing over at the Tibetans within a few feet of them. And the Lhasa General himself with his staff was on our side of the wall, among the sepoys.

The Tibetans outnumbered the British force by a large margin, but their antique matchlocks were no match for modern repeating rifles, artillery, and machine guns. General Macdonald consulted with Younghusband, then ordered a unit of Indian sepoys to cross the wall and disarm the Tibetans.

When the Indians tried to take away their weapons, the Tibetans resisted, and the two groups of soldiers began to scuffle. The Tibetan general in command suddenly spurred his horse forward into the melee. A Sikh soldier grabbed his bridle, the Tibetan shot him through the jaw with his pistol, and general firing broke out immediately. The Gurkhas and Sikhs fired across the wall at pointblank range, supported by the Maxims and the artillery. It was a massacre. The Tibetans turned but did not run. They walked slowly away with heads bowed as a rain of bullets mowed them down. Of an estimated fifteen hundred men, they left perhaps seven hundred dead on the field and more than one hundred fifty wounded. One British soldier, who manned a Maxim, later wrote to his mother, "I got so sick of the slaughter that I ceased fire, though the General's order was to make as big a bag as possible. I hope I shall never again have to shoot down men walking away."

Younghusband had hoped to avoid bloodshed. He had asked General Macdonald to order his men not to fire unless the Tibetans fired first, and the General had complied. If the Tibetan general had not suddenly lost his head, the massacre might never have occurred. Younghusband later called it the "Guru Disaster" and described it as "a terrible and ghastly business."

The mission moved forward, and another action was fought on April 8, leaving two hundred Tibetans dead. The British arrived at Gyantse on April 12 and paused to await the Chinese and Tibetan negotiators from Lhasa. Gyantse, a significant market town, was dominated by a huge masonry jong, or fort, overlooking the town from atop a high rock outcropping. It reminded some officers of Gibraltar, others of Mont-Saint-Michel, still others of Edinburgh Castle. It looked impregnable. The British realized that it was probably impossible to storm it with the forces they had been able to get as far as Gyantse and without heavy artillery, but they did not have to. The Tibetans evacuated the fort, and it was briefly occupied by British forces. But they did not remain, because of a lack of water. They camped about two miles away in a village called Chang Lo, next to the river.

During pauses such as the one at Chang Lo, members of the mission, some of them acknowledged scientific experts, explored the surrounding country to learn about Tibet, in particular about its unusual religion and government. One of the strangest and most bizarre of their discoveries was the "Cave of Happy Musing on Misery" at Nyang To-Ki-Pu. In a rocky ravine about fourteen miles from Gyantse lived a community of hermits. In the rocky sides of the defile were about twenty caves, their mouths sealed with stones. It was the practice of these hermits to be sealed up in these cave cells to "meditate." They did so voluntarily in three stages. The first stage lasted six months, the second three years, three months and three days, and the third lasted for life. They lived in total darkness, endlessly reciting spells in Sanskrit accompanied by certain gestures and attitudes of the fingers and limbs.

Their brethren outside fed them once a day through a small door in the wall of their cell, like the door in a rabbit hutch. They communicated with no one. The British visitors were told that one hermit had been in his cell thus for twenty-six years. One of the visitors asked how anyone could be sure someone was in a cell, so one of their hosts tapped very lightly on one of the small doors, as he did when food was left outside. After a short time the door slowly slid open, and a gloved hand shakily protruded a few inches and fumbled about, then withdrew, and the door closed again. The hermits were considered very holy, because the spells they chanted millions upon millions of times were thought to combat demons which the Tibetans feared constantly surrounded them. One of the British visitors later wrote:

> Glad was I to get away from this "Cave of Happy Musing on Misery," with its melancholy captives entombed and inarticulate, and to emerge again into the priceless freedom of the air and sunshine of God's splendid Earth.

Entombed hermits were to be found not only in Nyang To-Ki-Pu. It was a common Tibetan practice. Three years after the members of Younghusband's mission discovered them near Gyantse, Sven Hedin, on his third journey of exploration, came across a hermit who had been walled up for life near an isolated monastery called Linga-gompa that lies west of, in Hedin's words, "the infinitely beautiful and wild My-chu Valley."

The entombed monk was called by an honorary title, Lama Rinpoche (holy monk). The Swedish explorer's reaction to the bizarre occurrence differed from the Younghusband group's feeling of repulsion:

> The Lama Rinpoche fascinated me irresistibly. Long afterwards, I would think of him at night; and even today, though eighteen years have passed, I often wonder if he is still alive in his cave. Even if I had the power and the permission, I would not for the life of me have liberated him and led him out into the sunshine. In the presence of such willpower and holiness, I felt like an unworthy sinner and a coward.

After a few weeks in Chang Lo it became apparent to Younghusband that the Tibetans were still unwilling to enter into negotiations. In late April the British learned that the Tibetans had constructed another defensive wall across the road at the Karo-la

Pass which lay ahead and was, at 16,500 feet, the highest point on the road to Lhasa. On May 3 a force under Colonel Brander, the second in command of the escort, moved forward to engage it. Only one hundred fifty men were left at the British camp in Chang Lo. On May 5 before dawn Younghusband was awakened by shots just outside his tent. About eight hundred Tibetans had crept up in the darkness and were attacking. Younghusband grabbed his revolver and rallied his meager forces. The battle lasted two hours. The Gurkhas beat back the attackers who left two hundred fifty dead and wounded. The next day, in the narrow defile of the Karo-la Pass, Brander and his men faced a wall six feet high, four feet thick, and eight hundred yards long, defended by three thousand Tibetans. He had no way of breaching it, so detachments of Gurkhas and Sikhs climbed the steep sides of the gorge to an altitude of 18,500 feet to flank it. Their crossfire from the heights drove the Tibetans away in flight. It was, and presumably remains, the highest altitude at which a battle was ever fought.

The Tibetans meanwhile had greatly strengthened their forces around Gyantse and had reoccupied the jong. They began cannonade fire against the British camped on the plain below, so the British became, in effect, besiegers under siege. They were outnumbered by the Tibetans ten to one. Later, when Younghusband stood on a tower of the fort and looked down on the British camp, he realized why the Tibetans felt themselves to be in an unassailable position.

> They were in a lofty and seemingly impregnable fortress in the heart of their own country. We were a little dot on the plain below. The idea of making a treaty with us, if they did not want to, must have appeared ridiculous.

The cannon fire from the jong continued for seven weeks. The Tibetans ran out of lead and used stone cannonballs and, later, gleaming red-gold missiles of copper. But the cannonade was not effective. Only about a dozen of the Indian sepoys were killed or wounded.

On June 5 Younghusband received orders to return to Chumbi, several dozen miles to the rear, to confer with military leaders from India about future plans. With an escort of forty troops, he headed south. Early the next morning the small force was attacked in its camp by more than three hundred Tibetans. Younghusband himself grabbed a rifle and joined the defense. Sixty or seventy Tibetans were killed before the attack was broken off. At Chumbi the military authorities from India argued against an advance on Lhasa. The mission would have to cross the Brahmaputra River, in effect cutting themselves off from any possibility of support or reinforcement from India. They would advance over unknown terrain, and they might encounter overwhelming resistance at the Tibetan capital that even their superiority in firepower would be unable to overcome. Nevertheless, Younghusband decided to go forward to Lhasa if one last appeal for negotiations at Gyantse proved futile. On May 14 the Cabinet in London had reluctantly approved an advance to Lhasa if it proved impossible to conduct negotiations at Gyantse. Younghusband returned to his command resolved to complete his mission.

By early July British forces at Chang Lo had been greatly reinforced and Younghusband, in a last parley with the Tibetans, warned that the fort would be stormed if serious negotiations did not begin. They did not and, on July 6, the assault began. Artillery pounded the walls with solid shot (laboriously carried up the zigzag mountainous track all the way from the railhead at Siliguri 213 miles away) until a breach was made. Two companies of infantry—one of Gurkhas, the other of Royal Fusiliers—under heavy fire from the defenders scrambled up the face of the rock outcropping to the breach in the wall. The Gurkhas, under Lieutenant Grant, led the way into the fort. Grant, who was wounded, was awarded the Victoria Cross. The fort, long considered the key to Tibet, fell, and the road to Lhasa lay open to the British.

A year had passed since Younghusband had gone to Khamba Jong, six months since he took up winter quarters at Tuna. Events had been moving in India and Britain as the mission made its painful way into Tibet. In April Curzon had gone to England on leave. Since childhood, he had suffered from curvature of the spine which caused him great pain. His affliction flared up in England, forcing him to be hospitalized. His wife, long not well, became seriously ill. Though she recovered, her illness was a distraction. Curzon consulted briefly with Cabinet members and others about the mission but, distracted and in pain, he was unable to exert any real influence. His friend Brodrick, as Secretary of State for India, had opposed Curzon's forward policy in

Tibet with the telegram of November 6. The two men clashed on that and other matters of policy, and Curzon's relationship with Brodrick deteriorated.

The questions that now became paramount in London were how long the mission should remain in Tibet, how large an indemnity should be demanded from the Tibetans, and whether a British resident was to be left in Tibet after the mission departed, as Younghusband and Curzon wanted and the Government of India had recommended. The Cabinet, however, was haunted by the memory of Major Cavagnari who had been sent to Afghanistan as Political Agent in 1879 and two months later had been murdered by the Afghans. The British had fought a war to avenge him. The Cabinet did not want that episode repeated in Tibet. On July 6, the day the jong at Gyantse fell, the Cabinet telegraphed to India and Younghusband, "neither at Lhasa nor elsewhere is Resident to be demanded." The other questions remained to be decided.

The international backdrop, against which London viewed events in South Asia, by the summer of 1904 had changed as compared with a few years earlier when Curzon had persuaded London to send a mission to Tibet. The Russo-Japanese War had broken out in February and, to everyone's surprise, the Japanese were giving the Russian colossus a drubbing. Germany was building a high seas fleet which was obviously designed to challenge British naval supremacy, even in home waters. To many Britons, Germany was rapidly becoming the principal threat to Britain's security. Younghusband was fully aware of the growing indifference, even hostility, toward his expedition:

> The Government had to contend with many difficulties. They were in the face of a strong opposition in the House of Commons. There was no enthusiasm for the enterprise in the country. We had only recently emerged from the South African War. The Russo-Japanese War was causing anxiety. And we had not yet concluded the Entente Cordiale with France [which would allay some of the growing anxiety felt about Germany].

By August 1904 a Russian threat to Britain's Indian Empire via Tibet seemed to be rapidly receding, if it had ever actually existed. Even so, too much treasure and prestige had been expended to permit Britain to walk away from the situation. If there was little enthusiasm

The mission entering Lhasa following months of diplomatic skirmishes both in Tibet and with the India Office in London.

for having the mission continue on to Lhasa, with the possibility of further bloodshed, no one was ready to order Younghusband to retreat back to India. As the British column moved out of Gyantse on the road to Lhasa, the Cabinet telegraphed India that British influence "must be duly recognized in Lhasa, so as to exclude foreign pressure."

On August 3 the British column sighted the golden roofs and pinnacles of the Potala gleaming in the sunlight. That evening they camped under Lhasa's city walls. Accompanied by an escort of two companies of Royal Fusiliers and the Chinese resident's bodyguard, Younghusband rode through the center of Lhasa, the first Englishman in more than ninety years to do so. Crowds of Tibetans watched with apparent indifference. Younghusband decided they "did not seem to care a twopenny damn whether we were there or not." He also noted:

> Many a traveler had pined to look on Lhasa, but now we were actually in this sacred city, it was, except for the Potala, a sorry affair. The streets were filthy, and the inhabitants hardly more clean than the streets.

British troops marching into Lhasa with the Potala looming in the background. Younghusband wrote, "On the day of our arrival, I and my staff donned our full-dress uniforms, and with an escort of three hundred men, including some of the Royal Fusiliers and a sort of band from the Gurkhas, we marched right through the city of Lhasa making all the noise we could."

Younghusband's task now was to conclude a treaty with the Tibetans, and circumstances made that appear virtually impossible. The Dalai Lama had fled to Mongolia, and it seemed doubtful whether the four-member Council of Ministers who remained behind would or could enter into any agreement that would be binding. The Tibetan government appeared to be paralyzed. Five days after entering Lhasa, Younghusband telegraphed to Simla:

> Tibetan authorities all in confusion. . . . National Assembly sits permanently now, but only criticizes and is afraid to act without reference to Dalai Lama who is three days distant, and will not in his turn act without sanction of Assembly. Everyone is in fear not of us, but of each other. . . . General attitude of Tibetans, though exasperat-

ing, is probably more futile and inept than intentionally hostile.

There were other difficulties. Younghusband, anticipating lengthy negotiations, had wanted to stay the winter in Lhasa. Macdonald, citing military requirements and the difficulties of maintaining a supply line, wanted to limit the stay to six weeks and depart in September. London agreed with Macdonald. Lord Kitchener, the Commander in Chief in India whose disputes with Curzon caused an open break between the two men, favored forgetting negotiations and simply punishing the Tibetans, beginning with an assault on the monasteries. The Cabinet began to think along the same lines. On August 15 Arthur Balfour, the Prime Minister and a friend of Kitchener, informed the King that in the absence of an agreement, the British could not simply leave Tibet without striking some kind of blow:

> The Cabinet decided that, if the Lama refuses even to consider our very reasonable and moderate offers, we have no choice but to turn the expedition from a peaceful into a punitive one: and with every regard to the religious feelings of the Tibetans, to destroy such buildings as the walls and gates of the city, and to carry off some of the leading citizens as hostages. This course is painful; but apparently inevitable.

That the Cabinet should put forward such a barbarous proposal has been a matter for criticism ever since. In fact, it could not have been carried out. The expedition had not been equipped with anything like the amount of explosives needed to destroy the massive walls and gates referred to. Even the stock of explosives available in Calcutta, the depot nearest to the railhead at Siliguri, had been exhausted by the expedition's needs. It would have required months to manufacture and assemble enough, and transport it to Lhasa.

The cast of characters with whom Younghusband had to work to meet his deadline is worth noting. In the absence of the Dalai Lama, the Ti Rimpoche, the Chief Doctor of Divinity and Metaphysics, served as Regent. He was quite friendly to the British. Younghusband found him to be a

> pleasant, benevolent, genial old gentleman. But his intellectual attainments did not amount to much more than a knowledge by

rote of prodigious quantities of verses from the sacred books, and his religion consisted chiefly of ceremonial.

The Tongsa Penlop of Bhutan, that country's ruler, had accompanied the mission during most of the march to Lhasa and had acted as an intermediary with the Tibetans. He was a jolly individual, called the "Tonsil" by the British soldiers and "Alphonse" by the officers, because of his faintly Gallic air. He carried with him an impressive golden crown but customarily wore an uncloven Homburg hat pressed down around his head to his eyebrows. Beneath the Tonsil's comical exterior, however, worked a shrewd brain able to assess relative political and military power. Immediately after Younghusband's expedition ended, Bhutan placed itself under the British government of India as a protectorate, a direct result of Younghusband's dealings with the Tonsil and that worthy's observations of his dealings with the Tibetans.

Yu-tai, the Chinese resident, or Amban, had been appointed to the post in December 1902, but had arrived in Lhasa only in February 1904. He was the representative of the Suzerain Power, but had no real authority. "We found him," Younghusband wrote, "to be practically a prisoner and almost without enough to eat, as the Tibetans had prevented supplies of money from reaching him, and he had actually to borrow money from us." Yu-tai's strategy became obvious: he allied himself wholly with the British in order to use the British occupation to reassert Chinese authority.

The last member of the cast was Captain Jit Bahadur, the Nepalese Resident, who later became Maharajah of Nepal. Like the Tongsa Penlop, he acted as a friendly intermediary to the Tibetans, and his bringing the Ti Rimpoche together with Younghusband served to get negotiations going.

With the aid of these supporters, Younghusband was able to prevail upon the Council of Ministers and the National Assembly to enter into a treaty. The mission was due to depart in less than six weeks. There was no agreement between Simla and London, or among the principal players on the British side, as to what the terms of a treaty should be. For example, Simla strongly recommended placing a British Resident in Tibet, in Gyantse if not Lhasa. London opposed a Resident, but suggested the possibility of a British trade agent having access to Gyantse, but not Lhasa.

The Cabinet had recessed for the grouse-hunting season immediately after passing the "punitive expedition" motion, leaving matters in Brodrick's hands. His paramount interest was to obtain a large indemnity from the Tibetans but he had given no figure. As Younghusband frantically prepared for his meeting with the Tibetans to finalize a treaty text, messages flew back and forth between Simla and London arguing these and other details. The British had laid a telegraph line along their line of march to link the mission with Simla. But there was not enough time to reach agreement on all the outstanding questions and receive approval of a text before the mission was due to depart. Younghusband had to act on his own.

On September 1 he presented a draft treaty to the Tibetans. It called upon them to accept the agreement of 1890 and recognize the border with Sikkim set forth in that agreement. They accepted all terms and agreed to sign the treaty on September 7 in the great Audience Hall of the Potala. When the appointed day arrived, the British delegation found that the approach to the Audience Hall was an inclined ramp in a long corridor dimly lit by flickering butter lamps and paved with stones worn smooth over centuries by the bare feet of thousands of lamas. The British officers in their nailed boots skidded and stumbled on the glassy surface as they clawed their way up to the ceremony site.

Five copies of the treaty were signed in three languages in an atmosphere that fell considerably short of solemn or ceremonial. The Tibetans thronging the hall giggled and whispered, while the British spectators, according to one officer, "were rather a rowdy lot and made a beastly noise." Their exit from the hall down the slippery ramp was no easier or more dignified than their entrance had been. "It was the funniest sight imaginable to see officers hanging on to the walls, on to the Tommies, on to anything they could catch hold of," one officer wrote in his diary. The Tibetans grinned as they watched their uninvited guests depart.

The text of the treaty was telegraphed to Simla for onward transmission to London. The news that a treaty had, at long last, been signed with Tibet brought telegrams and letters of congratulation to Younghusband. The acting Viceroy in Simla telegraphed the appreciation of the Government of India and the King. Lord Kitchener and Lord [Frederick] Roberts, a former Commander in Chief and the most highly regarded British soldier of the day, telegraphed their congratulations. Lord Curzon sent a warm letter from London.

The official response from London was in a different tone. Brodrick immediately stated his objections to two clauses of the treaty: (1) The Tibetans were to pay an indemnity of £50,000 over a period of seventy-five years, during which time the British would occupy the Chumbi Valley. The Cabinet had specified that the indemnity, whatever the amount, should be paid over a period of three years, and the occupation should continue until the indemnity was paid. The Ti Rimpoche had made a special plea to Younghusband to extend the period of payment to seventy-five years, and Younghusband had agreed. (2) An annex to the treaty, signed separately, stipulated that a British trade agent be stationed at Gyantse and have the right to visit Lhasa to settle matters he could not settle in Gyantse. Younghusband had added this clause when he discovered that the Tibetans had no objection to a British trade agent resident in the country, but he placed it in a separately signed annex in deference to London's objections to a British resident. He included right of access to Lhasa as a result of his experiences dealing with mountain kingdoms in the 1890s. He had learned that it was always necessary to deal directly with the ruler in the kingdom's capital.

These two provisions brought a storm of protest from London. Simla defended Younghusband's actions but, as he later wrote, "I knew that I was not acting within my instructions." The problem had been the vagueness and contradictory nature of the instructions and the brief time he had been allowed to negotiate with the Tibetans. He later wrote:

> If I had not been rushed at Lhasa, but had had plenty of time to gauge and report the situation there, and to receive the orders of Government on any modifications which might be suggested by circumstances, I should have been able to conclude with both the Chinese and Tibetans a treaty which my own Government as well as they would have accepted.

As the mission prepared to depart Lhasa, a wrangle developed between London and Simla as to whether the negotiations should be reopened to modify the objectionable provisions. Finally, a message was sent to Younghusband authorizing, but not directing, him to re-open the talks. The message arrived on the eve of his scheduled departure. He decided that to approach the Tibetans about new negotiations would not only be futile, but could jeopardize the agreement already signed. So he ignored the message, and rode out of Lhasa on September 23, 1904. By early December he was back in London.

Brodrick now seemed determined to discredit Younghusband whom he suspected of having communicated with Curzon on his own throughout the negotiations. He also suspected Younghusband had a private line of communication into Buckingham Palace and had been secretly getting messages to the King; how else to explain the King's strong endorsement of the commissioner's actions? Brodrick charged that Younghusband had deliberately flouted London's instructions, and even before Younghusband departed India to return to Britain, he sent a sharply worded message of censure. Younghusband replied from Simla:

> I hope I shall be able to show that I have disobeyed no orders of His Majesty's Government which it was practicable for me to carry out and that the severe censure now passed by the Secretary of State . . . is wholly undeserved.

But Brodrick was able to persuade Balfour of Younghusband's transgressions. In a letter written even before the mission departed Lhasa the Prime Minister wrote, "Younghusband, by disobeying our explicit orders, has placed us in a very false position." In another communication a little later, he said, "Younghusband has got us into a most abominable mess. . . . I think [he] will have to be publicly repudiated."

When the time came to decide on a decoration for the commissioner, Brodrick argued that none should be given. That was unacceptable to everyone, but he was able to prevail in arguing that the lowest ranking appropriate decoration should be awarded.

Younghusband returned to India to take one last post as Political Resident in Kashmir, a plum assignment. Several people attached to the mission published accounts of it, and all were unanimous in their praise of Younghusband as a leader, as a negotiator, as a soldier, and as an unfailingly polite and considerate human being. They unanimously

*Younghusband meeting the Chinese Amban and his staff in Lhasa.
Though representing the ostensible Suzerain Power in Tibet, the Amban
had no real authority and had to borrow money from the British.*

argued that he had, in his mission to Lhasa, overcome incredible difficulties, both natural and man-made, to achieve a signal success by winning over the Tibetans and defusing a potentially ominous political dispute. Nevertheless, Younghusband was never able to disperse completely the cloud that Brodrick's actions placed over his career.

In 1910 he retired and wrote about the mission in *India and Tibet.* His reputation survived Brodrick's attacks and the disputes surrounding the Tibetan treaty. As President of the Royal Geographical Society he vigorously promoted the expeditions of the 1920s to conquer Mount Everest.

The mystical side of Younghusband's nature, always in evidence even during his years of exploration, became more prominent in his later years. He wrote several books and spoke frequently on religious subjects. He helped to organize the Conference on Religions of the Empire held in London in 1924. He had married in 1897, and he had a son who died in infancy, and a daughter. He died, full of years and honors, in 1942.

Lord Curzon resigned the Viceroyalty in 1905, also under a cloud, his tenure marred by disputes with Kitchener and Brodrick and the controversial results of the Tibet Frontier Commission. Although in 1919 he succeeded in becoming Foreign Secretary, the Prime Ministership eluded him. In 1923, when a new government was to be formed by the Conservatives, he was, as Foreign Secretary, one of several candidates for Prime Minister. The King finally called in Lord Balfour, regarded as a senior statesman and Curzon's old nemesis from his days as Viceroy, for advice. Balfour left a house party at his country house to travel to London to confer with the King. When he returned, the ladies at his party asked, "and will dear George get the Premiership?" "No," Balfour replied, "dear George will not." Curzon had made too many enemies.

China took over payment of the indemnity on behalf of Tibet and made the last payment in 1908, so British occupation forces were withdrawn from the Chumbi Valley in that year. A British trade agent was installed in Gyantse, and the position survived to be moved to Lhasa in 1936. After 1947 the newly independent Indian government retained the services of the last British agent who remained until the Communist takeover of the country.

The Tibet Frontier Commission found no Russians in Lhasa and no evidence of Russian influence. But some of the issues it was intended to resolve continue, after nearly a century, to lie below the surface of international politics, waiting to break out into open flame. Chinese authority over Lhasa waxed and waned in the 20th century as the authority of the central government ebbed and flowed after the 1911 revolution. After ousting the shaky Kuomintang government in 1949, the Communist government of Mao Tse-tung made reassertion of Chinese authority in Tibet a priority and did so in 1951. In 1959 the Dalai Lama fled in protest to India. In 1962 China and India fought a brief border war, in part over the eastern border established by the 1890 agreement. To this day, China remains in firm control in Tibet, India continues to give political asylum to the Dalai Lama, and India claims that China, as a result of the 1962 war, illegally occupies fifty thousand square miles of Indian territory.

Bibliography

There is no dearth of published firsthand accounts of Younghusband's expedition. Several by various people attached to the mission, including two journalists, were published within a few years of the mission's return from Lhasa. Biographies of Lord Curzon contain accounts of the mission in greater or lesser detail, depending upon the main focus of the biography. One of the titles cited below, "A Footnote," is a double entendre. The author's nom de plume, Pousse Cailloux, dates from Napoleon's army and means, literally, "pebble-pusher," French slang of the period for foot soldier.

Candler, Edmund. *The Unveiling of Lhasa*. London: 1905. A firsthand account by a journalist who accompanied the expedition.

Dilks, David. *Curzon in India*. 2 vols. New York: Taplinger Publishing Co., 1970. Perhaps the best account of Curzon's years in India. Includes details of the expedition.

Fleming, Peter. *Bayonets to Lhasa*. London: Readers Union, 1962. A scholarly, thoroughly researched account by the author of *News from Tartary,* Ella Maillart's traveling companion across Central Asia.

French, Patrick. *Younghusband: The Last Great Imperial Adventurer*. London: Harper Collins, 1994. A new, carefully researched biography. Despite the rather lurid subtitle, the author declares his purpose is "to expose the subject with ruthless clarity to the calm eye of the reader."

Landon, Percival. *The Opening of Tibet*. New York: Doubleday, Page & Co., 1905. Another firsthand account by a journalist who accompanied the expedition.

Ottley, W.J. *With Mounted Infantry in Tibet*. London: Smith, Elder & Co., 1906. A firsthand account from the "worm's eye" perspective of one of the private soldiers.

"Pousse Cailloux." "A Footnote." *Blackwood's* Magazine (February 1929), pp. 147-77 [the author was L.A. Bethell, a lieutenant of the 8th Gurkhas in 1904]. A firsthand account, written several years after the event, by an unabashed admirer of Francis Younghusband.

Seaver, George. *Francis Younghusband*. London: John Murray, 1952. An admiring biography with extensive material on Younghusband's mystical side.

Verrier, Anthony. *Francis Younghusband and the Great Game*. London: Jonathan Cape, 1991. A recent biography that focuses on Younghusband as explorer and political agent.

Bibliography continued next page

Waddell, L.A. *Lhasa and Its Mysteries.* London: John Murray, 1905. A first-hand account by the medical officer who accompanied the expedition. He was an expert on Tibet who wrote several scholarly studies.

Younghusband, F. *The Heart of A Continent.* London: John Murray, 1896. His account of the journey from Peking to India in the 1880s.

India and Tibet. London: John Murray, 1910. His account of the expedition. Includes extensive introductory material on earlier British contacts with Tibet and Younghusband's recommendations for British policy.

5
Sir Aurel Stein

The Caves of the Thousand Buddhas

But I will sit beside the fire,
And put my hand before my eyes,
And trace, to fill my heart's desire,
The last of all our Odysseys.

HILAIRE BELLOC

In the first decade of the 20th century, on those rare occasions when people in the West thought about Central Asia at all, the images they brought forth were few and limned in broad, vague strokes. Foremost was a picture of a vast land of extremes, of endless steppes, deserts, and mountains. The tones were harsh and stark, of sand, rock, ice, or seemingly limitless flat grassland baking under broiling sun or freezing in blizzards of unbelievable ferocity. If people were to be seen, they were a few primitive nomadic tribesmen, or perhaps even fewer small, settled populations clinging to the edges of isolated oases.

Of history, the images were equally few: caravans of camels along the ancient Silk Road, perhaps, the Mongol hordes of Genghis Khan, and Marco Polo. The images combined to produce a portrait of a large portion of the Earth's surface with few attractions and little to interest anyone except perhaps a few geographers, geologists, and other spe-

Aurel Stein at about age sixty. This brilliant archeologist revealed a long-lost civilization buried for a thousand years beneath "the worst desert in the world."

cialists who were probably a bit eccentric if they were interested in such a desolate part of the world.

The meager history that was generally known about Central Asia demonstrated that it was a place to be traversed, an unpleasant part of the world to be gotten across on the way to somewhere else. Traffic along the ancient Silk Road, Chinese Buddhist pilgrims like Hsüan-tsang in the seventh century, and Marco Polo—all were on their way to somewhere else. This mental portrait was based upon limited and fragmentary information but it was accurate, as far as it went. Did it go far enough?

Ninety years later the images in most people's minds are not much different. That is regrettable, because, thanks to the extraordinary efforts of a few unusual people, information about the great heartland of the Eurasian landmass is no longer so sketchy. Those people have revealed that Central Asia is, indeed, a forbidding land of terrible deserts and glacier-capped mountains. But it was also once the home of communities that for nearly a millennium combined in a unique manner three of the great civilizations of antiquity: Greece and Rome, India, and China. It was not only the avenue by which the ideas, products, and people of ancient Rome and the Near East, India, and China were exchanged, but also a meeting ground where those civilizations lived side by side, mingled, and influenced each other.

One of the earliest and most important of those extraordinary people who uncovered and documented the story of that ancient interaction of cultures was, appropriately, a man of many cultures. He was Hungarian by birth but British by choice, a scholar of Sanskrit who lived most of his life in India when he was not traveling in Central Asia and the Middle East on extended archeological expeditions, and whose body lies buried in Kabul, Afghanistan.

Mark Aurel Stein (apparently, he never used his first name) was born in Budapest on November 26, 1862. An uncle on his mother's side of the family was a member of the upper house of the Hungarian Parliament. He was educated at the universities of Vienna and Dresden and received a doctoral degree from Tübingen where he studied Persian and Indian archeology. He then went to England where he spent three years studying classical and oriental archeology and languages at Oxford and at the British Museum.

In 1887 he sailed to India to become Principal of Oriental College in Lahore and, simultaneously, registrar of Punjab University. But his real love and purpose in life was archeology and ancient oriental studies, and he spent his vacations in Kashmir and the Northwest Frontier area in geographical and historical research.

Early in life, Stein became fascinated with three historical figures who influenced much of what he did later. While still in school, he began to read about Alexander the Great, and many of his later archeological expeditions were concerned with tracing Alexander's routes and sites of his activities in India, Afghanistan, and Persia. Later to his pantheon of heroes and guides were added Hsüan-tsang, the seventh-century Chinese Buddhist pilgrim who crisscrossed Central Asia traveling to and from India and left a detailed account of his journeys; and the great Venetian, Marco Polo.

The writings of the latter two travelers became Stein's guides as he pursued his archeological quests. In particular, Hsüan-tsang became his "patron saint" to whom he constantly referred. His detailed knowledge of the great Chinese pilgrim's travels stood him in good stead on more than one occasion when he had to deal with Chinese officials and religious figures.

In 1897 Stein began to hear of documents and other relics from the region of Khotan in southwestern Chinese Turkestan that had begun to appear in antiquities collections in India and in Russia. They had been acquired by British and Russian representatives in Kashgar, and in Kashmir and Ladakh in the far north of India. The documents were of both Chinese and Indian origin and obviously of great antiquity. Sven Hedin's account of his journey through the Takla Makan Desert and his discovery of buried ancient cities there, which Stein read in 1898, confirmed that there were ancient sites near Khotan likely to reward systematic, scholarly investigation.

No part of Chinese Turkestan had been explored archeologically (Sven Hedin was a geographer and geologist), so in 1898 Stein submitted to the British Indian Government, which was his employer, a plan for a proposed expedition to Khotan and request for assistance to finance it. The proposal was approved and support provided. In March 1900 Stein, accompanied by three Indians from the Indian Survey Department, headed north from Kashmir through Gilgit and Hunza across the Pamirs into Chinese Turkestan. His first destination was Kashgar.

En route to Kashgar he passed through Tashkurgan, the "Stone Tower" of Ptolemy, the second-century astronomer and geographer. In ancient times, it had been the entrepôt on the extreme western border of China where traders from the West had exchanged Roman gold with Chinese merchants for the highly prized silk of the East. It had been the crossroads where traders from the Mediterranean, India, and China mingled. The ancient town had been destroyed by numerous earthquakes and several periods of neglect, so little was left of the settlement from the days of Han China and the Roman Empire, but Stein made a careful survey of the area anyway. It was the place where the commerce of the ancient worlds of East and West connected. Would he find other sites where their cultures and civilizations intermingled?

In Kashgar Stein was the guest of the British Agent, George (later Sir George) Macartney, in the spacious official British residence, "Chini Bagh." Macartney also hosted Sven Hedin on several occasions, and he became a close friend of both men. He and Stein became especially close, because they shared many interests. For example, the documents and artifacts from desert dwellers in Khotan that attracted Stein's attention and prompted him to undertake the expedition to Central Asia had, in fact, been purchased and sent to India by Macartney.

Macartney, who was the son of a Scottish father and Chinese mother, had spent the first ten years of his life in a Chinese household in Nanking. His mother died when he was twelve, and he had been educated in England and in France where he received a university degree. He had gone to India in 1887, the same year as Stein, to serve as Chinese interpreter with the Burma Commission. In 1890 he had been selected to accompany Francis Younghusband to Kashgar. Younghusband arranged for his appointment as an Agent of the Indian Government there, and he stayed on when his companions returned to India (this position was upgraded to Consul General in 1910).

Macartney, who remained in Kashgar until 1918, was especially suited for the position by temperament, background, and education. Fluent in both Chinese and French, he possessed competency in German and Russian, as well as Persian, Hindustani, and Turkish. His profound understanding of China and the Chinese was unusual for an official of a Western power and made him invaluable in a sensitive listening post like Kashgar. His friendship with the Chinese Amban, or resident governor, made it possible, despite great official reluctance on the part of the Chinese, to obtain the permits necessary for explorations in the deserts of Chinese Turkestan. His wife, who had never been outside Britain before she married him less than two years before Stein's arrival, made Chini Bagh a homelike oasis of comfort and rest for wanderers like Stein. The Macartneys, through their advice, support, and assistance provided to Hedin, Stein, and others, played an important role in the early geographical and archeological exploration of Central Asia.

Stein spent the summer in Kashgar enjoying the Macartneys' hospitality and preparing for his explorations. He left for Khotan in late September and arrived there a month later. After spending several weeks in the Kunlun Mountains mapping the sources of the Khotan River, he returned to Khotan in early December to launch his expedition into the Takla Makan Desert to the north. His first destination was the buried city discovered by Sven Hedin which Hedin had called Takla Makan but which Stein was told was called Dandan Oilik.

Dandan Oilik, where he spent three weeks, became his laboratory. Here he experimented with, and perfected techniques best suited to excavating ruins buried in sand and extricating and preserving what he found there. Altogether, he and his men cleared and examined fourteen buildings scattered among the sand dunes. He found, first, friezes of Buddhist paintings very much in the Indian Gandhara style which flourished in northwest India in the early years of the Christian era and which incorporates Greek influences; slips of paper with Sanskrit texts of Buddhist scripture; and paper with writing in an Indian Brahmi script, but in an unknown language. In a building nearby, he found wooden slats with Chinese ideographs and pieces of Chinese lacquer ware. On January 2, 1901, he sent a message to the Indian Government:

> The last weeks spent at this old site in the desert have brought interesting results in the form of ancient Sanskrit, Turki, and Chinese manuscripts, Buddhist paintings, etc., recovered from sand-buried ruins. I am keeping well, though the cold is semi-Arctic just now, and hope to do useful work elsewhere.

Stein had taken the first step in the archeological exploration of Central Asia by confirming that long-forgotten communities, where people of the ancient East and West had lived and worked side by side, had flourished in what are now absolutely desolate wastelands. But it was only the beginning.

Having by now heard rumors of other abandoned cities in the desert around Khotan, Stein was now convinced there must have been other cities in the flourishing ancient kingdom of Khotan. He headed east to Keriya, another oasis. In Niya, a village north of Keriya on the edge of the desert, he met a villager with two wooden inscribed tablets which electrified him. They contained writing in Karosti, the script of ancient northwestern India. The villager guided him to the site where he had found the tablets. It contained ruins of buildings even larger, more elaborate, and more solidly built than in Dandan Oilik.

A little digging in one of the buildings uncovered more than one hundred wooden tablets. Most were wedge-shaped, seven to fifteen inches long, and designed to be fastened together in pairs. Those remaining in pairs were still fastened with clay seals that held them together and obviously had served as a means of keeping their contents private. The writing on the inner surfaces of those still sealed was as fresh as when it had been written. The writing was in Karosti. Until then, the only pieces of Karosti writing from Central Asia had been on a very few early Khotan coins from the first and second centuries, and some fragments of birchbark found in 1892 by a French traveler. By the end of the first day's digging in Niya, Stein had uncovered a cache of documents in Karosti to equal "the aggregate of all the materials previously available for the study of Karosti, whether inside or outside India."

Other buildings yielded items of everyday life like a piece of rug, kitchen equipment, spindles, and a walking stick. Stein chose one ruin for excavation which turned out to be just what he was looking for: a rubbish heap. It contained all sorts of refuse—and hundreds of wooden tablets bedded among the rubbish, apparently discarded by their original owner. The rubbish had preserved them perfectly. But excavating them was a chore:

> For three long working days I had to inhale the odors of this antique dirt and litter, still pungent after so many centuries . . . [and] swallow in liberal doses antique microbes luckily now dead.

From the rubbish heap also came two dozen complete documents written on perfectly preserved sheepskin—the first example ever found of writing in an Indian language on leather.

Niya was a site even richer than Dandan Oilik, and showed the same mingling of ancient East and West. The wooden tablets were a writing material that originated in China before the invention of paper, but in Niya they contained writing in an Indian script. Paper had been invented in China early in the first century A.D., but the new invention had not penetrated to the far reaches of Turkestan by the third century. The old method of wooden tablets (which were erased by paring down the surface containing writing with a knife to produce a clean surface) had still been used in Niya. The clay seals on them were marked with impressions clearly based on Greek models. One contained a Pallas Athena, complete with aegis and thunderbolt, while another showed Heracles. Niya had been a city ruled by Chinese from the later Han dynasty, but settled even earlier by people from Taxila in the extreme northwestern corner of Punjab in India who had, in turn, been influenced by the Greeks of Alexander. It had been abandoned some time in the third century when Chinese authority was withdrawn as the Han dynasty ended.

Stein left Niya in mid-February 1901, having examined and excavated every ruin he could trace under its sand covering. He was convinced that other ruins lay buried nearby, and he had now heard stories about other sites. After crisscrossing the region for the next two months he was able to find a few sites which proved interesting, but not nearly as important or rich in yields as Dandan Oilik or Niya.

Winter was coming to an end, and it was now the season of the burans, or black sandstorms, that Stein found just as terrible as had Sven Hedin. There was also

> added the trying sensation of glare and heat all throughout the daytime. The sun beat down with remarkable intensity through the yellowish dust-haze and the reflection of its rays by every glittering particle made the heat appear greater than it really was.

By mid-April, when Stein was preparing to end his season of exploration and return to Khotan en route home, one of his men casually mentioned one more site on the route back to Khotan and called it "Rawak," or "High Mansion." His casual manner did not prepare Stein for what he found there.

A huge Buddhist stupa lay buried in the sand, surrounded by enormous stucco heads, obviously all that remained of massive statues. Stein spent eight days at Rawak and, with additional laborers sent urgently from Khotan, was able to remove enormous quantities of sand. Rawak had been a stupendous place. The court measured 164 feet long by 143 feet wide, with a wall three feet thick and eleven feet high. The stupa rose two stories to the top of its dome. Most awesome were the colossal statues that lined the walls of the court. Stein uncovered 91 of them that lined 300 feet of the inside walls. Some still had bits of paint adhering to their molded draperies, and remains of goldleaf still stuck in small, square patches to the knee of one image.

It would have been impossible to remove any objects from Rawak. The stucco statues were huge and fragile. Any attempt to move them would have reduced them to fragments. So, with some regret, Stein had the trenches refilled to protect the delicate antiquities from the devouring sand-laden wind:

> It was a melancholy duty to perform, strangely reminding me of a true burial, and it almost cost me an effort to watch the images I had brought to light vanishing again, one after the other, under the pall of sand which had hidden them for so many centuries.

Stein headed back to Khotan where he still had one final task to perform. He had embarked on his journey with three goals in mind: to survey the sources of the Khotan and Keriya Rivers in the Kunlun Mountains, which he and his Indian surveyor assistant, Ram Singh, had accomplished early in the journey; to discover and investigate sites of ruins in the desert, which he had done with spectacular success; and to investigate the origins of some "old books" written in an unknown language that had reportedly been found in the desert somewhere near Khotan.

The books first appeared in the mid-1890s when they were offered for sale in Kashgar and in Kashmir by travelers from Khotan. Macartney had bought and sent some on to India for study. The Russian Consul General in Kashgar had also purchased some and sent them to Saint Petersburg, and others had been bought in Kashmir. They could now be found in museums and libraries in India and England, as well as in Paris and Saint Petersburg. Scholars had been working for several years trying to decipher the unknown script, but without success. Stein was determined to ascertain during his expedition to Turkestan precisely where the mysterious books had been found.

Most of the books had been traced to one man, Islam Akhun, in Khotan, and Stein had tried to locate him during his first visit to Khotan, but without success. En route through Khotan on his return journey, Stein asked the Chinese Amban, with whom he had become very friendly, to locate Akhun to clear up the mystery of the books. The Amban, who shared Stein's interest in antiquities, enthusiastically agreed to find the missing "antiquarian." He was found in a nearby village where he was practicing as a hakim, or Muslim doctor.

By the time he confronted Akhun, Stein had uncovered large numbers of documents and manuscripts in numerous languages from several desert sites, but none in the mysterious unknown script. He had come to the conclusion that the "old books" were forgeries, but he wanted to make sure.

Questioned by Stein and the Amban for two days, Akhun admitted to some legal infractions: extorting money from ignorant hillmen under false pretenses, and passing himself off as an official using forged official documents. But he denied knowing anything about forged antique documents. He admitted having sold the books as a middleman, but claimed he had bought them from three nomads who, he said, had told him that they found them at sites in the desert. All three had long since run off.

Stein decided to set a trap for the "wily old scoundrel." Since Akhun stoutly denied that he had found the books or that he knew where they had come from, Stein confronted him with several depositions he, Akhun, had made toMacartney years earlier in which he had described in detail where he claimed to have found the documents.

> The effect was most striking. Islam Akhun was wholly unprepared for the fact that his lies told years before, with so much seeming accuracy of topographical and other details, had received the honor of permanent record in a scientific report to Government. . . . He appeared also greatly impressed by the fact that, with the help of the exact information recorded by Mr.Macartney . . . I could enlighten him as to what "old books" he had sold at Kashgar on particular occasions, what remarkable statements he had made about the manner of their discovery by himself, etc.

After he got over his initial surprise, Akhun also appeared to take some pride in learning that his "books" had received such treatment. Assured by Stein that he would not be punished, he broke down and admitted his "crime."

He had for a few years collected coins and other objects from desert sites to sell. Then he learned that "sahibs from India" also wanted to buy manuscripts. He decided that scouring the desert for them would be too much trouble; it would be much easier to manufacture them. At first, he tried to copy existing manuscripts, but when that proved too time consuming, he created his own script. Finding that a ready market existed, he hired others to write the manuscripts; in effect, he created a forgery factory. When that also proved too slow, he began to block-print books in his bogus script on paper made to look old by first staining it with a vegetable dye, then suspending it in smoke over a fire. But business had fallen off recently, as suspicions had begun to grow among the sahibs as to the authenticity of the "books." So Akhun turned to practicing medicine as a hakim.

It was obvious to Stein that old Akhun "was a man of exceptional intelligence for those parts, and also possessed of a quick wit and humor." But, with some amusement, he refused the old man's request to be taken to Europe. As they parted, he showed Akhun photographs of some of his forgeries that had been published as part of a scholarly report about them (before, of course, they were known to be forgeries):

> He was greatly impressed by seeing his own handiwork so perfectly reproduced in the photogravure plates . . . and was very anxious to learn how this feat could be accomplished. I had no doubt he was fully alive to the splendid opportunities for fresh frauds which this art might provide. How much more proud would he have felt if he could but have seen, as I did a few months later, the fine morocco bindings with which a number of his block-printed Codices had been honored in a great European library!

Stein traveled overland via Kashgar to Europe. He had been given leave by the Indian Government to remain in London for several months to unpack and begin to catalogue his huge collection of artifacts and documents. He then returned to India, and while pursuing archeological investigations in Kashmir, wrote his "personal narrative" of the Turkestan expedition entitled *Sand-Buried Ruins of Khotan*, published in 1903.

In 1904 Stein submitted to the Indian Government a proposal for a second expedition to Central Asia, this time extending eastward as far as the borders of China. He obtained approval as well as financial support, and on April 2, 1906, departed Srinagar in Kashmir on his second great expedition.

With Takla Makan desert ruins as a backdrop, team members pose during their second expedition. Aurel Stein sits behind his sweater-clad dog, Dash. Behind him are locally hired porters and on either side are cartographers from the Survey of India Department whose mapping expertise proved "enormously valuable."

He crossed the mountain barrier—a formidable journey in itself—and visited the Macartneys at Kashgar. Then, he turned southeast again to Khotan, where he undertook further investigations of sites he had visited in 1900. He returned to Rawak, the "High Mansion," where he had reburied the colossal statues, and found that a group of Chinese jade diggers had visited the site since his earlier visit. In their search for "treasure" they had destroyed the statues—"my care in burying these again under sand just as I found them had proved in vain." He revisited Niya and unearthed more artifacts and documents.

But Stein's principal interest on this trip lay to the east, and he traveled in that direction along the route he knew had been one of the Silk Road routes traveled by Marco Polo. He was able to trace the great Italian's travels by the landmarks which still existed. He passed through the oases of Charchan and Charkhlik. From the latter settlement, he planned to travel north to the ruins of Lou-Lan discovered by Sven Hedin. But he heard of ruins nearby at Miran, so he went there first.

He first found Tibetan ruins and documents in Tibetan, showing occupation after the eighth century. Then he found Buddhist artifacts of a much earlier period, including huge heads of what must have been enormous statues in the Greco-Buddhist style of Gandhara. While excavating one building, he began to uncover frescoes of winged angels:

> As in eager excitement I cleared head after head with my bare hands, I rapidly convinced myself that the approach to classical design and color treatment was closer in these wall paintings than in any work of ancient pictorial art I had seen so far. . . . Much in the vivacious look of the large fully opened eyes, in the expression of the small dimpled lips, etc., brought back to my mind the fine portrait heads of Greek girls and youths to be seen on painted panels from mummies of the Ptolemaic and Roman periods found in Egypt.

He was on the eastern side of the Takla Makan Desert, 600 miles from Khotan, nearly 1,000 miles from Kashgar, practically on the border of China proper. He had never expected to find evidence of the influence of ancient Mediterranean civilization so far east in such ancient artifacts:

> I felt completely taken by surprise. How could I have expected by the desolate shores of Lop Nor, in the very heart of innermost Asia, to come upon such classical representations of Cherubim! And what had these graceful heads, recalling cherished scenes of Christian imagery, to do here on the walls of what beyond all doubt was a Buddhist sanctuary?

He made a systematic written and photographic record of his startling discovery. His efforts illustrate the physical ordeals through which an archeologist in the deserts of Central Asia must suffer to amass the meticulously detailed information that alone will justify and reward his efforts:

> All day it was bitterly cold, and icy gusts from the north soon benumbed my hands as I kept crouching in cramped positions, busy with endless measuring and scribbling of penciled notes. . . . As I groveled amidst the sand and clay debris on the floor adjusting the levels of the camera, focusing the lens, etc., the

From a fresco of Western-style winged figures found by Stein at Miran.

temporary protection from the wind which the focusing cloth secured for my face seemed but a scant comfort; but even for that I felt grateful.

The frescoes were painted on brittle plaster, and to remove them meant removing the walls—a task that would require more time than Stein could afford. So he reluctantly re-covered them with sand, as he had the statues of Rawak. He returned to the site on his third expedition in 1914 to find that a young Japanese traveler had visited the site after his first visit, had tried to remove the frescoes, and had reduced them to shattered fragments. Only a small portion had been left undamaged:

> Of the greater portion of the paintings I had first brought to light here, my photographs, imperfect as they are, and my notebooks have alone preserved a record.

Now he could proceed north to Hedin's ruins of Lou-Lan. He found them, and was able to make systematic excavations which unearthed a large quantity of documents and artifacts. He was able immediately to identify the writing on wooden tablets, which Hedin had not been able to recognize, as Karosti script, and he was amazed to find so many documents in that Indian script here practically on the borders of China, so far from its origins. The tablets were found in a building which apparently had been the office of a minor official, and they contained various routine official records. Lou-Lan was controlled by China, so records kept in an Indian writing system suggested that the area had first been settled by people from the West, i.e., from northwestern India, and only later taken over by China which kept the indigenous writing system alongside their own. Stein had not been prepared for the idea that Indian settlement had progressed so far to the east before the thrust of the Chinese to the west.

Stein also found many artifacts of everyday life, including sandals woven from hemp and many pieces of fabrics, wrapped bundles of silk and pieces of carpet, as well as a great many examples of wood carving used to decorate houses. Beams as long as twenty feet were found. All the items showed a mixture of east and west which Stein sorted through in his tent on Christmas day:

> The "finds" of this ruin seemed like a Christmas present specially prepared to bring home to me in the desolation of the desert how this forgotten dead corner of Central Asia had once been linked by relations of art, trade, and culture with all the great civilizations of the ancient world.

His excavations at Lou-Lan were completed by late February, and he returned to Charkhlik and Miran. His next objective was Tun-huang, a major crossroads on the western border of the Chinese province of Kansu. He was again following the route of Marco Polo across absolutely empty wasteland. Even with forced marches, the journey took seventeen days. The group encountered no other human beings—or, indeed, life of any kind—along the way.

Stein knew he was following an ancient caravan route, and he expected to encounter "pao-tais," or small towers which served as signposts along Chinese roads. In early March he finally found a well-preserved watch tower, twenty-three feet high and solidly constructed of bricks. He was able to see immediately from its manner of construction that it was of great antiquity. He soon found another tower, and then ascertained that they were connected by the remains of a wall. Further on, he was able to find a stretch of wall sixteen miles long connecting towers at irregular intervals.

It recalled at once those Limes lines with which the Roman Empire protected its frontiers wherever barbarian inroads threatened them, from Hadrian's Wall in Northumberland down to the Syrian and Arabian Marches. It was a fascinating discovery which invited prolonged exploration.

These were more than mere signposts along the road. The walls, interspersed with watch towers, seemed to go on, endlessly:

> Never did I feel more the strange fascination of this desolate border than while I thus traced the remains of wall and watch stations over miles and miles of bare desert and past the salt marshes. There were, indeed, the towers to serve as guides from a distance. But what with the marshes and salt-encrusted bogs encountered between the tongues of the desert plateau, the strips of treacherous ground along the edges of the marshes, it seemed to me at times like an obstacle race.

He could even climb some of the best preserved towers:

> As I sat there amidst the debris of the small watch room usually provided to shelter the men on guard, and let my eyes wander over this great expanse of equally desolate marsh and gravel, it was easy to recall the dreary lives once passed here. No life of the present was there to distract my thoughts of the past. Undisturbed by man or beast for so many centuries, there lay at my feet the debris of the quarters which the men exiled to this forbidding border had occupied. . . . I soon grew accustomed to picking up records of the time of Christ or before within a few inches of the surface.

The wall Stein had discovered had been built in the second century B.C. by the Chinese Emperor Wu Ti who defeated the Huns and extended the power of the Han dynasty into the Tarim Basin. It was an extension to the westward of the earlier "Great Wall of China." It had been built to protect the trade route that was pushed into the interior of Central Asia as Chinese power and authority was extended westward. Stein found one large inscribed tablet bearing a date corresponding to 94 B.C. The towers and the settlements near them yielded rich finds of artifacts and documents. At one small post, which apparently had been a kind of regional headquarters, it was possible to reconstruct roughly life as it was lived at that isolated outpost more than two thousand years before:

> The arrangement of the modest quarters could be made out clearly.
> . . . The wooden door posts at the entrance were still in position;
> the fireplace or oven, enclosed by a thin clay wall burnt red, still
> retained its ashes. Yet among the wooden documents recovered in
> the room, which was probably meant to accommodate an officer,
> one bore a date corresponding to May 10, 68 B.C.

Stein found large quantities of documents and artifacts along the limes wall, but he could not pause for extensive excavations. His destination was Tun-huang, an important crossroads dating from ancient times. It lay along the Silk Road connecting East and West, but it also was an important way stop on the north–south route that connected Lhasa in Tibet—and through Lhasa, India—with Mongolia and Siberia to the north. A Hungarian expedition had visited Tun-huang from China as early as 1879 and had investigated sacred Buddhist grottoes nearby known as the "Caves of the Thousand Buddhas." Stein was eager to visit the site. Within a few days of his arrival at Tun-huang in March 1907, he was able to do so.

The caves were carved in a precipitous cliff overlooking a barren valley twelve miles from Tun-huang. There were hundreds of grottoes, large and small, extending for more than half a mile. Two shrines had been excavated to an unusual height to accommodate huge statues of Buddha more than ninety feet high. All the grottoes contained fresco paintings on the walls. Some of the higher grottoes were inaccessible, the stairs originally built to reach them having crumbled away. Stein passed rapidly through several on the lower levels and, once again, saw the mingling of East and West:

> The Chinese artists seemed to have given free expression to their
> love for the ornate landscape backgrounds, graceful curves, and
> bold movement. But no local taste had presumed to transform the
> dignified serenity of the features, the simple yet expressive gestures,
> the graceful richness of folds with which classical art, transplanted
> to the Indus, had endowed the bodily presence of Buddha and his
> many epiphanies.

The crumbling façade of one of the Caves of the Thousand Buddhas at Tun-huang.

The caves were still in use as places of pilgrimage by the devout. Some were in a state of decay, while others had been damaged by well-meant, but clumsy, efforts at restoration. Chinese monks were in charge of some, and Stein wondered whether any systematic archeological investigations could be undertaken at a site still in use as a place of worship and under the control of monks. This was his first encounter with a site not isolated and abandoned.

But Stein was more interested in a report he had just heard in Tun-huang from an itinerant Muslim trader who had told him that a huge cache of old manuscripts had recently been found in a sealed-up room of one of the cave temples. Stein learned that the temple was in the charge of a Taoist monk, Wang Tao-shih, who had collected money to restore his temple. In the restoration process, a crack in what had been thought to be a solid stone wall proved to be an opening into a room full of documents and artifacts. Wang had reported it to the Chinese authorities who had ordered the room locked. Stein learned that Wang was away in Tun-huang seeking more money for his restorations, so it was impossible to pursue the matter further.

Stein spent the next several months tracing the limes walls to

the east of Tun-huang. When he returned to Tun-huang, he immediately sought out Wang Tao-shih who proved to be

> a very queer person, extremely shy and nervous, with an occasional
> expression of cunning which was far from encouraging. It was clear
> from the first that he would be difficult to handle.

If Stein was to examine the hidden documents—never mind acquiring any of them—he would have to succeed in delicate negotiations with Wang Tao-shih who was reluctant to reopen the sealed chamber, both because of religious scruples and fear of the Chinese authorities. The person Stein knew he would have to depend upon in this
effort was his Chinese secretary, Yin Ma Chiang, or Chiang-ssu-yeh,
his secretarial title by which Stein customarily referred to him. He was
a cultured, well-educated assistant whom Stein had hired in Kashgar,
dependable and trustworthy. Stein was a scholar of ancient Asian religions and cultures, intimately familiar with the Buddhist scriptures,
but in their Indian guise. He often lamented his inability to make out
anything in the Chinese documents he discovered. But Chiang-ssu-yeh
had proven to be a superb interpreter, translator, and all-around advi-
sor on things Chinese. Stein knew he must now depend upon Chiang
to obtain the cooperation of the Chinese monk, Wang Tao-shih and, if
they had an opportunity to examine the documents, to assess their
importance.

Stein and Chiang sought out Wang immediately upon their return to Tun-huang. Wang proudly showed them his restored cave
temple. When Stein spoke of his "patron saint," Hsüan-tsang, Wang
responded immediately. He, too, revered the great traveler and displayed as much knowledge as Stein about him. This mutually held
interest and respect became the first step in gaining Wang's cooperation. Stein departed the cave, leaving Chiang alone with the monk.
Chiang found his way that night to Stein's tent with a bundle of Chinese
rolls which Wang Tao-shih had finally agreed to lend him. However,
Chiang needed time to decipher them, and he took them to his tent.

> He turned up by daybreak, and with a face expressing both tri-
> umph and amazement, reported that these fine rolls of paper con-
> tained Chinese versions of certain "sutras" [scriptures] from the

Buddhist canon which the colophons [notes at the end of the manuscript] declared to have been brought from India and translated by Hsüan-tsang himself!

A few hours after Chiang informed the monk of this news, the wall was opened, and Chiang got a glimpse of a room crammed with manuscript bundles. He hurried to inform Stein, who returned with him to the temple.

> The sight of the small room disclosed was one to make my eyes open wide. Heaped up in layers, but without perfect order, there appeared in the dim light of the priest's little lamp a solid mass of manuscript bundles rising to a height of nearly ten feet, and filling, as subsequent measurement showed, close on five hundred cubic feet.

Further inspection revealed "paintings on fine gauze-like silk and linen . . . all kinds of silks and brocades, with a mass of miscellaneous fragments of painted papers and cloth materials." Stein was able to deduce that the room had been sealed more than a thousand years earlier to preserve the religious texts and artifacts from a Tibetan invasion. They dated from the early 5th to the 10th century A.D. Among the items was a large block-printed roll dated A.D. 868, which scholars later confirmed as the oldest specimen of a printed book ever found.

Many of the documents were well worn, obviously having been used many times before being hidden. But there had obviously been no damage while sealed up. The room must have been absolutely dry with no seepage of moisture. The fragile items appeared to be in exactly the same condition as when they had been hidden away. Documents and artifacts of such fragility would never have survived if buried in abandoned, sand-filled ruins. Indeed, they would never have been left behind in settlements abandoned to the desert sands. What had been found in the sealed cave chapel was therefore unique.

Wang Tao-shih was still reluctant to allow Stein to take any document away, fearing punishment from the Chinese authorities. However, Chiang, pleading the need for "closer inspection" and "further examination," was able to persuade the monk to allow him to remove armloads to Stein's camp.

*Wang Tao-shih, caretaker priest at Tun-huang who
opened the sealed chapel for Stein to reveal the enormous cache of documents and
art treasures stored and forgotten for one thousand years.*

Stein would have liked to carry away the entire cache, but he knew that was impossible. He made a generous offer to the monk for the entire collection, but Wang was obviously too frightened of possible reprisals from the Chinese government to accept. Stein and Chiang spent more than a week sorting through thousands of rolls, documents, paintings, and fragments. They were able to persuade Wang Tao-shih that making at least some of the material available to the outside world's scholars would be much like Hsüan-tsang's bringing the Buddhist scriptures from India and translating them into Chinese, rather than allow-

A printed Buddhist text dating from 868 A.D., found in the sealed chapel at Tun-huang. It was the oldest printed text discovered until that time. In 1966, a printed text was discovered in Korea that dates from about one-and-a-half centuries earlier.

ing them to languish in darkness and secrecy, unknown to devout Chinese Buddhists.

> He was almost ready to recognize that it was a pious act on my part to rescue for Western scholarship all those relics of ancient Buddhist literature and art which were otherwise bound to get lost sooner or later through local indifference.

That argument, and the promise of a substantial donation for Wang's cave temple restorations, finally brought the monk around, and he nervously permitted Stein to pack up a selection of materials. Seven cases of manuscripts totaling about three thousand complete rolls and six thousand separate documents, and five cases of paintings and other artifacts totaling more than three hundred pieces, were carefully packed and loaded onto camels for the long journey to India and thence to the British Museum in London where they arrived safely sixteen months later.

Stein finished his work in Tun-huang in the early summer of 1907, but he continued his explorations and travels for another eighteen months. He first traveled south for geographical exploration in the Nan Shan, or Southern Mountains, on the edge of Tibet, then north and west completely around the Tarim Basin. Traversing the feared Turfan Depression, in places more than 1,000 feet below sea level, he was able to undertake some excavations of ancient tombs there. Ranging as far west as Bokhara and Samarkand, he finally arrived in Yarkand and back in Khotan in the early autumn of 1908. He headed south again into the Kunlun mountains in Tibet for more geographical exploration of the sources of the rivers that flowed north and finally disappeared in the Takla Makan Desert.

In the mountains, while climbing on a glacier, Stein suffered severe frostbite in his feet which rendered him practically unable to walk. During the next three weeks he was mostly carried in a litter across the Karakorums to Leh in Kashmir, the first location at which he could receive medical attention. Here some of the toes of his right foot, which had become gangrenous, were amputated. But by January 1909 he was well enough to travel to London.

Now a celebrity at the British Museum, Stein spent several years sorting out and cataloguing his finds, and wrote *Ruins of Desert Cathay*, published in 1912.

By 1914, when Stein began his third, and longest, expedition to Central Asia, the Chinese revolution of 1911 had removed all the Chinese officials with whom he had become acquainted, and political conditions were unsettled. Although this time he was concerned with geography rather than archeology, he did revisit Tun-huang to see his friend, the monk Wang Tao-shih.

He learned from him that the eminent French scholar, Paul Pelliot, had visited Tun-huang about a year after Stein's first visit. A distinguished sinologist, with total command of written and spoken Chinese, Pelliot could evaluate the scrolls and manuscripts himself and persuaded Wang Tao-shih to part with more of the documents. On his way to Europe, however, he disclosed in Peking the news of the presence in Tun-huang of important manuscripts. This had prompted the revolutionary government to order that the entire collection be sent to the capital. As a result,

> the whole collection of manuscripts was taken away in carts, packed in a very perfunctory manner. A good deal of pilfering occurred while the carts were still waiting at Tun Huang, for whole bundles of fine Buddhist rolls of Tang Dynasty times were in 1914 brought to me there for sale . . . so one may wonder

Yin Ma Chiang, or Chiang-ssu-yeh, Stein's invaluable secretary who persuaded Wang Tao-shih to open the sealed chapel and entrust to Stein some of its treasures.

how much of the materials thus carted away actually reached Peking in the end.

Wang had been sent a large sum of money for his temple as compensation from the government, but none of it reached him; all had been absorbed by various offices in fees en route. He told Stein his feelings had now changed:

> In view of the official treatment his cherished store of Chinese rolls had suffered, he expressed bitter regret at not having previously had the courage and wisdom to accept the big offer I had made . . . for the whole collection en bloc.

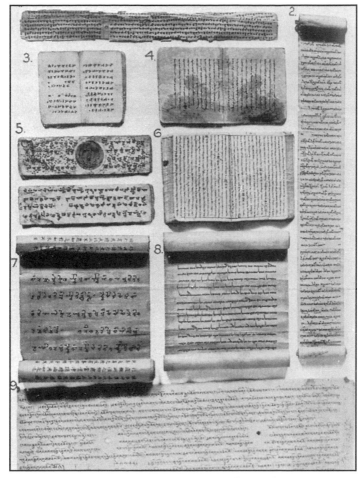

Documents, in various ancient Central Asian languages,
from the sealed chapel.

However, Wang had not sent the whole collection to Peking. In exchange for a generous donation to his temple, he turned over to Stein six hundred of what he, Wang, considered the choicest of the items he had secretly withheld from the Peking shipment. Five more cases were soon on their way to London.

On a visit to Tun-huang in the 1920s, an American archeologist, Langdon Warner, discovered that White Russian soldiers quartered in the caves had defaced many of the paintings with graffiti. He was able to remove a few of the paintings from the caves' walls and ship them back to the United States where they found a resting place and a display worthy of their merit at the Fogg Museum of Harvard University.

Today, what remains of the paintings is threatened with final destruction from another source: tourists. Tun-huang has become an attraction for groups of tourists, and their numbers increase every year. The very breathing of crowds of visitors has raised the level of humidity in the caves and affected the paintings. The Chinese government is finally following the example of the French government's decision to save the famous cave paintings at Lascaux by building a replica for tourists to view and sealing off the original. The Chinese are building a replica, and when it is finished, the Tun-huang caves will be closed to visitors. It is too late to rescue the scrolls and wall hangings retrieved from the sealed chamber, then lost. Let us hope it is not too late to preserve what remains of the unique paintings on the walls of the Tun-huang caves.

There is no narrative by Stein of his third expedition. A fourth expedition to Chinese Turkestan in 1930 proved to be abortive because of political unrest.

After his second Turkestan expedition, Stein began to turn his attention from India toward the northwest in connection with his early hero, Alexander. He made several expeditions into Persia and Baluchistan tracing Alexander's activities. He was also electrified, as was the world's entire archeological community, by the spectacular discovery in India in the early 1920s of the Indus Valley civilization, a discovery which pushed back the early horizons of ancient Indian history by more than a millennium. Stein became interested in tracing possible connections between the Indus Valley communities and the ancient world of the Tigris and Euphrates valleys, and his expeditions in Persia and Iraq between 1927 and 1936 focused on that thesis. He early saw the value of air reconnaissance in archeology, and with the help of the Royal Air Force surveyed Roman ruins in Syria from the air in the 1930s.

Stein was a gregarious man with numerous friends in several parts of the world, but he never married. He lived most of his life in India, and his favorite place was Mohand Marg, a high alpine meadow in Kashmir, where he liked to pitch his tent between expeditions in the summer and work on his writings. He was a complete nomad who never had a fixed address and never owned a residence. When he died, to prove his will, the court ruled that although he had for many years been a British subject, he had never lost his domicile of birth in Budapest.

Stein worked literally until the end of his life. When more than 80 years old, he embarked on an archeological expedition to Afghanistan. But two days after arrival in Kabul he caught a chill and died at the American Legation there on October 26, 1943. He was buried in the Christian cemetery in Kabul.

Stein and other early archeologists of Asia have been criticized for removing documents and artifacts from the countries where they were found and placing them in libraries and museums in Europe and the United States. Stein shipped thousands upon thousands of documents in a variety of ancient Asian languages, and hundreds, if not thousands, of exquisite pieces of ancient Asian art to the British Museum. It is fair to ask what would have happened to those priceless relics if he had not done so.

John Otway Percy Bland was an Irishman who lived in China for many years before and after the turn of the century. He witnessed first-hand such momentous events as the Boxer Uprising and the Revolution of 1911 and wrote reports of them for the *Times* in London. He also wrote several books based upon his years in China. Most notably, he collaborated with the famous sinologist, Sir Edmund Backhouse, the "Hermit of Peking," to produce two historical studies that have become classics, *China under the Empress Dowager and Annals and Memoirs of the Pekin Court.*

Bland viewed events as they unfolded in China with the realistic and unsentimental eye of a veteran journalist, and he saw much he considered worthy of censure. He deplored not only the rapacious imperialism of the West that threatened to dismember China after 1895, but also the decadence and corruption of the social and political institutions in China that invited the inroads of imperialism. From his residence in Peking, he watched the wholesale removal literally by the ton of the accumulated treasures of China to countries abroad, mainly in Europe (in 1912 his collaborator Backhouse donated twenty-nine cases of rare Chinese books and manuscripts weighing forty-two tons to the Bodleian Library at Oxford).

A small part of the treasure trove of manuscripts
from the sealed chapel at Tun-huang

In 1914, while on a visit to London, Bland wrote in a letter to a friend:

> As things are in China, and as they are likely to be for many years to come, every work of art recovered and brought away in safety is preserved for the future edification of the whole world, whereas left in China it must always be in danger. For instance, Aurel Stein's barefaced looting of the Cave of the Thousand Buddhas has been no loss to China and a great gain to scholars and antiquarians in this country. . . . Nine-tenths of ancient China's treasures are at this moment in Europe and America. If they had not been thus preserved, it is quite certain that most of them would have been destroyed in the upheavals of recent years.

What happened at Rawak and Miran and Tun-huang even as Stein was making his expeditions is but one indication that, had he not rescued them when he did, the treasures he shipped to the British Museum might well not have survived. Most of the numerous sites he excavated had already been damaged by local "treasure seekers" before he arrived. But their damage was slight compared to the destruction later wrought by travelers looking for souvenirs or well-meaning but amateur archeologists making clumsy excavations. The indifference or corruption of local officialdom contributed to the destruction or disappearance of documents and artifacts. Rather than criticism, Stein deserves thanks, not only from the British Museum, but from the people and governments of Asia whose heritage he worked so hard to preserve and interpret.

Stein's name has always been linked most closely with the spectacular discovery of the sealed chapel's treasures at the "Caves of the Thousand Buddhas." It was by no means his only contribution to archeology or to the study of ancient oriental religion and culture, but it was the most dramatic. The importance of what he found, and rescued, there for the study of Buddhism and its development across Asia can be compared with the importance of the Dead Sea Scrolls for the study of Judaism and early Christianity. When his other discoveries are added to his Tun-huang achievement, his contribution to Asian archeology and the study of contacts among the ancient worlds of East and West must be considered unique. In his introduction to *Sand-Buried Ruins of Khotan*, Stein himself cogently summed up the meaning and significance of what his long, difficult years of exploration in Central Asia accomplished:

> These ruins throughout reveal to us a uniform and well-defined civilization. It is easy to recognize now that this bygone culture rested mainly on Indian foundations. But there has also come to light unmistakable evidence of other powerful influences both from the West and from China, which helped to shape its growth and to invest it with an individual character and fascination of its own.

Bibliography

Aurel Stein was a prolific writer, and his collected works are extensive. He wrote two kinds of books about his archeological expeditions and discoveries: the "detailed report" intended for scholars and specialists; and the "personal narrative" intended for the general reader. The following include titles from the latter category that relate to his first three expeditions to Central Asia.

Hopkirk, Peter. *Foreign Devils on the Silk Road*. London: John Murray, 1980. An entertaining account of early archeological discoveries in Central Asia which includes chapters on Sven Hedin and Aurel Stein. By the author of *The Great Game*.

Macartney, Lady. *An English Lady in Chinese Turkestan*. London: Ernest Benn, Ltd., 1931. A very readable account of the author's years as wife of the British Consul General in Kashgar.

Mirsky, Jeannette. *Sir Aurel Stein*. Chicago: University of Chicago Press, 1977. A rather pedestrian but thorough and scholarly biography.

Skrine, C.P. and P. Nightingale. *Macartney at Kashgar*. London: Methuen, 1973. A very readable account of Macartney's twenty years in Kashgar.

Stein, M. Aurel. *On Ancient Central Asian Tracks*. Chicago: University of Chicago Press, 1964. An account of all his Central Asian expeditions.

Ruins of Desert Cathay. 2 vols. London: Macmillan Co., 1912. An account for general readers of the second Central Asian expedition. Describes the discoveries of the Great Wall and the art treasures at Tun-huang.

Sand-Buried Ruins of Khotan. London: Fisher-Unwin, 1903. The author's account of the first Central Asian expedition.

Walker, Anabel. *Aurel Stein: Pioneer of the Silk Road*. London: John Murray, 1995. A new biography, carefully researched and beautifully written. Heartening evidence that a revival of interest in Stein and his contemporary travelers may be underway.

6
Alexandra David-Neel

Rational Mystic Among the Lamas

Learn from this information not to cavil
At slight mistakes in books on foreign travel.
HILAIRE BELLOC

In October 1923 four travelers set out from the French mission of
Abbé Ouvrard in western China on the bank of the Mekong River in
northwest Yunnan province near the junction of the borders of Yunnan,
Tibet, and Burma. Their plans, as communicated to the abbé, were
vague; they were headed, they said, for the Kha Karpo mountains.
Two of the travelers were coolies, or porters, hired locally to look after
the baggage. Their employers were a young man and an older woman.
Both were dressed in ordinary Chinese clothing, but neither was Chinese. Once out of sight of the mission house, the coolies were given
their pay and sent away, and the two remaining travelers reduced their
baggage to loads they could easily carry, which meant that they carried
only the barest necessities beyond the clothes on their backs. They
assumed the guise of mendicant Tibetan pilgrims, but anyone who
might have been able to see what the woman carried under her robes
would have seen things no poor pilgrim would ever carry: a watch, a
compass, a cache of exquisite gold jewelry which had been a present
from the Maharajah of Sikkim. Her short brown hair was dyed black,

with a black braid of dyed yak hair attached to simulate the ordinary hair style of Tibetan women. Both travelers carried loaded pistols concealed under their ragged robes.

The young man was, indeed, Tibetan, a lama of the conservative Red Hat sect. His name was Aphur Yongden, and he was the adopted son of his companion with whom he had spent the past ten years traveling, mostly on foot, through Asia. The woman was French, and her name was Alexandra David-Neel. Their secret destination was the "forbidden city" of Lhasa. Their journey was the final, and most remarkable, chapter in an Asian odyssey as remarkable as any undertaken in this century.

Almost twenty years after Francis Younghusband and his armed expedition reached Lhasa, Tibet's capital was still a forbidden city in a forbidden land. The treaty Younghusband signed with the Tibetans established a British presence in Tibet—a trade representative in Gyantse—and made southern Tibet a sphere of British influence. But it warned all other powers away from the country and thereby confirmed and continued Tibet's self-chosen isolation. The Anglo-Russian agreement of 1907, which formalized the neutralization of Central Asia and Tibet and ended the Great Game, further codified the arrangements that kept the forbidden land cut off. Finally, the Chinese Revolution of 1911 began a decades-long evolution of power in China that weakened Chinese authority in the peripheral regions of the Celestial Kingdom and left Tibet with an independence that was de facto, if not de jure, under the rule of the Tibetan theocracy headed by the Dalai Lama.

The Tibetans, protected after 1911 by British power based in India rather than Chinese power based in Peking, could continue to exercise their chosen policy of isolation that they felt was the only way to protect their religion and religion-based government from foreign influence that would weaken and debase them. In the 1920s, with China deprived of an effective government and torn by civil war among local warlords, Tibet, perhaps to an even greater degree than at the turn of the century, was an isolated country hostile to any intrusions by foreigners. A few British officials and travelers had penetrated the screen erected by the Tibetans to reach Lhasa, but they had been only a handful of people whose travel was sanctioned by the British Indian government and backed by British power.

Now, in 1923, a French woman with a will of iron and a knowledge of Tibet as profound as that possessed by any non-Tibetan, was determined to defy the Tibetan and British governments and become the first European woman to enter Lhasa. To do so, she had to assume a disguise and travel for months in the forbidden land undetected as a foreigner—as a Tibetan among Tibetans.

Louise Eugénie Alexandrine Marie David was born in Paris on October 24, 1868, the daughter of a radical journalist. Among her earliest memories were the Franco-Prussian War and the Paris Commune. As a toddler, she was bounced on the knee of Victor Hugo, a friend of her father. Very early in life she became fascinated with two pursuits: travel to faraway, exotic places, and the study of mysticism and oriental religions. She later wrote:

> Ever since I was five years old, a tiny precocious child of Paris, I wished to move out of the narrow limits in which, like all children of my age, I was then kept. I craved to go beyond the garden gate, to follow the road that passed it by, and to set out for the Unknown.

She also proved to be gifted with an excellent singing voice, so she studied music seriously. Last, but not least as a precursor of things to come, she began to follow the maxims of Epictetus, the Stoic Greek philosopher, whom she called "the revered master of my youth."

Her interest in mysticism brought her into contact, at the age of sixteen, with something called the Society of the Supreme Gnosis, based in London. She avidly read its journal which contained a crackpot pastiche of occultism and oriental religious teachings. At age twenty she was given an opportunity to travel to London to study at the Supreme Gnosis, an opportunity she enthusiastically accepted to the consternation of her parents who wanted her to continue her musical studies. She spent a year in London where she met an assortment of spiritualists, mystics, mediums, and others versed in occult and paranormal phenomena. She also spent hours in the library of the Supreme Gnosis, and in the British Museum, reading deeply in oriental philosophy and religion. After a year she returned to Paris where she continued her interrupted musical studies, but also continued her reading in the occult at the Theosophical Society of Paris and at the Sorbonne.

A young Alexandra in costume for one of her operatic roles.

In 1891 Alexandra inherited a modest sum from her "godmother," whose identity is unknown, and used it to make a journey to India, a country she had wanted to visit ever since her introduction to Sanskrit and Buddhism at the Supreme Gnosis. She spent more than a year in the subcontinent, traveling on foot from Ceylon northward across the entire length of India to the Himalayas in the far north. She stayed at hostels maintained by the Theosophical Society, and she interviewed Annie Besant, the President of the Theosophical Society, who had been one of the founders of the Indian National Congress, the political party which under Gandhi and Nehru would achieve Indian independence.

In the spring of 1893 Alexandra returned to Europe. She was now faced with the problem of choosing a career and earning a living. She decided to pursue a musical career, and studied in Brussels and in Paris. Chosen in 1895 to tour Indochina with the road company of L'Opéra-Comique, she was a hit in Hanoi and Haiphong as the premier chanteuse of the company, especially in the roles of Violetta in *La Traviata* and Manon Lescaut in *Manon*. But when she returned to Paris in 1897, she discovered that her success in Asia did not ensure success in the more demanding operatic world of Europe, and she was forced to perform in the provinces. In 1900, while in Marseilles, she felt compelled to accept an engagement with the municipal opera in Tunis, a further decline in her fortunes as a singer. But in Tunis, her life took another abrupt turn. She got married.

Philip Neel was the chief engineering officer of the French railway line that had recently been constructed to link Algeria with Tunisia. He was thirty-nine years old, a bachelor with a large home in Tunis, a yacht, and a string of mistresses. Alexandra apparently became one of his mistresses but, unlike the others, she finally moved in with him in his beautiful house. In August 1904, they married.

Their marriage must rank as one of the oddest on record. The first years were stormy, and Philip on more than one occasion threatened divorce. Alexandra loved their spacious, airy Moorish-style house in Tunis overlooking the Mediterranean, but she chafed at her restricted life as the wife of a French colonial bureaucrat. She took to journalism, often traveling to Europe to cover stories. She began writing what today would be called feminist articles on the status of women. She was gone for long periods, and her absences finally drove Philip to threaten divorce. But they remained married, and Alexandra, in addition to her journalistic writings, renewed her interest in oriental religions, and began to write books on that subject.

She had already written an autobiographical novel, which was never published. In 1907 her biography of one of her favorite oriental philosophers, *The Philosophy of Meh-ti and the Idea of Solidarity*, was published. In 1910 she lectured to large crowds at the Theosophical Society in both Paris and London. Another book, *Modern Buddhism and the Buddhism of Buddha,* was published in 1911. By 1911 she was gaining a reputation as an expert on Eastern religions, but her first-hand experience in the East was limited to a year's travel in India many years before (not counting her operatic tour of Indochina). Philip now made a proposal that would set the future course of their marriage until it was ended by his death more than a quarter-century later. He proposed that Alexandra visit India again to perfect her knowledge of oriental languages. He offered to bear all the costs for a one-year trip. Alexandra accepted the offer with delight and in August 1911 boarded a steamer for India.

Alexandra would remain in Asia for fourteen years. She maintained a continuous correspondence with Philip, who continued to provide financial support, sending her bank drafts whenever she was in need of money. The life Alexandra led required minimum financial support, but when she needed money, as she did regularly, Philip never refused her pleas. He also acted as her literary agent, relaying manuscripts and dealing with publishers on her behalf as she continued her writing. Alexandra spent long periods in remote places, often during periods of upheaval and anarchy. Nevertheless, she and Philip were able to continue their correspondence, and she was able to receive the drafts of money that he sent periodically, with few if any hitches. Her letters to him eventually totaled more than three thousand typewritten pages.

In August 1911 Alexandra arrived in Colombo, Ceylon, and traveled north through India, as she had in her earlier visit, to arrive in Calcutta, the capital of British India, by December. She found she was well known there, because several of her articles had been reprinted in the leading Anglo-Indian newspapers.

Irresistibly drawn to the solitude and vastness of the mountains to the north, after a few months she left behind the stuffy British colonial society of Calcutta and the city's sticky, suffocating heat. In March 1912, she traveled north to the tiny kingdom of Sikkim, wedged in the Himalayas between India, Nepal, Tibet, and Burma.

En route, at a dak bungalow, or rural rest house, she met Sidkeong Tulku, the thirty-three-year-old Crown Prince of Sikkim. He had been educated at Oxford and by English tutors, had made a grand tour of Asian capitals, and was a sophisticated man of the world, not at all what Alexandra had expected to find in a tiny, isolated Himalayan

Philip Neel, Alexandra's husband, never failed to respond to her requests for money during her years of travel in Asia.

kingdom. She was his guest at the royal palace in Gangtok, the Sikkimese capital, and the two apparently quickly developed a close relationship. Whether it remained platonic is uncertain, but each apparently was much taken by the other. Alexandra and the prince made treks into the mountains to the border of Tibet. Her first view of the vast tableland stretching beyond the snowy peaks of the Himalayas awakened in her an immediate, overpowering desire to visit the forbidden land:

*Sidkeong Tulku, the Maharaja of Sikkim, whose relationship with
Alexandra David-Neel may have been more than platonic.*

The path . . . starts from a low point in Sikkim, amid tropical
vegetation, wild orchids, and the living fireworks of fireflies. Gradually, as one climbs, the scenery changes, nature becomes severe, the
singing of birds and the noisy buzzing of insects subside. The huge
trees, in their turn, are unable to struggle in the rarefied air of the
summits. With each mile the forest becomes more stunted, till the
shrubs are reduced to the size of dwarfs creeping on the ground
while still higher up they cannot even continue to exist. The traveler is left amidst rocks richly embroidered with brightly colored
lichens, cold waterfalls, half-frozen lakes, and giant glaciers. Then
. . . one suddenly discovers the immensity of the trans-Himalayan

tableland of Tibet, with its distant horizon of peaks bathed in strange mauve and orange hues, and carrying queerly shaped caps of snow upon their mighty heads. What an unforgettable vision! I was at last in the calm solitudes of which I had dreamed since my infancy.

Her objective in going to Sikkim was to interview the Dalai Lama. This was the same Dalai Lama who had fled Lhasa in 1905 to avoid Younghusband. He had returned to his capital when the British expedition departed but a few years later he fled again in the face of an invading Chinese army sent by the dying Manchu dynasty to reassert Chinese authority. In 1912 he was living in exile in Kalimpong, twenty miles from the British hill station of Darjeeling, under the protection of his former enemies.

Alexandra interviewed the "living Buddha" twice, with Sidkeong acting as interpreter. She impressed him with sophisticated questions about Buddhism, and he left her with a ringing bit of advice: "Learn Tibetan!" Instead, she decided to expand her knowledge of Sanskrit and spent a year in Benares, the holy city of the Hindus on the Ganges, studying that ancient Indian language. In December 1913 she returned to Gangtok to a huge welcome arranged by Sidkeong. He treated her with great deference as well as affection, and showered her with gifts of costly pure gold jewelry. She began to study Tibetan, which she found easier than Sanskrit, and to spend more and more time in the mountains. She spent the summer months in Gangtok, then in the autumn of 1914, as the Great War in Europe settled into a grim bloodbath of attrition, Alexandra entered into one of the more remarkable phases of her unusual life.

In 1912, in the royal palace in Gangtok, she had met the Gomchen of Lachen, a revered hermit associated with a monastery at Lachen, a tiny village at an altitude of 8,000 feet near the Tibetan border. The Gomchen had gone to Gangtok to perform a religious ceremony at the request of the Maharajah. Over the next two years Alexandra visited him at the monastery a few times. But the Gomchen spent most of his time in a cave, high above the monastery at 12,000 feet, where he permitted no one to visit him. Alexandra, against the advice of everyone at Lachen, decided to seek him out in his cave retreat, and scrambled up the mountain to the hermit's remote dwelling. She had

*Alexandra David-Neel with the Gomchen of Lachen with whom she studied
for two years while living in a mountainside cave in Sikkim.*

impressed the lama with her sincerity and knowledge of Buddhism
during their conversations at the monastery, and he did not turn her
away. To her delight, he agreed to take her on as a disciple. She settled
down in her tent attached to a cave slightly below the Gomchen's, to
enter into a life of severe austerity, difficult study, and meditation. She
was not alone; she was accompanied by several Tibetan servants who
stayed in a rude hut nearby. But her life was reduced to absolute essen-
tials. Every day she ascended to the Gomchen's cave to study Tibetan
and Buddhism. Every night was spent in solitary meditation.

Alexandra spent two years with the Gomchen. For the first winter, he descended from his cave to the monastery before the snows
came to isolate the cave from all contact with the outside world until
spring. Alexandra followed and pitched her tent just outside the walls
of the monastery where she, as a woman, was not permitted to stay. In

December, as she was living in her tent pitched in deep snow outside the monastery, she received shocking news. Sidkeong, who had recently succeeded his father as Maharajah, had suddenly died after a brief, mysterious illness. Whether he died of natural causes was never established; as Maharajah of the tiny mountain kingdom, he lived amid swirls of intrigue and could easily have been the victim of an assassination plot. Alexandra grieved for months.

For the second winter of her period as a disciple to the Gomchen, the hermit decided to remain in his solitary retreat and Alexandra remained with him. She had built a rude wooden house extending outward from the mouth of her cave. She lived there, climbing each morning through knee-deep snow to her teacher's quarters, and returning in the late afternoon. Their long conversations during the months of winter isolation were not restricted to the exotic realm of Tibetan Buddhism, although Alexandra became deeply versed in that esoteric subject:

> He would often stop our reading to tell me about facts he had himself witnessed. . . . He would describe people he had known, repeating their conversations and telling me about their lives. Thus, while seated in his cabin or mine, I visited the palaces of rich lamas, entered the hermitages of many an ascetic. I traveled along the roads, meeting curious people. I became in that way closely acquainted with Tibet, its inhabitants, their customs and their thoughts: a precious science which was later to stand me in good stead.

By the summer of 1916 Alexandra decided that her period of study as a disciple should end. She later wrote, "I never let myself be taken in by the illusion that my anchorite's home might become my final harbor." Before parting from her teacher, she broached to him the idea of writing a book about the Buddhist teachings she had mastered. He dissuaded her:

> "Waste of time. The great majority of readers and hearers are the same all over the world. . . . If you speak to them of profound Truths, they yawn, and if they dare, they leave you; but if you tell them absurd fables they are all eyes and ears."

Alexandra David-Neel in Sikkim. At far left is sixteen-year-old Yongden.

When she parted from the Gomchen, Alexandra was accompanied by Aphur Yongden who at age fifteen had joined her as a servant shortly before she attached herself to the Gomchen. She had first met him at the home of a Sikkimese nobleman who had given the young man an education. Alexandra and Yongden developed a close relationship, and he was to remain with her until he died in 1955.

As he emerges in the pages of Alexandra David-Neel's writings, Yongden is one of the more fascinating characters in the travel literature of Asia. He was, according to Alexandra, an "authentic Tibetan lama" of the older, more conservative Red Hat Sect (the more recently created reform group being called the Yellow Hats). He was always immediately recognized as such by any fellow Tibetans he met, and they accorded him the respect and deference his position demanded. Yet he fully supported his foreign "mother" when she deliberately circumvented the policies and laws of Tibet and abetted her in her deceptions of his fellow countrymen.

In the many anecdotes Alexandra recounts in her writings about Yongden, he comes across as someone of quick, perceptive intelligence, shrewd judgement, and a fine sense of humor. The many charades into which he entered with Alexandra during their trek across Tibet to Lhasa in order to maintain their disguises as mendicant pilgrims are sometimes poignant, more often hilarious. He often comes close to becoming a parody of his religion, but he always stops short. He became indispensable to Alexandra in many ways. Without him, it seems unlikely that she could have spent the many years she spent in Asia in the manner in which she spent them.

In July 1916, having parted from the Gomchen in Lachen, Alexandra and Yongden headed north to cross the border into Tibet. They were bound for Shigatse, a market town, and more specifically Tashilumpo, a monastery nearby where the Panchen Lama, second in authority in Tibet to the Dalai Lama, resided. He had invited Alexandra, so she interviewed the great lama whom she found to be sophisticated, well-educated and altogether impressive.

When Alexandra and Yongden returned to Sikkim, they found their hut at Lachen sacked and the Gomchen in seclusion, seeing no one. Their trip to Tibet had not been authorized by the British authorities. The British Resident in Gangtok had fined the villagers near Alexandra's retreat, because they had not reported to him her unauthorized journey (of which they were, in fact, not aware). The villagers, in revenge, had looted her house. Alexandra and Yongden were given two weeks to leave the country. Alexandra vowed revenge:

> These uncivilized proceedings made me wish to retaliate, but in a witty way, befitting the spirit of the great city in which I had the privilege of being born.

Alexandra was determined to return to the Land of Snows, but she chose a roundabout route that took several years to complete. From Calcutta, she and Yongden sailed via Burma and Vietnam to Japan where they spent six months studying Zen methods of meditation. In August they moved on to Korea, then in October to Peking. Their objective was Mongolia, where Alexandra felt she could find Tibetan lamas with whom to continue her studies. In Peking she met a lama from the famous Kum Bum monastery in the Koko Nor district of northeastern Tibet, then under Chinese control. He offered to take her to his monastery, in exchange for her help in writing a book on astronomy. She accepted and, in January 1918, they left Peking.

In the chaos of warlord China the 1,600-mile trip from Peking to Kum Bum took six months. The countryside was torn by banditry and warfare between troops of the weak central government and local armies, among the warlords, and between Chinese and Tibetan armies. At one point, Alexandra became ill in a small, remote, filthy village. She feared the illness was fatal, and seriously considered suicide, but then began slowly to recover. In Tungchow she took shelter in a Swedish mission during an attack by rebel soldiers. Finally, in July 1918, she arrived at Kum Bum.

Kum Bum is a very old and large complex of temples and monasteries, one of the most revered in Tibet. Sven Hedin had visited it more than twenty years earlier, and it is interesting to compare his impressions of it with Alexandra's. He thought some of the temples were magnificent, but his overall reaction was not favorable:

> The Buddhist architecture leaves a peculiar "mythical" impression upon the mind. It conforms to the rules of Tibetan taste; but in the end it becomes wearisome to a European, who is accustomed to the sound and genuine forms of the West. In such interiors you cannot possibly experience that sense of calm serenity and well-being which you feel in a Christian temple.

He was positively repelled by the

> swarms of idle lamas, who did nothing all day long but grovel on their hands and knees, muttering their stupid parrot-like repetitions before those gilded blocks of wood or clay. . . . They sat about the cloisters, and yawned, and told their beads. Whenever I stopped to make a sketch or drawing, they started like rats out of their holes and lurking places, and swarmed thickly around me, infesting the very air with the ill-savor of their presence.

The Swedish explorer stayed only a few days to tour the complex. Alexandra stayed more than two-and-a-half years, although she spent part of that time making expeditions into the region around the monastery. She and Yongden lived in a comfortable house. She spent the time translating rare Tibetan Buddhist manuscripts into French and English, while Yongden completed the studies required to pass a special examination to attain the rank of full lama.

When they departed Kum Bum for the last time in February 1921, Alexandra did so with regret:

> I would willingly have spent the rest of my days in the lulling calm of the monastic citadel where I . . . lived for two years and eight months. . . . I valued the serenity of the hours passed in following the thoughts of ancient Buddhist sages, in the books that had been taken down for me from the sealed bookcases, where they lay in wrappings of iridescent yellow brocade. It was delightful to study and meditate in such surroundings; the mind experienced, to the point of intoxication, the subtle voluptuousness of solitude and silence.

However, her attitude toward the swarms of monks may not have been so different from Hedin's:

> In the large monasteries, the gathering monks number several thousands. A strange, shabby, ill-smelling crew . . . .

As had happened when she parted from the Gomchen, she felt the time had come to move on. More importantly, she had come to a definite decision: she would go to Lhasa, whether or not the Tibetans or the British or anyone else granted permission. But it would be two-and-a-half years before she would even begin the journey directed toward the Tibetan capital. She would spend that time crisscrossing western China in an incredible journey of thousands of miles that would take her and Yongden as far north as Mongolia; south to Chengtu, the capital of Szechwan province; and as far west as Jyekundo, a market town of mud houses at 12,000-foot altitude under the control of a Chinese warlord where the travelers stopped for ten months. In the middle of winter, they tried to leave Jyekundo and travel north to Mongolia. They struggled in the mountains for ten days in snow drifts to their waists. Their horses' hooves froze, and they were attacked by wolves. They finally turned back, and spent several more months in Jyekundo. The trip from Kum Bum to Jyekundo is described in Alexandra's book entitled *Tibetan Journey* in its English edition.

So when Alexandra and Yongden bid farewell to the Abbé Ouvrard at his mission on the Mekong and set out for Lhasa in October 1923, more than seven years had passed since they had departed Sikkim under an expulsion order from the British Resident. Since their departure from Kum Bum two-and-a-half years had elapsed, and they had traveled during that period perhaps 8,000 miles through western China across deserts and snow-choked mountain passes; in freezing cold and burning heat; eluding bandits and renegade soldiers. Alexandra had also spent months on end translating Buddhist scriptures and treatises and studying the most esoteric aspects of the Tibetan religion. It had been a journey of epic proportions, but the journey that would make her famous had only just begun.

Alexandra was fifty-four when she departed the abbé's mission. Her travels over the previous seven years had been difficult by any yardstick, but those challenges were mild compared with the privations she was to suffer over the next four months. She and her companion carried with them a small tent, but they seldom were bold enough to pitch it, since poor pilgrims, such as they pretended to be, would never have had such a luxury. Most often, they slept in the open on the ground with the tent covering them like a blanket. Like pilgrims, they often stayed in the homes of Tibetans in villages or on farms. Sometimes, they slept in caves. Their route led them almost directly west, through eastern Tibet across several high mountain passes. They traveled in the depths of winter, as pilgrims did, in order to arrive in Lhasa for the spring festival in February.

During the first week or two, they traveled mostly at night to avoid detection by Tibetan border guards until they were well across the border. The second night's experience was a taste of things to come:

> I felt exhausted and walked mechanically, half-asleep. . . . At last utter exhaustion compelled us to rest. . . . We lay down on a rocky mattress whose roughness we unpleasantly felt through our clothes and endeavored to remember even in our sleep that we were perched on the edge of a precipice whose depth was unfathomable at night. In such wise we spent the second happy night of our wonderful adventure.

They often encountered other groups of pilgrims traveling to or from Lhasa as well as the residents of villages and farms along the way. Yongden was always recognized as a "authentic lama," and almost always asked to tell fortunes or predict the future, called the art of mo:

> It is regarded as an unpardonable sin for a lama to refuse such a request. "Red Hat" sect lamas, in particular, who are credited with a profound knowledge of occult lore, can only with difficulty avoid acting as fortune-tellers, astrologers, exorcists, and the like. My companion endeavored to combine each of his consultations with some simple words about the true Buddhist doctrine which might lead his hearers away from their deep-rooted superstition. He also added, according to circumstances, some advice about cleanliness—as far as hygiene can be understood by Tibetans.

Alexandra recounts many anecdotes of Yongden making mo, and the lama's ingenuity as a soothsayer was often admirable. Early in their trip they encountered a group of pilgrims, among whom was a young girl with feet so sore she could no longer walk. She feared being left behind by the others and begged Yongden to tell when she would be able to walk again. Her mother demanded to know which demon had caused her daughter's trouble and how to exorcise it.

> Yongden, with impressive gravity, counted the beads of his rosary, threw some pebbles in the air, caught them again in his hand before they touched the ground, and performed a few other ceremonies, accompanied by an unintelligible muttering in broken Sanskrit. My adopted son is really gifted for such ritualistic work and, had he continued his life in a lamasery, he might have become quite famous as an oracle or exorcist.

Yongden told the group they would soon encounter a chorten, a small monument to hold religious articles—"a prophecy that could not but be fulfilled, for chorten are numerous in Tibet." They were to have the girl lie down there for three days; three times a day have her walk around the monument while chanting a spell; her feet and legs then to be massaged with water (into which a pinch of holy sand was to be placed); and she was then each time to be fed well. A few other spells and incantations were prescribed.

Alexandra David-Neel and Aphur Yongden in Tibet.

Moreover, the lama taught the mother another spell which would protect everyone from the demon, so long as they remained together until they reached their destination.

> The poor fellows felt as if in Heaven. The lama had spoken long, and what he had said they could neither well understand nor remember, which meant that he was exceedingly learned.

Alexandra and Yongden left the group with the old mother "bowed down with the utmost gratitude." The two travelers chuckled.

"What does it matter?" said Yongden, smiling. "The girl will get three days' rest, a little massage, and good food, and as the mother has the precious zung [spell] and will not leave her daughter, the other people will not abandon her, either. That is good honest work and, moreover, I learned such tricks from you."

On another occasion a week or two later, they encountered an old couple leading a goat very badly overloaded with their belongings. Yongden spoke to them.

"Be careful," he said, "to be very kind to that beast. It has been related to you in a previous life when it was a human being. On account of some bad deeds it has been reborn in the sorrowful animal kingdom . . . it will be once more a man in its next life, and you three will meet again, so do your best in order that feelings of friendship may be cultivated between you which will bear good fruits in the future."

The villagers were impressed by this oracular announcement, and they expressed their gratitude.

Before we started, I saw the woman taking a few packages out of the goat's load to lighten it, while the old man patted it. "The little thing will be happy now," Yongden told me as we continued down the hill. "They will treat it kindly now."

They often went for twenty-four hours at a stretch, or much longer, without any solid food. For sustenance, they depended mainly upon two Tibetan staples: buttered tea, in which hot, strong tea is laced liberally with butter and salt; and tsamba or barley flour, which was usually mixed with tea to form a dough which was then rolled into balls and eaten, or added to soup to thicken it. Both reportedly are acquired tastes. Alexandra very early in her Asian travels developed a liking for both. Later, when they reached the lower elevations approaching Lhasa, where the population was more numerous and they stayed more often with Tibetans, they had a few gastronomical adventures in poor Tibetan huts that even Yongden had never before experienced.

In one village they were invited into a hut of a family that obviously had no extra food for guests. Yongden gave the man some money to buy more food. The man hurried off and returned to the smokey room, dimly lit by a flickering fire, carrying a bag.

> Ugh! A most fearsome odor suddenly fills the room, the smell of a charnel house. It is sickening.
>
> "Oh," says Yongden, in a voice that trembles slightly, concealing the nausea that he is obliged to repress. "It is a stomach!"
>
> I understand now. The Tibetans, when they kill a beast, have a horrible habit of enclosing in the stomach the kidneys, heart, liver, and entrails of the animal. They then sew up this kind of bag, and its contents go on decaying inside for days, weeks, and even longer.
>
> "Yes, it is a stomach," repeats its purchaser, whose voice also trembles somewhat, but with joy, seeing the mass of foodstuff falling out of the now-opened bag. He has placed the horror on the floor, is plunging his hands into it, taking out the gelatinous entrails. Three children who were asleep have awakened, and are squatting in front of their father, watching him eagerly with covetous eyes.

Alexandra is able to plead illness and lie down in a corner to feign sleep, but Yongden cannot avoid swallowing at least one full bowl of the evil-smelling soup their hostess has concocted. He then sincerely pleads feeling ill and retires.

> The others feast long and gluttonously upon the broth, smacking their lips in silence, overcome with joy at this unexpected bonne bouche, and I am overtaken by sleep whilst the family is still masticating noisily.

The travelers crossed several high, snow-choked mountain passes. On one, which Alexandra estimated to be 19,000 feet high, occurred one of the few incidents she describes in her account of the journey to Lhasa that could be called supernatural. At one o'clock in the morning they were at the height of the pass, exhausted, wet, and nearly frozen. Yongden discovered that his flint and steel, the only means they had to light a fire, were also wet. Alexandra sent Yongden to gather some firewood, while she undertook the practice of thumo reskiang to warm herself and dry out the flint and steel.

Thumo reskiang is described by Alexandra as "the art of warming oneself without fire up in the snows." She had studied it on several occasions, though she had not done it for several years when she attempted it on the road to Lhasa. It requires a long initiation.

The most important qualifications required are: to be already skilled in the various practices connected with breathing; to be capable of perfect concentration of mind, going as far as the trance in which thoughts become visualized; and to have received the proper angkur from a lama possessed with the power of conferring it [angkur: the rite by which a peculiar power is communicated by the master to his disciple].

Initiates who have completed the study are given an examination which consists of going outside on a frosty winter night, sitting naked on the ground, and wrapping oneself in a sheet dipped in ice water. The internal heat generated by thumo must dry the sheet which is then dipped again. The examination lasts until daybreak. It is said that as many as forty sheets are thus dried in a single night. Lamas completely adept at the practice are said to be able to live for years through winters at extreme altitudes wearing only a single thin cotton garment, constantly keeping warm through the art of thumo.

Alexandra had studied this practice, and on the road to Lhasa she undertook to do it. It was the middle of the night, and she was exhausted and cold.

> I began to doze. Yet my mind continued to be concentrated on the object of the thumo rite. Soon I saw flames arising around me; they grew higher and higher; they enveloped me, curling their tongues above my head. I felt deliciously comfortable.

She was awakened by a loud report of ice cracking in the river.

> I opened my eyes. The wind was blowing hard and my body burned. The flint and steel were dried, and Yongden returned with wood, so a fire was kindled.

Another paranormal occurrence took place one night as the travelers camped outdoors. An ascetic lama suddenly appeared out of the darkness and sat down next to the fire. After a long period of silence, he suddenly addressed Alexandra, asking her questions that demonstrated he knew who she was and had met her before. But she could not recall ever having seen him, and she stared at his face. Yongden went off to gather firewood.

"Do not try to remember, Jetsunma [honorific address to an older woman]," said the ascetic to me when we were alone. "I have as many faces as I desire, and you have never seen this one."

They conversed for a long time on Tibetan mysticism, and then the visitor disappeared silently into the night. In other books, Alexandra describes many other even more startling paranormal occurrences she not only heard about but said she witnessed or even experienced herself.

For four months they had a string of adventures that were in turn exciting, funny, frightening, startling, or simply grueling tests of fortitude and physical endurance. While crossing one mountain pass, Yongden sprained his ankle, and they had to retreat into a cave to wait until it healed. It snowed without letup, their food ran out, and they wondered if they would ever be able to leave. He fashioned a makeshift crutch and they slowly and haltingly made their way down the mountain. Villagers in the valley were amazed that they had crossed the pass, which was considered closed by snow. They were convinced that the lama had used his supernormal powers to do so.

In February they arrived at Lhasa. As they prepared to enter the city, a sudden sandstorm enveloped everything in a blinding yellow curtain of swirling sand, thus providing a welcome screen for the disguised travelers.

> I interpreted it as a symbol promising me complete security, and the future justified my interpretation. For two months I was to wander freely in the lamaist Rome, with none to suspect that, for the first time in history, a foreign woman was beholding the Forbidden City.

They toured the Potala and other public buildings. They stayed in a caravansery "where the strangest specimens of humanity were to be met . . . every act, even every thought, was public." It was packed with other pilgrims visiting the city for the New Year festivities. They became embroiled in a domestic quarrel between two families that finally came to blows, and they were summoned as witnesses in a law suit that the head of one family brought against the other. Fearing that their disguise would be revealed in court, they were able to avoid appearing in court for awhile. But finally, fearing exposure, they left the city.

They traveled for a few weeks through southwestern Tibet to col-

Personal effects carried by Alexandra during her journey to Lhasa. They are on display in her home at Digne, now a museum.

lect rare Buddhist books and manuscripts. But the trip had taken its toll on Alexandra, and they finally appeared in late April in Shigatse at the residence of the British Trade Representative, David Macdonald, to seek shelter and help in reaching India. He later wrote of his amazement at the two ragged and worn travelers appearing so suddenly and unexpectedly at his house. Alexandra looked completely worn out. "She appeared very frail," he wrote. "She must have undergone incredible hardships." Given rest and some new clothes, the travelers continued south to India. After resting in Calcutta, they sailed to Europe, arriving in Valencia, Spain, on May 4, 1925.

Alexandra remained in Europe eleven years. The story of her Asian exploits had preceded her, and she was a celebrity. She did not meet Philip until Christmas, and then they quarreled over Yongden whom Alexandra was determined to adopt legally as her son. She and Philip continued to live apart while she became a traveling lecturer and writer. Several books were published in the next several years. She was awarded the Gold Medal of the Geographical Society of France and was made a Chevalier of the Legion of Honor. In 1928 she purchased a house in Digne, a cathedral town in the Alps, where she and Yongden settled down. Philip visited them occasionally.

Alexandra David-Neel and Yongden in front of the Potala in Lhasa.
Alexandra's face is blackened as part of her disguise.

In January 1937 Alexandra and Yongden again set out for Asia, this time overland across Europe and Russia to Peking. When the Japanese invaded China later that year, she retreated up the Yangtse River to Tachienlu in western Szechwan where they stayed at the French Catholic Hospital until mid-1944 when the renewed Japanese offensive drove them further south to Chengtu. In mid-1945 they flew over the Himalayas from Kunming to Calcutta. In July 1946 they returned to Europe by air.

Alexandra spent the rest of her life at her home in Digne, writing more books and receiving visitors. Philip had died in 1941 while she was in China. Yongden remained with her collaborating with her on some of her books. Some neighbors who became acquainted with him later said that he was unhappy and depressed away from his homeland and that he lapsed into alcoholism. He died in 1955 at the age of fifty-six. In her last years, Alexandra's legs became swollen and she was barely able to walk, stumping around her house leaning on a cane. She hired a young female secretary upon whom she depended more and more as she became increasingly infirm. She was reportedly a demanding and ever more irascible employer. She died at Digne in 1969, less than two months short of her 101st birthday.

There can be no doubt that Alexandra David-Neel acquired an amazing store of knowledge about Buddhism, especially the northern Mahayana, or "Greater Wheel," variety, and even more especially, the Tibetan version of that tradition. She collaborated with Yongden to write a book entitled *The Secret Oral Teachings of Tibetan Buddist Sects* (which was published after his death when she was ninety-nine years old). It was described by one Western authority on Buddhism as "the most direct, no-nonsense, and down-to-earth explanation of Mahayana Buddhism which has thus far been written." She could acquire that knowledge and understanding because she was fluent in Tibetan. David Macdonald, the British Trade Representative in Tibet at whose house Alexandra appeared after her journey to Lhasa, was half Sikkimese and fluent in Tibetan. He wrote that she "spoke Tibetan like a native." Yet, it is not easy to sort out from her writings what her true feelings and beliefs about Tibet and its religion must have been.

Alexandra described herself as a "rational Buddhist." Moreover, she said, she had "inborn tendencies to distrust and incredulity." She considered Buddhism eminently rational; indeed, its rationality was what attracted her to it. She repeatedly distinguished between what she considered "true Buddhism" and the religion practiced by most Tibetans which she considered shot through with ignorance and superstition. The picture she draws of the average Tibetan—certainly, the uneducated masses, but often members of the educated elites as well—is far from flattering: he is credulous to the point of almost unbelievable gullibility, but at the same time suspicious almost to the point of paranoia. He may be goodhearted and generous at times, but he is also hopelessly stupid. He believes ghosts and demons rule his life. He lives in filth and eats offal.

Yet, the "rational Buddhist" chose to study Buddhism through the Tibetan variety with Tibetan teachers. She would have found it much easier to study the religion in any of a half-dozen or more other Asian countries with predominantly Buddhist populations (she did study briefly in Burma and Japan, but those were only brief interludes compared to the years she spent studying Tibetan Buddhism). To choose Tibet, and stick with it, required determination, perseverance, and bravery, traits Alexandra possessed in abundance.

Even so, why choose it when there were so many other more hospitable places to go, if simply study of Buddhism was her objective? It seems fairly certain that Alexandra's lifelong fascination with mysticism and the occult accounts to a large degree for her parallel fascination with Tibet, the land above all others with traditions of mystical and supernormal phenomena.

In various books, but especially in *With Mystics and Magicians in Tibet*, Alexandra recounts numerous stories she heard of paranormal or occult occurrences: telepathy, reincarnation, clairvoyance, necromancy, psychic phenomena, and the like. More startling are the many other occurrences she said she witnessed or even took part in herself. Reference has already been made above to her engaging in thumo reskiang, the art of warming oneself without a fire. Another of what she called "psychic sports" was lung-gom.

Lung-gom is "a kind of training which is said to develop uncommon nimbleness and especially enables its adepts to take extraordinarily long tramps with amazing rapidity." What is involved here is something much more than running a marathon in two or three hours, although to call it the art of flying, as some writers have done, is not fair to the Tibetans who do not go that far in making claims for it. It is, according to Alexandra, "tramping at a rapid pace and without stopping during several successive days and nights." It is accomplished after long training and involves maintaining a trance. In one account which has been recounted by some of her biographers, she described watching a lung-gom.

She first saw him through binoculars, a man moving "at an unusual gait and . . . with extraordinary swiftness." As he approached, her servants identified him as a lung-gom and warned Alexandra not to stop him or speak to him, as she wished to do, because it would break his trance and perhaps thereby kill him.

> By that time he had nearly reached us; I could clearly see his perfectly calm impassive face and wide-open eyes with their gaze fixed on some invisible far-distant object situated somewhere high up in space. The man did not run. He seemed to lift himself from the ground, proceeding by leaps. It looked as if he had been endowed

with the elasticity of a ball and rebounded each time his feet touched the ground.

Four days after encountering the lung-gom, Alexandra met some herdsmen who had also seen him. Based upon where she had seen him and where the herdsmen had seen him, and the elapsed time between the sightings, she calculated that he must have continued at the same speed after she sighted him for the rest of the day and night and the whole of the next day. On another occasion she was able to speak with a lung-gom who had attached himself to her caravan. The anecdote is humorous, because the lung-gom went into his trance almost involuntarily as he hurried to arrive at camp before nightfall, spurred by thoughts of the hot dinner awaiting him.

> When he reached us, the man stood quite still for a while staring straight before him. He was not at all out of breath, but appeared only half-conscious and incapable of speaking or moving. However, the trance gradually subsided and the arjopa [novice] came back to his normal state. . . . The novice regarded himself as a sinner. The mixture of gluttony, holy mystic words and lung-gom exercises seemed to him sacrilegious.

Many anecdotes, some involving death and necromancy, reflect the Tibetans' preoccupation with those subjects. One incident apparently occurred soon after Alexandra's arrival in Sikkim, although she does not identify the time or place. In a village where she was staying, she heard two boys mention that someone had died. Later the same day, she came upon two monks seated under some trees near a hut. She watched them from behind a bush.

> Hik! cried one upon a peculiar abnormal shrill note. Hik! repeated the other after a few minutes. And so they continued, with long intervals of silence, during which they remained motionless between shrieks. I noticed that a great effort seemed required to produce this sound, which apparently came up from their very entrails. After having watched them for some time, I saw one of the trapas put his hands upon his throat. His face expressed suffering, he turned his head to one side and spat out a stream of blood. His companion said a few words that I could not hear.

> Without answering, the monk rose and went towards the cabin.
> I then noticed a long straw standing straight up on the top of his
> head. What did this ornament signify?

She withdrew and returned to her house where she asked a lama with whom she was studying what the men were doing. He explained that the peculiar cry she heard was part of a ritual a lama performs while seated next to a person who has died. The purpose of the ritual is to allow the spirit to escape the body of the dead person. The cry opens a small hole in the top of the skull in which a straw is placed. When the straw stands up straight, the lama knows the hole is large enough for the spirit to escape. In some cases, the opening becomes large enough to introduce the little finger. Thus, if the story is accurate in all its particulars, Alexandra saw a corpse walking and talking.

Interestingly, reviews of *With Mystics and Magicians in Tibet* in such leading British periodicals as the London *Times Literary Supplement* and *The Spectator* expressed no skepticism about these and the many other similar occurrences described in the book. The reviewer in *The Saturday Review* simply seconded Alexandra's plea, made at the end of the book, that more scientific effort be directed toward investigation of hitherto unexplainable psychic phenomena.

It is difficult to avoid the conclusion that Alexandra, like Arnold Henry Savage Landor, on many occasions "drew the long bow" in her accounts of her travels. There is no evidence that those two travelers in the forbidden land ever met, or even that either knew of the other's existence. They seem very different personalities in so many respects; one wonders how they might have gotten on together if they had met. Admirers of Alexandra might resent comparing her with Landor; her accomplishments greatly exceeded his. Yet both appreciated the value of a good anecdote, and both wrote vastly entertaining accounts of some truly astonishing experiences. Whatever doubts one might harbor about the accuracy of some of Alexandra's stories, one must conclude that, like Landor, she had enough adventures to fill the lives of twenty people.

Bibliography

Alexandra David-Neel wrote a great many books and periodical articles in both French and English. Some of her books written in French have never been translated into English. The following include only her best known books that relate directly to her Asian travels and that have appeared in English.

David-Neel, A. *My Journey To Lhasa.* New York: Harper & Bros., 1927. √ Her account of the remarkable 1923 journey.

The Secret Oral Teachings in Tibetan Buddhist Sects. San Francisco: City Light Books, 1967. The author's version of what Tibetan Buddhism is, or should be.

Tibetan Journey. London: John Lane, 1936. An account of the author's wanderings in the 1920s. Originally published in French √ as *Grand Tibet.*

With Mystics and Magicians in Tibet. London: John Lane, 1931 (later reprinted as *Magic and Mystery in Tibet*). A collection of accounts of paranormal experiences—some that Alexandra heard about, some she claimed to have witnessed, and some she said she experienced herself that stretch the reader's credulity to the limit.

Foster, Barbara and Michael. *Forbidden Journey: The Life of Alexandra David-Neel.* San Francisco: Harper & Row, 1987. A thoroughly researched, uncritically admiring biography.

Macdonald, D. *Twenty Years in Tibet.* Philadelphia: J.B. Lippincott Co., √ 1932. A fascinating firsthand account of a British official's life in Tibet when it was still almost totally unknown to the outside world.

Middleton, Ruth. *Alexandra David-Neel: Portrait of an Adventurer.* Boston: Shambala, 1989. An admiring and uncritical biography.

Miller, Luree. *On Top of the World: Five Women Explorers in Tibet.* Seattle: Mountaineers, 1984. Includes a chapter on Alexandra with emphasis on her journey to Lhasa.

7
Roy Chapman Andrews

Dinosaur Eggs and Warlords

The camel excels in a number of ways,
And travellers give him unlimited praise—
He can go without drinking for several days.

HILAIRE BELLOC

The road across the Mongolian desert reflected shimmering heat rays into the crystal air. Though smooth, the road was really no more than a trail, used for centuries by camel caravans traveling between Kalgan, the entry point to Mongolia at the Great Wall of China, and Urga, the capital of Mongolia. The driver of the open touring car speeding along the trail was alone. He had just begun to apply the brakes as he approached a spot where the road abruptly dipped into a valley, when he spotted a man on horseback emerging from behind a hill just off the road. Sunlight gleamed on a rifle barrel.

The driver knew this was neither the time nor the place to take chances, and he grabbed the .38 revolver on the seat beside him. He dropped a shot in front of the rider who disappeared into the valley. As the car swept over the valley rim and started down the slope, the driver saw four more horsemen straight ahead, rifles slung across their backs. He opened the cutout and jammed the accelerator to the floor. The car roared down the hill toward the horsemen. Their ponies took fright,

Roy Chapman Andrews in Mongolia in 1928, at the height
of his fame as an explorer.

rearing and plunging, preventing the men from unslinging their rifles. As the car swept past, three of the riders raced off. The driver fired several quick shots at the remaining rider, whose pony momentarily appeared too frightened to move, but deliberately aimed to miss him. The four bandits, for such they were, disappeared in a cloud of dust.

Fifty miles further on, the driver came upon a detachment of Chinese soldiers. He reported the incident to their commander, who was furious because the driver had not even tried to kill at least one of the bandits. The driver replied that he was a peaceful explorer, and it was the soldiers' duty to kill bandits, not his.

Bandits were an old story in Mongolia, but what about an automobile? The year was 1923, and Central Asia was no longer the terra incognita it had been when Sven Hedin plunged into the Takla Makan Desert in the 1890s. Automobiles were by no means commonplace, but by 1923 there was a regular motor service in operation between Peking and Urga. Even so, Mongolia was no place for the timid or fainthearted, and a traveler took his chances with bandits and with groups of renegade soldiers, who were the same thing, if he made the trip.

The "peaceful explorer" who had the brush with bandits was Roy Chapman Andrews, and this was not his first, nor his last, automobile trip across Mongolia. Neither was this his first or last brush with bandits; in some other encounters the shooting was more bloody. He was already famous in the United States as a lecturer and writer whose thrilling accounts of adventures in remote parts of the world had made his name familiar to armchair travelers and stay-at-home adventurers. His scientific achievements were probably less generally known in 1923, but he was on the threshold of a discovery that would splash his name across newspapers all over the world.

Roy Chapman Andrews was born in Beloit, Wisconsin, on January 26, 1884, the son of a wholesale druggist. The woods and rivers of southern Wisconsin offered plenty of hunting and fishing, and the young Andrews early in life became an avid outdoorsman. He received his first shotgun when he was nine years old and, before he finished grammar school, he was an accomplished taxidermist. He studied at Beloit College in his hometown where he was a mediocre student. He graduated in 1906.

Among his favorite childhood books was *A Handbook of North American Birds* by Frank M. Chapman, a naturalist at the American Museum of Natural History in New York. While still in college, Andrews wrote to the Director of the Museum seeking a job. The Director sent an offhand reply inviting the young job-seeker to come see him if he was ever in New York. Upon graduation from college, Andrews went to New York and called on the director who, surprised, said he had no job to offer except mopping the floors. Andrews told him he would take it. Thus began his thirty-seven-year association with one of the world's leading natural history institutions.

Andrews soon became involved in other activities in the museum besides cleaning the floors. He assisted in the construction of a model whale, and he determined to learn more about the mammoth creatures. Although whales had been hunted for centuries, much was still unknown scientifically about their living habits and physiology. In 1908 he was sent to accompany a whaling expedition to Vancouver Island and Alaska. Soon after his return, he jumped at an opportunity to sail aboard the *U.S.S. Albatross*, perhaps the premier American oceanographic vessel, on a voyage to the Dutch East Indies to study whales and collect specimens of mammals from the tropical islands. He joined the ship at Manila and spent several exciting months cruising among the islands of the Philippines, an American possession recently acquired from Spain, and the Dutch-ruled islands of the fabled East Indies. While sailing north to Japan after completing its explorations in the southwest Pacific, the *Albatross* sailed through a typhoon off the coast of Formosa, and was saved from foundering only by seeking shelter in the port of Keelung on the island's north coast.

Andrews left the *Albatross* in Japan, but obtained permission from his employers in New York to remain in Japan to observe Japanese whaling activities. He spent several months in a remote whaling port. He collected tons of specimens for the museum, and was able to identify among the whales being caught by the Japanese the California gray whale, long thought to be extinct. He also gained a useful knowledge of Japanese. He returned to the United States in a long roundabout, leisurely journey via Singapore, the Suez Canal, and Europe.

In 1911 he was made an Assistant Curator of Mammals in the Museum. He wanted to return to the Far East, specifically to Korea. In Japan he had heard about a strange whale in Korean waters called a devilfish. His imagination was also fired by a book by Francis Younghusband about a "Long White Mountain" on the border of Korea and China which Younghusband had visited during his explorations of Manchuria in the 1880s. Andrews wanted to explore the deep forests on the Korean side of the mountain which Younghusband had sighted from the mountaintop but had not entered. So far as Andrews could learn, they had never been explored by a European.

Andrews received permission from the Museum to make the trip, in exchange for a promised collection of mammal and bird specimens (the museum had virtually nothing from Korea) and provided he could raise the necessary funds. It was his first experience in fundraising, an activity at which he later became an expert. Since his arrival in New York just a few years earlier, he had been away more than he had been in the city, and during his brief stays between journeys, he had worked long hours in the Museum while pursuing graduate studies in zoology at Columbia University. Nevertheless, he had somehow found time to meet many of the "right people."

> By that time, I knew a good many people of wealth in New York and I set about selling the expedition. The price was $10,000. . . . Eventually, I got the money.

In Korea he spent several months in whaling ports and obtained two complete skeletons of devilfish whales which he shipped to New York. When the whaling season ended, he headed north toward the Long White Mountain forests. In Seoul he hired a cook and an interpreter. The trip was not easy.

> The traverse through the larch forests to the base of the Long White Mountain was a mixture of elation, discouragement, utter exhaustion, and final satisfaction.

He reached the base of the mountain Younghusband had climbed, and pushed on to the headwaters of the Yalu River on the Manchurian border.

> Dense forests, swamps and drizzling rain . . . not far from the Yalu, I stumbled into the camp of eight Manchurian bandits, but talked my way out of a ticklish situation.

On the train back to Seoul he met an American missionary and they discussed their respective plans for traveling back to America. Andrews, who had been out of touch with the world for months, said he had read before embarking on his journey about a great new ship being built in Britain, and he hoped to book passage on it. Its name was *Titanic.* His traveling companion "jumped as though from an electric shock. `You mean you haven't heard about her? She's at the bottom of the sea!' "

He returned to the United States via Peking, where the Chinese revolution had just occurred, and the Trans-Siberian railway. By coincidence, he arrived in New York just when Younghusband was lecturing at the American Museum of Natural History, and was able to tell the English explorer about his trip to the Long White Mountain.

In 1913 Andrews received his M.A. degree from Columbia University with a thesis about his rediscovery of the California gray whale in Japan. He also was given the chance to sail to Alaska aboard a yacht, the *Adventuress*, which a sportsman from Chicago had built and planned to use to hunt a bowhead whale in the Arctic. The Museum wanted one to complete its collection. The trip "turned out to be nothing more than a big game hunt, which under ordinary conditions would have been delightful, but I had a job to do." They shot caribou, emperor geese, mountain goat, duck, and Kodiak bear. Andrews did not get a bowhead whale, but he spent three weeks alone on a island in the Pribilofs, obtaining the first motion pictures of the great seal herds there.

Back in New York, Andrews decided to give up whales in favor of land exploration, although he was by now a recognized authority on whales. World War I had begun, but the United States was not involved, and he could pursue a plan that had been forming in his mind. He wanted to test a theory advanced by Professor Henry Fairfield Osborn, the President of the Museum. Many years earlier, Osborn had published a paper arguing that Central Asia was the home of primitive man and the mother of much of the animal life of Europe and America.

His arguments were brilliant and based upon solid scientific reasoning, but he had never been able actually to visit Central Asia to find evidence to support them. Andrews proposed to find the evidence in a long series of expeditions. He broached his idea to Osborn, who was understandably sympathetic. Andrews proposed first to go to Yunnan province in China on the edge of the Tibetan plateau on a purely zoological trip. Again, he had to raise funds, and again he was successful among his rich New York friends to the tune of $10,000.

Accompanied by his wife and one other scientist, Andrews sailed for China in March 1916. They spent more than a year roaming from above the tree-line in mountains on the frontier of Tibet to the hot, malarial jungle valleys of northern Burma. It was largely a hunting expedition, and they brought back many specimens to be mounted for display in the Museum.

By the time they returned to the United States, the country had entered the war. Andrews went to Washington "to offer my services to the Secretary of War whom I had known for years." To his disappointment, his offer was accepted, but for a desk job in Washington—his knowledge of Asia would be useful to the intelligence services—rather than a field assignment in France. But then he happened to meet another influential friend who was in Naval Intelligence and who offered him an assignment in Peking. A week later, he was off again to China.

> I arrived to find Peking a city of intrigue. No one believed that anyone else was what he said he was or that his presence in China did not have some underlying secret significance. New faces were continually appearing at the Club or the Wagon-Lit Hotel, sending a flurry of gossip through the foreign community. Money was being made in undreamed-of quantities. . . . Political chaos reigned. . . . The republic was a joke. . . . Warlords controlled every province.

Even twenty-five years later he wrote that he could not reveal what his secret assignment was.

> Suffice it to say that it was exceedingly unimportant although interesting and at times exciting.

His headquarters was in Peking, but he traveled extensively:

> My peregrinations took me over much of China and Manchuria, twice across the Gobi Desert from Kalgan to Urga, and northward, on horseback, through the vast unexplored forests into Siberia.

He made his first automobile journey across Mongolia and had his first encounter with Chinese bandits. He and his companion killed two of them, and Andrews narrowly escaped being hit by a bullet which shattered the lower part of the steering wheel of the car he was driving.

When the war ended, Andrews requested and received permission to stay on in China to spend the summer in Mongolia collecting specimens for the Museum and continuing preparations for the major expedition he wanted to lead to test Osborn's thesis. He and his wife spent the summer of 1919 roaming through Mongolia. As in Yunnan, it was largely a hunting expedition. When they returned to Peking in the autumn, they had fifteen hundred animal specimens for shipment to New York. Andrews later wrote, "never, I think, have I been happier in the field than during that summer in Mongolia."

Soon after his return to New York, Andrews again sought out

*The caravan of Dodge automobiles that enabled Andrews
and his Expedition to range widely over Mongolia.*

Osborn and outlined his plan for the expedition to Mongolia to test Osborn's thesis. It was breathtaking in its scope and audacity. He proposed to assemble what today would be called a multidisciplinary team, a group of recognized authorities in paleontology, geology, topography, meteorology, zoology, and botany. Their principal purpose would be to test Osborn's theory, but they would gather data about Central Asia in an immense range of fields.

Their base would be Peking, and they would remain in Asia for several years. To extend the range of their explorations to the maximum, Andrews proposed to use a fleet of automobiles and one-ton trucks. He had already proven that motor vehicles could be usefully employed in the deserts and grasslands of Mongolia. To supply the expedition with food, gasoline, and other necessities, he proposed to send out caravans of camels to pre-position caches of supplies in strategic locations. He calculated the cost, at least initially, at $250,000—this in the days when a new car cost about $1,000, a new suit cost $35, and a good seat at a Broadway show could be had for $2.

Osborn was understandably enthusiastic about Andrews'simaginative proposal which he pronounced scientifically sound. He could assure the Museum's scientific sponsorship, but could guarantee only a small fraction of the required funds. It was up to Andrews to find most of the money. The explorer once again approached his wealthy New York friends.

He started with J.P. Morgan. He simply telephoned, asked for an appointment, and the next day met the financier in the Morgan Library. Andrews reasoned, correctly, that if he could immediately obtain one large donation, others would follow. He had told Osborn:

> My only chance, I believe, is to make it a "society expedition" with a big S. You know that New York society follows a leader blindly. If they have the example of someone like Mr. Morgan, for instance, they'll think it is a "must" for the current season. "Have you contributed to the Roy Chapman Andrews' expedition? If not, you're not in society." That's the idea.

He was correct on all counts. After hearing Andrews outline his plans for fifteen minutes, Morgan pledged $50,000, and sent Andrews on to the president of the Chase National Bank with his, Morgan's, recommendation for a contribution.

Andrews spent the winter at lunches and dinners with captains of industry and finance, raising funds. He finally reached his goal with a $50,000 contribution from John D. Rockefeller, Jr. The list of contributors eventually totaled two hundred twenty-nine individuals and institutions, plus one identified only as "a friend." With the money in hand, Andrews moved to seek publicity for his project. He held a press conference, and got stories on front pages and wire services all over the country. To his chagrin, the newspapers dubbed it the "Missing Link Expedition," focusing on the search for evidence of primitive man and ignoring other scientific aspects of the project. The publicity produced a flood of letters from would-be adventurers and scientists seeking places on the expedition team.

By March 1921 Andrews was ready to sail to China with an advance team to set up his headquarters in Peking. The brash explorer knew he was embarking on an enormous gamble, made all the greater, with tremendous potential for failure and embarrassment, by the intense publicity the Missing Link stories had produced. No fossils had ever been found in Central Asia, except for one doubtful rhinoceros bone found by a Russian explorer in the 19th century. Sven Hedin and Aurel Stein had both found scattered evidence of Stone Age man, but neither had found any fossils. Both had been interested in other matters and had not investigated further. Some scientists scoffed at the idea of finding fossils in Central Asia; one reportedly said Andrews might just as well look for them in the Pacific Ocean. Andrews knew he might fail, and if he did, the failure would be on a grand scale and would probably ruin his scientific career at the American Museum of Natural History. But he and Osborn felt certain the fossils were there to be found.

In Peking Andrews leased a large, rambling house, which he dubbed "my Peking palace," to serve as the expedition's headquarters. It belonged to a Manchu prince, and had earlier been leased by a famous British sinologist, Dr. George E. Morrison. Andrews brought in an army of carpenters and plumbers to renovate the place completely. It contained forty-seven rooms clustered around eight courtyards. Andrews added a garage for six cars, stables (he was an expert polo player), a laboratory, and a complete photographer's dark room. Andrews grew to love the place, and it must have been wonderfully attractive. Existing photographs show a long, low building of Chinese design, fronted with spreading shade trees and Chinese "moongates" opening into courtyards. When he was in Peking, Andrews entertained a good deal, and the house often was thronged with guests at elegant dinners and cocktail parties.

Andrews spent the whole of 1921 completing preparations in Peking. On April 17, 1922, the expedition in its fleet of seven automobiles piled high with baggage left Peking and headed for the Great Wall and Mongolia.

> Roaring like the prehistoric monsters we had come to seek, our cars gained the top of the last steep slope and passed through the narrow gateway in the Wall. Before us lay Mongolia, a land of painted deserts dancing in mirage; of limitless grassy plains and nameless snow-capped peaks; of untracked forests and roaring streams. Mongolia, a land of mystery, of paradox and promise!

The Central Asiatic Expedition of the American Museum of Natural History was underway.

Their immediate goal was to locate formations of sedimentary rocks where fossils might be found. In igneous or metamorphic rocks, any bones or other remains of living tissue would have been destroyed. Sedimentary strata cut by gullies were what they sought. The geologists rode in a separate automobile, and often left the group to examine outcroppings that looked promising. The chief paleontologist of the expedition was Walter Granger, a long-time friend of Andrews, who also served as second in command. He would be responsible for identifying any fossils they might find, determining which should be collected, and supervising their removal, preservation, and packing for shipment.

Shortly after entering Mongolia, they camped near the spot where the first advance cache of gasoline had been left by their camel caravan. The geologists and paleontologists fanned out over nearby rock outcroppings. Soon, their two cars roared back into camp. Andrews and his wife hurried out to meet them.

> Granger's eyes were shining and he was puffing violently at a very odious pipe. . . . Silently he dug into his pocket and produced a handful of bone fragments; out of his shirt came a rhinoceros tooth and the various folds of his upper garments yielded other fossils. . . . "Well, Roy, we've done it. The stuff is here. We picked up fifty pounds of bone in an hour."

It was a moment to savor and remember, a historic moment in paleontology. They laughed and shouted and pounded each other on the back. The next day Granger uncovered a large bone, and Dr. Berkey, the chief geologist, ran to summon Andrews to the site. They found Granger wielding a camel hair brush to uncover the bone. Even Andrews, who was not a paleontologist, could see it was neither mammal nor bird.

> "It means," said Berkey, "that we are standing on a Cretaceous strata of the upper part of the Age of Reptiles—the first Cretaceous strata, and the first dinosaur ever discovered in Asia north of the Himalaya Mountains!"

In the ensuing months they found literally tons of fossils, both of mammals and reptiles, at several different locations. Some lay exposed on the surface of the desert. They were astonished that no one had ever reported finding fossils in the Gobi Desert before.

Their next significant discovery occurred on August 4. Again, it was evening, and the expedition was camped when Granger, this time accompanied by "Shack" Shackelford, the photographer, entered camp with startling news. He had found parts of a skeleton of a Baluchitherium.

The Baluchitherium—the "Beast of Baluchistan"—had first become known in 1914 when a few vertebrae and neck bones had been found by an American paleontologist in Baluchistan in western India. Nothing more had been found anywhere until Granger's discovery in the Gobi. Granger had discovered part of a jaw and an upper leg bone. The next day Andrews himself, while accompanied by Shackelford and a Chinese chauffeur, found a complete Baluchitherium skull.

> At six o'clock, while the men were having tea, we burst into camp, shouting like children. Granger is not easily stirred but our story brought him up standing. He was as excited as the rest of us. Even though we had realized the "Baluch" was a colossal beast, the size of the bones left us astounded.

The Baluchitherium was the largest mammal ever to walk the Earth. The following summer the expedition found a complete skeleton and, for the first time, the museum in New York was able to reconstruct how the animal looked. It was a huge, hornless rhinoceros, twenty-four feet long that stood seventeen feet high at the shoulders, several feet higher than the largest African elephant of today. Andrews and the others could not help but wonder what fossils of other little-known, or totally unknown, ancient animals they might find.

By early September they were in the middle of the Gobi, and Andrews decided it was time to return to Peking. The expedition could not usefully work in the desert during the frigid winter months when it was swept by violent blizzards.

They were in unexplored territory; old Russian maps that they used, the only ones in existence, showed a range of mountains where, they discovered, none existed. As they headed back towards Kalgan, they came upon a badlands area, a vast basin ringed by cliffs of brilliant red sandstone that seemed to shoot out tongues of fire when touched by the late afternoon sun. The basin was almost literally paved with white fossil bones of animals unknown to anyone in the group. They named the area the Flaming Cliffs, and vowed to return the following summer when they would have time to explore it thoroughly. Before they pushed off for the return journey to Kalgan and Peking, Granger, while poking around the basin floor, picked up a few small bits of fossil egg shell which he identified as being from some long-extinct birds.

Roy Chapman Andrews and Walter Granger, the Expedition's chief paleontologist, with bones of "the monster," the Baluchitherium, *the largest mammal ever to walk the earth.*

Some members of the team returned to America for the winter. Andrews remained in Peking to prepare for the next year's activities. The staff would be larger, and more planning and more supplies and support were needed. He threw himself into the work. But he was not too busy to throw himself also into the social life of Peking. The expatriate and diplomatic communities lived gay, active lives, and Andrews was delighted to join in. He was a popular host at his elegant "Peking palace" and a sought-after dinner guest.

He was also an enthusiastic polo player; he later wrote, "polo was a passion with me." He played on the Peking team in matches against teams representing Shanghai, Tientsin, and Hankow as well as regimental teams from all over the Orient.

> The matches were brilliant affairs with gay crowds, bands, and military trappings. I don't think I ever had more excitement than when I waited, every muscle tense, for the referee's whistle to start play.

During that winter he attended the wedding of the last Chinese emperor, Pu Yi. It was a bitter cold winter night, the night of St. Andrew's Ball which the British expatriate community celebrated boisterously. Andrews and a small party went from the ball to the Forbidden City. It was a poignant event; everyone knew that even if the struggling republic did not survive, a Manchu emperor would never again rule China. Afterwards, Andrews reflected:

> We had lived through one of the great moments of history. . . . I had witnessed the last act in the age-old drama of imperial China.

On April 17, 1923, exactly one year after their first departure from Peking, the expedition again left the Chinese capital for Mongolia. The first year had been spectacularly successful, but it had been intended mainly as a reconaissance. The second year was devoted to exploring more fully the sites discovered the previous year. Their destination was the Flaming Cliffs. They found there had been absolutely no rain for a year. The tracks their cars had made ten months earlier were still sharp and fresh.

The second day after their arrival, George Olsen, Granger's assistant, reported he had found some fossil eggs, recalling Granger's discovery of a few bits of fossilized shell the previous autumn. The whole group returned with him to the site. There were three eggs, beautifully preserved and unlike any other any of them had ever seen. They were elongated, like a loaf of French bread, about nine inches long. Two of them, broken in half, showed the white fossilized bones of unhatched baby dinosaurs. They were the first dinosaur eggs ever seen by modern human eyes. Indeed, until that day in the Gobi, no one could be certain that dinosaurs laid eggs, although it was assumed that they, like modern reptiles, reproduced in that fashion.

Just a few inches above the eggs they uncovered the skeleton of a small dinosaur of a type new to science. It was only four feet long but fully grown. They speculated that it was a type of dinosaur that fed upon the eggs of other dinosaurs and that it had been somehow killed—perhaps suffocated by a sudden, violent sandstorm—while in the act of digging up the eggs just beneath it. The next day twenty-five more eggs were found in several clusters in different locations.

The second expedition produced a great many more fossils and, when the group returned to Peking in September, they decided to suspend operations for a year to raise more money in the United States to extend operations beyond the five years originally planned. In October 1923 Andrews sailed for New York.

Back in the United States, he found the expedition on the front pages of newspapers across the country.

> "Dinosaur eggs! Dinosaur eggs!" That was all I heard during eight months in America. . . . Vainly did I try to tell of the other, vastly more important discoveries of the expedition. No one was interested.

But the publicity was invaluable in raising more funds. Some of the original donors who had contributed the largest amounts, like Morgan and Rockefeller, doubled their donations. An idea occurred to Andrews. He explained it to Osborn, who agreed they should try it: they would auction off one dinosaur egg to the highest bidder to call attention to the need for contributions. Thus began "The Great Dinosaur Egg Auction." Bids started at $2,000 and quickly escalated to $4,000. More importantly, the publicity was enormous and produced a flood of contributions. The egg finally went for $5,000 to a bidder who donated it to Colgate University. But the publicity stunt proved to be a boomerang:

> Up to this time, the Chinese and Mongols had taken us at face value. Now they thought we were making money out of our explorations. We had found about thirty eggs. If one was worth $5,000, the whole lot must be valued at $150,000 . . . the other fossils probably, too, were worth their weight in gold. Why should the Mongols and the Chinese let us have such priceless treasures for nothing? I had to combat this idea throughout all the remaining years of the expedition.

Offers came in from promoters to make casts of eggs and sell them as paperweights and other knickknacks, but Andrews declined them. The *New York Times* asked for exclusive rights to stories about the expedition, but Andrews refused, as he did a $250,000 offer from William Randolph Hearst for exclusive publication rights. He knew that granting exclusive rights would reduce the number of stories that would appear. He did, however, enter into an agreement with the Dodge

Roy Chapman Andrews and George Olsen, the assistant paleontologist, examine the nest of "an even dozen" dinosaur eggs at the Flaming Cliffs.

Brothers Automobile Company, whose cars the expedition had been using, by which the company provided a new fleet of cars in exchange for an endorsement. The advertising was dignified, and the arrangement continued after the company was sold to Walter Chrysler. Andrews calculated that it saved the expedition $50,000.

Andrews returned to Peking in the autumn of 1924. The 1925 expedition was the largest and most ambitious of the series. The number of sciences represented was increased. Fifty scientists took part using eight cars and one hundred fifty camels. They returned to the Flaming Cliffs and found more dinosaur eggs as well as a treasure trove of new fossils. They discovered the remains of a hitherto unknown Stone Age culture they called the Dune Dwellers who had occupied the area for thousands of years and left numerous stone implements. Among the Stone Age artifacts they found were bits of fossilized dinosaur eggshell neatly drilled with holes. Andrews had to admit that the Dune Dwellers were really the discoverers of the dinosaur eggs; they had used the fossilized shell to make necklaces millennia before Andrews and his expedition came on the scene.

While they were camped in the desert, a letter with startling news arrived from New York. During the first year's explorations, Granger had found the remains of a small animal, about the size of a rat, that he had labeled a reptile, because the remains were found in strata from the Age of Reptiles. The remains had been sent on to New York and forgotten by members of the expedition. Study by the staff in New York, however, showed that they belonged to a mammal that coexisted with the dinosaurs. Until then, only a single skull of a mammal from the time of the great reptiles had ever been found, in Africa. The expedition searched for more and found seven skulls and parts of skeletons. Andrews, though not a paleontologist, realized the significance of the discovery:

> After the dinosaur eggs have been forgotten, these little skulls will be remembered by scientists as the crowning single discovery of our paleontological research in Asia.

Andrews returned to the United States in the autumn for more fundraising and lecturing. When he returned to Asia in March 1926, he found northern China embroiled in civil war. Feng Yu-hsiang, the "Christian General," controlled Peking while Chang Tso-lin, the Manchu warlord, controlled the port of Tientsin. Heavy fighting had occurred in January and February but by March, when Andrews arrived, there was a lull. As he traveled the familiar road from Tientsin to Peking, Andrews passed through the no-man's land between the lines of the two armies.

> No active fighting was going on at the time, but it was a decidedly unsafe road to travel. Soldier stragglers roamed all along the way robbing whenever they had the opportunity.

A few days later, Andrews and three others tried to drive back to Tientsin. They passed through the lines of the troops occupying Peking, but soon came under machinegun fire from troops on the other side. Andrews, who was driving, swung the car around and headed back toward Peking.

The troops around the city, who had let them pass only a short time before, upon hearing the firing down the road, opened up on the car when it came in sight. The Americans ran a gauntlet for three miles, with soldiers firing at them, sometimes in squads, sometimes singly.

No one in the car was hit, but bullets struck all around them. They were stopped by a group of soldiers who demanded a ride and climbed aboard. One fell off, and his arm was mangled by the rear wheel passing over it. The others yanked the Americans out of the car and appeared on the verge of shooting all of them when an officer appeared. He sent the soldiers away, but warned the Americans he could not guarantee their safety and advised them to get off the road. They finally returned to the city by driving over the plowed ground of the fields beside the road.

A plane belonging to Chang Tso-lin's forces was bombing the city daily. Soon after he arrived, Andrews was caught in a bombing raid at the railway yards as he tried to arrange shipment of supplies to Kalgan in preparation for that season's explorations. He took cover under a railroad car. A piece of shrapnel buried itself in the earth two inches from his face. He burned his fingers digging out the red-hot piece of metal for a souvenir.

It became obvious that the expedition could not go into the field that year. The staff, except Andrews and one other man, returned to the United States. Supplies and equipment were sold to reduce expenses to a minimum. The question became: when would the expedition be able to return to Mongolia?

Andrews sailed to the United States in the autumn of 1926 and returned to China in the following spring. The situation still prevented any resumption of explorations in Mongolia, but he began to make plans for the following year.

By the spring of 1928 the expedition was able once again to go into the field. They pushed into new areas and made useful finds, but none were so spectacular or significant as the discoveries at the Flaming Cliffs.

By 1929 the forces of the warlord Chang Tso-lin, which had replaced the Christian General's forces in Peking, had, in turn, been pushed out of the capital by the Kuomintang army under Chiang Kai-shek. A new wave of nationalism was sweeping the country. For Andrews and the Central Asiatic Expedition, it took the form of suspicion and opposition to the expedition's activities. The group was accused of violating China's sovereign rights and of spying. No field activity was attempted during 1929. In 1930 the last field campaign went out, but it was a disappointment.

It was restricted only to paleontology for we were not allowed to make maps, and were so handicapped with stupid restrictions that our whole plan of operations was crippled. It simply wasn't good enough. I decided to quit even though we had only scratched the surface of the Gobi.

The Central Asiatic Expedition was dismantled. All equipment and supplies were sold, the local staff was paid off, and the Americans returned to the United States.

Andrews stayed on in Peking to write a narrative history of his great enterprise. Interestingly, Sven Hedin was living at that time in Peking, also at work on a book. Like Andrews, he tended to work at night. The two explorers often met at three o'clock in the morning to go off to "night cafés of dubious reputation, have scrambled eggs, dance with the Russian girls, and then go home to bed." Andrews's book, entitled *The New Conquest of Central Asia*, was completed by the end of the summer of 1932. His work in Asia was finished. The Peking palace was given up, and he returned to New York. Although he did not know it at the time, his days as an explorer had ended.

Andrews lived the rest of his life in the United States. He continued his career at the American Museum of Natural History. In 1934 he was appointed the Museum's director, thus capping a career that had begun as a janitor mopping the floors. He had long been a successful writer with several best-selling titles to his credit since his first book, based upon his whaling experiences, had been published in 1916. He continued to turn out popular books based upon his travels and explorations.

In 1941 he retired as director. In early 1942 he moved from New York to a farm in Connecticut he had bought a few years earlier as a weekend retreat. During the last years of his life he lived in Carmel, California, where he died of a heart attack on March 11, 1960.

The members of the Central Asiatic Expedition never found any remains of the "Missing Link." Although they found artifacts from the Stone Age culture of the Dune Dwellers, and numerous fossil remains of animals, they never found any ancient human remains. But the idea of finding the fossilized remains of primitive man in Central Asia was by no means farfetched, as was demonstrated by the experience of another group of scientific explorers who were at work in northern China at precisely the same time that Andrews and his group were busy in nearby Mongolia.

The Chinese for centuries have ground up the fossilized bones of ancient animals, which they call "dragon bones," for use as medicine. By the late 19th century European scientists in China had learned to hang around the Chinese "drugstores" that dispense traditional drugs and medicines to learn about locations where "dragon bones" could be found. One such scientist, a Swedish geologist named Johan Gunnar Andersson, learned at a Peking "drugstore" about a location some thirty miles southwest of Peking called Chou-kou-tien, where fossils could be found.

Excavations there by Andersson and his assistants uncovered, in 1921, a tooth which they identified as belonging to an early primitive human, or hominid. Andersson predicted that further evidence of primitive man would be found there, an announcement that attracted the notice of paleontologists to the site. Andersson's excavations continued, and his finds were sent to Sweden for analysis.

In October 1926, in a well-publicized announcement to a group of scientists in Peking, Andersson revealed that two more teeth had been found at Chou-kou-tien. They were, in his opinion, definitely of hominid origin. Many scientists were skeptical. Andrews heard the news of Andersson's announcement in London where he had gone to address the members of the Royal Geographical Society. He was already quite familiar with Andersson's efforts, and he was not skeptical:

> Personally, I got very excited. Those two teeth represented the first human fossil material accompanied by certain geological data, that had ever been discovered on the Asiatic continent north of the Himalayan Mountains. That meant more to me, perhaps, than to the usual investigator, because I had banked on northern Asia as a theater of human origin.

When he had first sought permission from the Chinese government to conduct explorations and excavations of fossils, he had wanted to include northern China, along with Mongolia, in his sphere of operations. But the Chinese Geological Survey wanted to conduct its own explorations in China proper, and Andrews had agreed to limit his activities to Mongolia. Andersson was attached to the Chinese Geological Survey and could therefore conduct excavations near Peking. Granger had accompanied Andersson on his first visits to Chou-kou-tien in 1921. Moreover, the anthropologist who took over from Andersson in the late 1920s and '30s and whose name became most closely associated with the Chou-kou-tien discoveries, Dr. Davidson Black, had accompanied Andrews on the first push of the Central Asiatic Expedition into Mongolia in 1922.

Further excavations at Chou-kou-tien over the next few years uncovered more fossilized remains, including parts of skulls. They were attributed to a hitherto unknown primitive ancestor of modern man that was dubbed Sinanthropus pekinensis or Peking Man who lived approximately 500,000 years ago. They were therefore among the oldest human fossils found until that time. In December 1929 in Peking Dr. Black invited Andrews to take a look at a skull that had just been discovered at Chou-kou-tien:

> There it was, the skull of an individual who had lived half a million years ago, one of the most important discoveries in the whole history of human evolution. He couldn't have been very impressive when he was alive, but dead and fossilized, he was awe-inspiring . . . when I thought of the pitiful fragments of other early primitive human types which scientists had studied for so many weary hours, this superb uncrushed specimen seemed an embarrassment of riches.

When excavations were finally suspended in 1937 because of the Japanese invasion of China, remains of an estimated forty separate individuals, including males and females, as well as adults and children, were included among the bone fragments and teeth that had been collected. There were one hundred forty-eight teeth, thirteen jaws, fragments of fourteen skulls, and four nearly complete crania, as well as a few fragments of arm and leg bones. Scientists were able to establish that Peking Man walked nearly erect and was the earliest hominid known to use fire. It was the largest collection of human fossils ever found at a single site, and the largest collection of fossils from a single hominid population. The collection was, in short, a scientific treasure of the greatest possible significance to the ongoing search for the origins of man on Earth.

The subsequent history of the fossil remains of Peking Man discovered by Andersson, Black, and their colleagues constitutes a tantalizing mystery that remains unsolved. The fossils were kept at the Peking Union Medical College. By the autumn of 1941, all-out war in Asia appeared imminent, and the scientists responsible for the collection decided the precious fossils should be shipped to the United States for safekeeping. They were packed in two wooden boxes and turned over to the detachment of U.S. Marines in the port of Tientsin. The Marines were scheduled to return to the United States because of the expected outbreak of war with Japan, and the fossils would go with them. But the attack on Pearl Harbor occurred before the Marines could depart, and the Americans were taken into custody by the Japanese to be interned for the duration of the war. In the confusion, the fossils disappeared. The wooden boxes in which they were packed were, according to some accounts, packed inside a Marine footlocker, although other accounts described the boxes as being as large as desks and obviously too big to fit inside a footlocker. Whatever their size, they were last reliably reported to be lying in storage in a room in the Marine barracks at Camp Holcomb near Tientsin when the Marines were taken into custody by Japanese soldiers. They have never been found, despite strenuous efforts by several scientists to trace them after the war. Fortunately, plaster casts had been made of all the fossils and sent to the American Museum of Natural History in New York, so their scientific value was not completely lost. In the 1960s further excavations at Chou-kou-tien uncovered a few more Peking Man fossils, but nothing to equal what was lost in the collection that mysteriously disappeared.

Although Andrews's expedition found no fossilized remains of primitive man, he nevertheless reached the conclusion, based upon the discoveries made by his expedition and by others, that Asia was the birthplace of the human species. During the three-quarters of a century since then, much more evidence of primitive man has been found in several parts of the world that has pushed back the horizons of man's origins millions of years. Discoveries made in East Africa in the decades since World War II led scientists to conclude that man originated in Africa, then spread to the other continents. However, precisely when primitive hominids migrated from Africa—if that is, indeed, where our earliest ancestors originated; not everyone agrees that it is—to the other continents is a matter of debate among paleontologists and anthropologists. Some scientists argue that homo sapiens developed after the migration and developed separately in several different parts of the world, while others believe that the modern species appeared first in Africa, then migrated. In view of the meager amount of ancient human remains that have been found to date, a conclusive answer is still impossible.

In 1992 two skulls, about as old as Peking Man, were discovered in China. They show characteristics of both homo sapiens, or modern man, and homo erectus, modern man's more primitive immediate ancestor which includes Peking Man. This discovery lends support to the theory that the earliest primitive man may have originated in Africa, but modern man evolved from that common ancestor independently in Africa, Europe and Asia. Final, definite proof is not yet in and may never be. Perhaps the theories about the origins of man in Asia, put forth so many years ago by Andrews and Osborn, may yet prove to be correct, at least in part.

The members of the Central Asiatic Expedition never found any of the human fossils they wanted so much to discover, but they amassed a huge quantity of data about the heartland of the Eurasian landmass that has been of enormous scientific value. They established that Central Asia is an enormous granite bathylith, probably the largest in the world. Moreover, it is the oldest continuously dry land in the world, never having been covered by the glaciers that encased much of North America and Europe. The expedition discovered fossil remains of numerous dinosaurs never before known, as well as the oldest true mammal, and they established that Asia was the motherland of much of the animal and plant life that later migrated widely to both Europe and America.

Andrews closed down the Central Asiatic Expedition with reluctance and regret. He was correct when he said it had "only scratched the surface." The Soviet Union sent an expedition into Mongolia immediately after World War II. It spent several years further exploring the sites Andrews had found and locating others. A joint Polish-Mongolian expedition made still more discoveries in the mid-1960s. Since the end of the Cold War, the American Museum of Natural History has begun collaboration with the government of Mongolia to send expeditions once again in Central Asia to locate new sites. In early 1994 an expedition sponsored by the Museum discovered a treasure trove of fossils at Ukhaa Tolgod on the Mongolia-China border. It includes excellently preserved fossils of hitherto unknown dinosaurs and remains of a creature thought to be a transition from dinosaurs to birds. The fossils were described as "extraordinarily important," being the best preserved collection of vertebrate animals from the Cretaceous period ever found anywhere. So subsequent exploration in Mongolia has confirmed that Andrews and his team could have made more, perhaps even greater, discoveries if they had been allowed to continue their explorations.

The Central Asiatic Expedition made Andrews famous, and his fame was further increased by his many popular books about his experiences. Written in an almost conversational style, his books combined accounts of hair-raising adventure in exotic places with solid, if rather elementary, scientific information. He supplemented them with a steady flow of popular magazine articles and lectures. His name was indissolubly linked with paleontology, because of the fossils and dinosaur eggs his expedition discovered. But he never studied paleontology formally and was by profession a zoologist. He admitted he lacked the patience to be a paleontologist, not being content to spend hours painstakingly brushing dirt away from delicate fossils. He wanted to go after them with a pick and shovel. He claimed that his colleague, Walter Granger, the chief paleontologist, would not allow him near an important fossil find, even if Andrews had discovered it. Granger feared that in his impatience to uncover the fossils, Andrews would damage or destroy them.

Andrews received numerous scientific honors and awards, especially in the 1920s and '30s when he was most famous. But he has never been accepted by the scientific community as one of its own. At Beloit College he majored in English, not science, and he never earned a doctoral degree, although he was customarily called Doctor Andrews by his staff at the Museum. He held honorary doctorates conferred by Brown University and Beloit College during the 1920s when his fame as an explorer was at its height. He has been called "superficial," a "promoter," and "a marvelous public relations man." His books have been criticized as simplistic and lacking in scientific merit.

Roy Chapman Andrews in camp, silhouetted against the Gobi Desert.

Andrews usually called himself an explorer, and he said he was born to follow that calling:

> Almost every day someone asks me: "How did you start explor-ing and digging up dinosaur eggs in the Gobi Desert?" I can answer simply enough: "I couldn't help it. I happen to have been born to do it. I am sure that I would have been a rotten failure doing anything else."
>
> Ever since I can remember, I always intended to be a natu-ralist and explorer. Nothing else ever had a place in my mind. . . . To enter the American Museum of Natural History was my life ambition.

During his seven years as director of the Museum he may not have been a failure, but he was not successful either. Osborn, his pow-erful patron as president of the Museum, retired after seeing Andrews installed as director, then died. The Great Depression forced the wealthy captains of industry who had so lavishly supported the Museum to curtail their contributions, and Andrews's tenure as director during the late 1930s was marked by chronic budgetary shortfalls. A report commissioned by the Board of Directors in 1941 found much wrong with the Museum's administration, and it resulted in Andrews's forced retirement under less than amicable circumstances. Despite his enormous contributions to the Museum, his death nineteen years later was allowed to pass unnoticed in the Museum's annual report.

A reading of Andrews's books suggests that he was really not a scientist or an administrator by temperament. He was by inclination an outdoorsman, a man of action, rather than a scholar happy to sift evidence in a laboratory or an executive content to work behind a desk in an office. He possessed an inborn talent for public relations, as his critics have maintained. To judge from his own writing, his real passion in life, at least until he reached middle age, was hunting. He must have killed literally thousands of animals with gun or trap, many of them belonging to rare species. He always gave as the reason for his hunting the collection of specimens for the Museum or the need for meat for the table, but his writing reveals that he hunted for the pure pleasure of it, too.

He devotes hundreds of pages to descriptions of hunting expeditions, from harpooning whales in the North Pacific, to shooting big cats in Yunnan, to chasing gazelles and stalking bighorn sheep in Mongolia. Nowhere does his writing come more alive and convey more emotion than when it describes the tension of the stalk, the exhilaration of the chase, the thrill of the killing shot, or the triumph of confirming possession of a record trophy. However, in *On the Trail of Ancient Man*, published in 1926 about the first years of the Central Asiatic Expedition, he wrote:

> Years of shooting have bred a change within me, and I care less and less to kill. I was born a sportsman. . . . But now that satisfaction comes less often. . . . My triumph leaves a vague unhappiness. I wish it could be undone. I would give back life to the creature against whom I have matched my skill—and won.

During his first years in Mongolia, he felt wild exhilaration while chasing and shooting antelopes from an automobile. He found that the animals could, incredibly, accelerate to sixty miles an hour. But by 1928 he felt differently about that kind of hunting.

It isn't sport, that is true. . . . New men always get a tremendous thrill out of hunting antelopes, and it surely is exciting at first. I've had too much of it.

But he did not give up hunting altogether after he left China. During his retirement years in Connecticut, he continued shooting birds and small game.

Andrews married in 1914 and became the father of a son. His wife accompanied him on the hunting expeditions to Yunnan during World War I and to Mongolia during the idyllic summer of 1919. She was with him during the first weeks of the Central Asiatic Expedition in Mongolia in 1922, but returned to live in Peking while her husband spent months in Mongolia and shuttled back and forth across the Pacific between China and the United States. Andrews devoted himself wholly to his expedition, and he became separated from his family. His wife took Andrews's son, and another boy she had borne in Peking, to England to live. In 1931 the couple divorced. Andrews remarried in 1935, and apparently his second marriage was a happy one. But although he wrote extensively about his own experiences, there is little in his books about his private life, except during the few years immediately after his retirement when he lived on his farm in Connecticut with his second wife. His biographers have supplied very little additional information.

During the 1920s, '30s, and '40s practically every schoolboy in America heard or read about Roy Chapman Andrews in the Gobi Desert, and dreamed, at one time or another, of emulating the adventures of the dashing explorer-scientist. Today, hardly anyone remembers the great fossil-hunter. One writer recently reported that a "persistent rumor" had it that Andrews was the real-life model for the film character, Indiana Jones. The producer of the films featuring the daring archeologist denied that he was. If he was not, he could have been.

Bibliography

Roy Chapman Andrews wrote numerous books, all based upon his travels and explorations, and all popularly written for general audiences or juvenile readers. The following include only his best-known works about his travels in Mongolia.

Andrews, Roy C. *Across Mongolian Plains.* New York: Blue Ribbon Books, 1921. An account of the 1919 hunting trip in Mongolia, Andrews' first extensive contact with Central Asia. One of his first books.

Ends of the Earth. New York: G.P. Putnam's Sons, 1929. Covers his travels and adventures until the late 1920s. A sort of early autobiography.

On the Trail of Ancient Man. Garden City: Garden City Publishing Co., 1926. An account of the first forays into Mongolia, apparently written when Andrews still hoped to find prehistoric human remains.

The New Conquest of Central Asia. New York: American Museum of Natural History, 1932. His definitive account of all the Central Asiatic Expeditions. The first segment of a compendium of technical papers by the scientists reporting the expedition's discoveries.

This Business of Exploring. New York: G.P. Putnam's Sons, 1935. Intended for juvenile readers.

Under a Lucky Star. New York: The Viking Press, 1943. His autobiography, written when his exploring days were long past.

Archer, Jules. *Science Explorer: Roy Chapman Andrews.* New York: Julian Messner, 1968. One of the two barely passable biographies. Very little about Andrews' private life.

Green, Fitzhugh. *Roy Chapman Andrews, Dragon Hunter.* New York: G.P. Putnam's Sons, 1930. Hagiography, written when Andrews' fame as an explorer was at its height.

Hellman, G. *Bankers, Bones and Beetles.* New York: The Natural History Press, 1968. An anecdotal history of the American Museum of Natural History. Fun to read.

Pond, Alonzo. *Andrews: Gobi Explorer.* New York: Grosset & Dunlap, 1972. The best existing biography, written by someone who knew Andrews and visited him in Mongolia.

Preston, D.J. *Dinosaurs in the Attic.* New York: St. Martin's Press, 1986. Half a history of the American Museum of Natural History, half a tour of the building, written by a former editor of the museum's magazine.

Rainger, R. *An Agenda for Antiquity.* Tuscaloosa: The University of Alabama Press, 1991. A scholarly account, probably an expanded Ph.D. dissertation, of Henry Fairfield Osborn's association with the Museum.

Shapiro, Harry. *Peking Man.* New York: Simon and Shuster, 1974. A fascinating and solidly researched account of the discovery and the loss of the remains of Peking Man.

8
The Houston Expedition

Flying Over the Roof of the World

As one who hath sent forth on a bold emprise
Into some distant land his Argoses
Watches in dread the fitful changing breeze,
And as now soft, now rude, its voices rise.

HILAIRE BELLOC

Where, exactly, is the Roof of the World? The term has been associated with more than one piece of the Earth's surface, but all lie somewhere along that great arc of mountain and plateau that stretches southeast from Central Asia more than 2,000 miles to shield Tibet's southern flank and separate the Indian subcontinent from the rest of Asia.

Marco Polo coined the expression to describe the Pamirs, the knot of mountain ranges that come together at the extreme northwest end of the arc. He presumably was not aware of the even higher mountains stretching to the southeast, the Karakorums and the Himalayas. Nor could he know about the high plateau of Tibet which today is often called the Roof of the World though, on his journey to China, he passed just to the north of it. But, inevitably, the expression is used most often today to describe the highest spot of Earth, the summit of the tallest mountain on the planet—Mount Everest.

The Marquess of Douglas and Clydesdale, chief pilot of the Houston Expedition.

Everest was first discovered in 1849 by the Great Indian Trigono-metrical Survey, and it was identified as the world's highest known mountain in 1852. However, for several decades thereafter, no one could be sure that it was, indeed, the highest on Earth, because there were still large portions of the Earth's surface, notably Tibet and the mountainous interior of New Guinea, that were so little known that geographers speculated that they might hold a mountain even higher. Only after the advent of the 20th century had exploration established with reasonable certainty that Everest is, indeed, the absolute king of mountains. Its officially accepted height has varied by a few feet over the years since its discovery. Originally, it was given by the Indian Survey as 29,002 feet. In the 1930s it had become 29,141 feet. Today, it is given as 29,028 feet. Through all the variations, Everest's height has always been given as being in excess of 29,000 feet, making it the only mountain in the world to top that figure.

Once it was established as the world's highest mountain, Everest naturally attracted the attention of European mountaineers who wanted to be the first to reach its summit. As mountaineering developed as a sport, the highest Himalayan peaks became the "property" of various countries, each "reserved" for expeditions sponsored by a particular country. Everest, named after a British Surveyor General of India, became a "British" mountain.

Lying astride the Nepal-Tibet border, it was not only the world's highest mountain, it was also one of the most inaccessible ones, protected by formidable barriers both natural and man made. During the 19th century and much of the 20th, Nepal and Tibet were hermit kingdoms that excluded foreign intrusions. Tibet's isolation was breached by the Younghusband expedition in 1904, but politics was not all that shielded the mountain. It lies in some of the most rugged, inaccessible topography in the world. By 1914 no European had been able to approach closer than forty miles from its base, let alone climb it.

After World War I ended, British mountaineers began planning in earnest for an assault, led by Francis Younghusband who lent his fame as an explorer and mountaineer to the organizing efforts. An expedition intended to be reconnaisance reached a point only 6,000 feet from the top in 1921, and an attempt to reach the summit was undertaken, and failed, in 1922.

A second attempt in 1924 also failed, but it became enshrined in mountaineering lore as one of the most famous climbs ever attempted. The final assault on the summit was made by two men, George Leigh-Mallory and Andrew Irvine. Mallory was a handsome, athletic, charismatic young man, respected as perhaps the most accomplished mountain climber of his day. He is remembered for his answer to a questioner who asked why he wanted to climb the mountain: "because it is there." He had been a leading member of the 1921 and 1922 expeditions, and he regarded Everest as his own personal challenge.

When Mallory and Irvine were last seen by other members of the expedition, they had reached a point only a few hundred feet below

Everest's peak (measured vertically; they had still to cover a much longer distance to reach the top, some of it requiring difficult and dangerous climbing). A bank of mist closed over them, and they were lost to view. They were never seen again. What exactly happened to them has never been determined, and whether they actually reached the summit has remained a mystery ever since. When last seen, they were reportedly "going strongly." After the expedition's tragedy, no further attempts on Everest were made during the 1920s.

Today, mountain climbers by the dozen, including rank amateurs, have reached the top of Everest. The well-defined route up the mountain is studded by garbage heaps of equipment and supplies discarded by the battalions of climbers. But today's successful climbers stand on the shoulders, as it were, of Leigh-Mallory and his fellow mountaineering pioneers. Those early Everesters lacked most of the sophisticated equipment used today. They did sometimes climb with oxygen, but the available equipment was bulky, heavy, and subject to frequent malfunctions. Many mountaineers in the 1920s and '30s argued that using oxygen was actually counterproductive, because the weight of the equipment and its unreliability more than offset the benefits of the gas itself. Perhaps most importantly, those early mountaineering trailblazers on Everest were boldly forging into the unknown, a piece of the Earth's surface never before trodden by the foot of a living being. There was no known, well-defined route to the top of Everest in 1924.

By 1932, then, no one had yet succeeded in reaching the summit of the world's highest mountain and returning to tell the tale. In Britain, another mountaineering expedition was being organized for an attempt in 1933. But in early 1932 an expedition of a rather different sort was also being assembled in Britain with Everest as its objective. It planned to attempt an airplane flight over the world's highest mountain.

The idea of flying an airplane over the top of Mount Everest in 1932 was not one to be dismissed out of hand, but neither was it something to be undertaken lightly. Pilots had flown over lower surrounding peaks in the 1920s, but their airplane engines could not cope with the altitudes needed to top Everest. The American daredevil, Richard Halliburton, tried to fly over the mountain in the 1920s in his plane, the *Magic Carpet*, but his engine failed before he could reach the required altitude. Aeronautical technology made great strides in the 1920s and 1930s, however, and by 1932 a flight appeared much more feasible than it had only a few years earlier.

The world altitude record by 1932 was 43,166 feet, set by an American Navy pilot in 1930, and it would be broken in September of that year by a British flyer who reached 43,976 feet. So the technology to reach an altitude sufficient to pass over the summit of Everest existed by then. Reaching an altitude higher than Everest was a surmountable, though daunting, problem, but it was not the only problem that made such a flight dangerous and scary.

The peaks of the Himalayas are swept by gales of incredible force, and the weather can change from clear and calm to blinding blizzard in minutes. The enormous mountains create updrafts and downdrafts of frightening velocity, sometimes in excess of 100 miles an hour. The summit of Everest is often obscured by a plume several hundred feet high composed of snow and ice crystals driven by winds of gale force. A pilot flying much higher than Everest's summit might suddenly be enveloped and blinded by a blizzard and, in 1932, he had no radar to guide him through the maze of peaks surrounding him. His frail airplane, powered by an engine puny by today's standards, might be suddenly sucked down in an unsuspected downdraft to crash into the side of the mountain. In 1932 there were no weather satellites to provide meteorological information about what was occurring on the peaks of the high Himalayas. No one knew for sure exactly how turbulent the air surrounding them might be, or the true force of the gales that were known to swirl around them. In sum, flying over Everest in the kind of airplane that existed in 1932 was every bit the challenge and as much a plunge into the unknown as a mountaineering assault on its summit.

The expedition was the creation of two men, only one of them a pilot, who were familiar with the Himalayas and whose lives were already filled with adventurous exploits. Colonel Percy T. Etherton had served in the Indian Army and fought in the Boer War and in World War I in Europe and the Middle East. In 1918 Etherton was assigned to serve as Consul General in Kashgar, to replace the legendary Sir George Macartney. Etherton remained in the post until 1924. Thereafter, he became known as a traveler, explorer, and big-game hunter, and by 1932 as the author of several bestselling books about his travels and adventures in Central Asia, South America, and the Orient. Already in his mid-fifties, he became the organizing secretary of the expedition.

Latham Valentine Stewart Blacker, Etherton's colleague, had also begun his career as an officer in the Indian Army serving on the northwest frontier, Persia, Afghanistan, and Russia. He early developed an interest in aviation and obtained his pilot's license in 1911, being awarded British flying certificate number 121. When war broke out in 1914, he transferred to the Royal Flying Corps and engaged in combat in France, being shot down and severely wounded three times. After the war, he became interested in developing designs for various kinds of armaments, while maintaining an interest in aviation.

Etherton and Blacker faced some difficult obstacles in turning their adventurous idea into reality. They had, of course, to identify and obtain an airplane capable of making the flight and recruit a pilot, or pilots, willing and able to fly it. They had to recruit the mechanics and other technical personnel needed, and they had to find some source of funding. They also had to gain official backing for the project. The plane, or planes, would have to fly from an airfield somewhere in northern India, so approval would have to be obtained from the Indian government, and they would probably have to use a Royal Air Force airfield. They would have to fly over Nepal to reach Everest, so agreement by the government of that country would have to be obtained.

The two originators spent the spring and summer of 1932 recruiting a committee of prominent people to organize the expedition and seek the official support and financial backing they needed. They were joined, for example, by Sir John Buchan, M.P., who later served as Governor General of Canada as Lord Tweedmuir. He was also, among other things, the author of many bestselling books (his best-known, the novel *The Thirty-Nine Steps*, became one of Alfred Hitchcock's earliest hit movies).

The committee obtained the sanction of the Royal Air Force which permitted it to use RAF facilities in Britain to prepare for the flight. Communications were sent off to India and Nepal requesting those governments' cooperation and support. The committee members began to consider which airplane and which engine should be used.

However, the search for funds was less successful. Etherton and Blacker decided the flight would make a good movie, and they began negotiating with the Gaumont-British Picture Corporation for financial support in exchange for rights to film the event. Unfortunately, the negotiations with the hardnosed businessmen of the movie company threatened to turn what was being described as a scientific endeavor into cheap entertainment.

In June Etherton and Blacker were able to recruit into the committee, through Buchan, the man who would not only become the expedition's chief pilot but who would also solve their financial problem. The Marquess of Douglas and Clydesdale was the eldest son of the 13th Duke of Hamilton and Brandon, one of the United Kingdom's most distinguished peers. A handsome and dashing figure in his Air Force uniform, Clydesdale was twenty-nine years old, a squadron leader in the Auxiliary Air Force and a Member of Parliament. He was not a man to jump immediately into such an undertaking, and he considered it coolly and carefully before agreeing to join the group:

> During the last few years many exciting enterprises had been laid before me by enthusiasts of all sorts. They were of a great variety, some erratic and quite impossible, others sound but obstructed by many difficulties. Some of the proponents were intelligent, some were stupid. . . . The world is full of ideas of this type, and many men receive such proposals. . . . The scheme to fly over Mount Everest appealed to me, but I viewed it much in the same way as the other ventures—to be carefully considered but not to be rushed at blindly.

He was not awed by the potential dangers:

> I had no thought of playing the heroic impersonator of British youth, nor had I looked on the expedition as likely to be particularly dangerous or spectacular.

By the end of summer, despite the committee's best efforts, the expedition's prospects were looking dim because of the difficulty of finding adequate financial backing. However, the addition of the dashing Clydesdale prompted publicity, and the expedition came to the attention of a friend of the young Marquess' mother, a rather remarkable woman named Fanny Lucy Houston.

Lady Houston was seventy-five years old, childless, possessed of a large fortune and a fond regard for the son of her friend, the Duchess of Hamilton. She is described in the *Dictionary of National Biography* as a "philanthropist and eccentric." Born the daughter of a warehouseman in Lambeth, she had grown into an unusually beautiful woman and had for a time earned her livelihood on the stage. She had married three husbands, all peers of the realm, the last of whom had bequeathed to her a fortune of several million pounds when he died in 1926. She became famous for unusual philanthropies which included large donations to such groups as Welsh coal miners, tramwaymen in Hull, and persecuted Russian Christians. In 1931, she provided £100,000 so a British flying team could compete for the prestigious Schneider Trophy.

In September Lady Houston summoned Clydesdale to one of her homes in Scotland to hear about the planned Everest expedition. The conversation resulted in her agreeing to contribute £10,000, with a guarantee of an additional £5,000 if needed. Clydesdale rushed back to England with the good news.

> I found Blacker and Etherton in gloomy conference at the College of Aeronautical Engineering with the representatives of an air operating company. They had been driven by the financial difficulties to contemplate hiring an ordinary commercial aeroplane for the job, and the representatives of the company, recognizing the situation of these two gentlemen, were dictating terms which would have placed the vital part of the undertaking in their hands.

Clydesdale's news brought the gloomy conference to an abrupt end. The committee shifted into high gear, and the enterprise was officially dubbed The Houston-Mount Everest Expedition. In November, a senior Royal Air Force officer, Air Commodore P.F.M. Fellowes, was appointed chief executive officer to take command of the expedition. A second RAF officer, Flight Lieutenant D.F. McIntyre, was appointed second pilot.

The committee spent the final months of 1932 acquiring planes, engines, and other equipment and having them modified for the special requirements of the flight. They settled on the Westland PV3 as the best aircraft and obtained two of them. One of the avowed purposes of the expedition was a dramatic demonstration to the world of the excellence of British aircraft design and construction. The two planes were described as "standard Royal Air Force general purpose aircraft,"

Starting the Pegasus engine of one of the Westlands at Lalbalu.
A British plane powered by a Pegasus engine had broken the world altitude
record a few months earlier.

thirty-four feet long with a wingspan of forty-six feet. To a modern
eye, the two Westlands used for the flight look remarkably like the
planes that fought over the Western Front in 1918. They were biplanes
with fixed landing gear and an open cockpit for the pilot. Behind the
cockpit was a closed compartment that could be used for a passenger
or two or for freight. It was modified for use by an observer who would
operate several cameras.

Actually, the planes were a good deal larger than World War I fighters and more solid, being of all-metal, aluminum construction. The expedition members considered them large, strong, and powerful. For the all-important choice of an engine, they settled on a Bristol Pegasus S.3. A British pilot had set a new altitude record in September, and his plane had been powered by a Pegasus engine.

There would be four crewmembers for the flight, a pilot and an observer/cameraman in each plane. Clydesdale would fly the lead plane with Blacker as observer, while McIntyre would pilot the second plane with the expedition's chief cinematographer, a man named S.R. Bonnett, as observer. They would wear special electrically heated flying suits and oxygen masks.

All the equipment was checked at RAF facilities where the four men tested the flying suits and oxygen equipment in a pressure chamber that simulated the temperature, air pressure, and oxygen supply that exist up to an altitude of 39,000 feet. Blacker was a pukka sahib who was never seen without a monocle screwed tightly into one eye. He insisted on wearing it under his oxygen mask in the pressure chamber. The diminishing pressure succeeded in dislodging the monocle, which had never before been known to happen, and it fell loose into the mask, affecting the flow of oxygen. Blacker's fumbling efforts to replace it without losing consciousness from loss of oxygen became a source of amusement to his companions.

Clydesdale decided to use the opportunity afforded by the pressure chamber test to experience firsthand the effects of oxygen deprivation at extreme altitudes:

> I had heard that at a height of 30,000 feet or above a man deprived of extra oxygen usually became unconscious in about thirty seconds. This I believe was due to the tendency to gasp and so to empty the system very quickly of oxygen. I removed my mask when the pressure was of 25,000 feet and found there was a temptation to gasp, but I hung on for nearly four minutes. Then I began to lose consciousness, rapidly replaced the mask and turned the flow of oxygen full on. On taking a few deep breaths, my senses immediately returned. Again at 35,000 feet, I took off the mask, and this time I could hardly avoid the temptation

to gasp. At the end of thirty-five seconds my sight was going wrong and I was on the verge of becoming unconscious. . . . Putting on the mask I soon had my supply of oxygen flowing again and was surprised once more at the rapidity of my recovery. I took no more liberties at greater heights.

He would be flying in an open cockpit, and there could no doubt that the least problem with the oxygen system could spell disaster within minutes. A mountaineer can become acclimated to the effects of extreme altitudes as he toils up the mountain over a period of weeks or even months, but the crewmembers of the Houston Expedition would take off from near sea level and reach an altitude in excess of 30,000 feet within an hour or two.

To gain official approval and support, the expedition committee emphasized the scientific value of the undertaking and played down its adventurous aspects. They would test planes, equipment, and crew reaction at extreme altitudes. They would investigate the meteorological phenomena in the turbulent air surrounding the giant peaks. Perhaps most importantly, they would take pictures, both still photos and movies, and the observer compartment of each plane would be loaded with several cameras. In particular, they hoped to take strips of still pictures, using a camera focused directly down through the floor of the plane, of the approach to the mountain and its south face. The planes would approach from the south over country never explored. The mountaineering expeditions had attacked the mountain from the northeast, and the expedition hoped to use the film to create a map of the unknown southern approaches and south face.

By February the testing was complete, and the expedition was ready to move to India. They had acquired use of a small RAF airfield at Lalbalu, a village in northern Bihar state about 250 miles northwest of Calcutta and less than 200 air miles from Everest. The two Westlands were crated and shipped by sea to Karachi, there to be assembled and flown to Lalbalu. The expedition had also acquired a small, light plane, called a Fox Moth, to serve as an auxiliary aircraft. It was complemented by two other small planes, a similar plane called a Gypsy Moth which belonged to Clydesdale, and a larger cabin plane, a Puss Moth, on loan from a wealthy British industrialist. The three pilots—Fellowes,

A local Maharaja aboard a caparisoned elephant inspects the planes at Lalbalu.

Clydesdale, and McIntyre—decided to fly the three small planes, loaded with some of the equipment, to India, and that flight became a minor adventure in itself.

The three small planes were slow, with cruising speeds of less than 100 miles per hour, and had limited range. They therefore had to fly in slow, short legs. The trip took weeks. They flew south across France and Italy to Sicily, across the Mediterranean to North Africa, through Egypt, Jordan, and Iraq to Karachi and Delhi in India. They encountered difficulties created by suspicious officials in several countries, notably in Mussolini's Italy, who confiscated their cameras and films. They were held up for days at several stops by bad weather. In India, after arrival at Lalbalu, one of the small planes was wrecked on the ground by a storm.

Meanwhile, the ship containing the Westlands docked at Karachi. The planes were uncrated and assembled, and Clydesdale and McIntyre flew over from Lalbalu to ferry them to the airfield in Bihar. They first spent a few days testing the aircraft and equipment at altitudes up to 35,000 feet, and everything worked perfectly. Even the Westlands cruised at only about 120 miles per hour, and the trip across India to Lalbalu took several days with stops at Hyderabad, Jodhpur, Delhi (where Lord Willingdon, the Viceroy, examined the planes with sharp interest), and Allahabad. The planes were stored in temporary canvas hangars erected by the RAF, and the expedition settled down to make last-minute preparations for the flight.

They spent several weeks in Lalbalu waiting for favorable weather. Every day their meterologist would send balloons aloft. If the weather was clear, they could be tracked to a height of 25,000 feet to measure wind velocities. The pilots learned, to their consternation, that wind velocities at that altitude were seldom less than 70 miles per hour and often topped 100 miles per hour. Earlier, it had been determined that a 40-mile wind would be the greatest in which it would be safe to make the attempt with the Westlands. The wind usually blew from the west, which meant the planes would have to fly a course to the north-west to compensate for the sideward drift the wind would cause. This meant flying a course a good deal longer than a straight line from Lalbalu to the mountain, against a strong headwind which would cut airspeed, causing more fuel to be burned.

Every day they waited for the evening weather forecast to arrive by telegram from Calcutta. They found the weather moved in ten- or twelve-day cycles, beginning with a disturbance which might be a rain-storm followed by several days of clear weather and little wind at the airfield and over the foothills. But on those days the mountain peaks were wreathed in clouds. As the cloud caps dissipated until the peaks stood out clearly etched against the sky, wind velocity rose. Within a few more days, another disturbance began the cycle again. Every day one of the small Moths went aloft a few thousand feet to check whether the mountains were free from clouds and to measure wind velocity. By early April their own observations and the Calcutta forecasts indicated that weather conditions for the next few days might permit a flight. On April 3 an early morning flight by Air Commodore Fellowes in one of the Moths revealed that the atmosphere surrounding the peaks was crystal clear, although he discovered the dusty haze that always hangs over the Indian plains and foothills at that time of year extended even higher than usual. The meteorologists reported wind velocity at 25,000 feet as fifty-seven miles per hour, high but not so high as to prevent a flight. Fellowes decided "go!," and the crews hurried to the airfield and donned their heavy suits. They loaded the delicate photo-graphic equipment (which had to be kept carefully wrapped against

The crews rush to man the Westlands for the first Everest flight.

the pervasive dust of the Indian plains). At 8 A.M. the two Westlands took off.

They found that the perpetual dust haze over the plains, which often hampered meteorological observations, had indeed risen higher than usual, and they broke out of it only after topping 19,000 feet. They had hoped to use landmarks on the ground to aid navigation, but the thick haze obscured the surface. After a half-hour's flight, they passed over the village of Forbesganj, on the Nepal border, the site of their forward emergency landing field. They began to pass over the ragged valleys and ravines of the Himalayan foothills. There would be no more possibility of an emergency landing. An engine failure would mean a crash and certain death.

The observers spent the first half-hour or so of the flight checking and making ready the several cameras they carried. Blacker had compiled a list of forty-six separate operations that he must perform to prepare the equipment and ensure that everything was ready (e.g., that the lens caps were removed). Soon after takeoff, they began to experience mechanical glitches that affected both crews. Clydesdale and Blacker discovered that their telephone link was plagued by a mysterious buzzing that increased as the plane gained altitude until the communication system was rendered useless. For the entire flight, they could communicate only by passing notes through a window in the bulkhead that separated their compartments. Blacker discovered that the dynamo which supplied electric current for their flying suits refused to work.

> Almost in a panic, I had to take off the cover of the cutout of the electrical system, undo the screws with my thumbnail, pressing the platinum contacts together by hand.

The dynamo began to hum and their suits warmed up comfortably.

Blacker opened the hatch in the roof of his compartment and thrust his head, protected by helmet, goggles, and oxygen mask, into the icy slip-stream. Straight ahead, over Clydesdale's shoulder and the pulsating rocker arms of the engine, he could make out Everest.

> Just a tiny triangle of whiteness, so white as to appear incandescent, and on its right, a hand's-breadth, another tiny peak which was Makalu . . . three incredible peaks—Everest and Makalu just to the right of the engine, and Kanchenjunga behind the right wing.

To his dismay, he saw an immense ice-plume streaming away from the crest of Everest, evidence of gale force winds sweeping the summit. But they pressed on toward the mountain, and Blacker ducked back into his compartment to open the hatch in the floor and make ready the vertical camera.

> Without getting up from a prone position, I could move myself back a little on my elbows, open the hatchway in the floor, and look vertically down on the amazing mountainscape, bare trees, seamed with great glaciers, and interspersed with streaks of scree and shale. This was the beginning of the range.

He stood up and again thrust his head through the overhead hatch. They were nearing the mountain at an altitude above 30,000 feet.

> Then, to my astonished eyes, northwards over the shoulder of the mountain, across the vast bare plateau of Tibet, a group of snow-clad peaks uplifted itself. . . . The scene was superb and beyond description. The visibility was extraordinary and permitted the whole range

to be seen on the western horizon. It seemed that the only limit to the view along the mountain was that due to the curvature of the Earth's surface. The size of the mountains stunned the senses; the stupendous scale of the scenery and the clear air confounded all estimates of size and distance.

As they approached Everest's summit, he again moved to operate the vertical camera through the floor.

I crouched down again, struggling to open the hatchway to take a photograph through the floor. Everything by now, all the metal parts of the machine, was chilled with the cold, the cold of almost interstellar space. The fastenings were stiff and the metal sides had almost seized. I struggled with them, the effort making me pant for breath, and I squeezed my mask on to my face to get all the oxygen possible. I had to pause and, suddenly, with the door half-open I became aware, almost perceptibly, of a sensation of dropping through space. The floor of the machine was falling away below us. I grasped a fuselage strut and peered through my goggles at the altimeter needle. It crept, almost swung, visibly as I looked at it in astonishment, down through a couple of thousand feet. Now I had the hatchway open, and the airplane swooped downwards over a mighty peak of jagged triangular buttresses which was the South Peak.

They were caught in one of Everest's hurricane-like downdrafts. Clydesdale revved the engine to full power and fought to bring the plane's nose up as the wind-scoured rock of the summit loomed in front of him. They were flying through the great plume of wind-driven ice and snow. Ice crystals from the plume pelted him in the open cockpit.

Blacker remained crouched on the floor of the observer's compartment, staring transfixed down through the open hatch.

Our airplane came to the curved chisel-like summit of Everest, crossing it, so it seemed to me, just a hair's breadth over its menacing summit. The crest came up to meet me as I crouched peering through the floor, and I almost wondered whether the tail skid would strike the summit.

The lead Westland, piloted by Clydesdale, approaching the summit of Mt. Everest five miles away. The plume of wind-blasted snow and ice crystals can be seen streaming away from the summit.

They cleared the jagged peak with perhaps 100 feet to spare. The second plane flew over the summit with a margin of safety only slightly greater. As it did so, the observer, S.R. Bonnett, began to feel faint and experience stomach cramps. He sank to the floor of his compartment as he began to lose consciousness. He discovered that the pipe feeding oxygen to his mask had broken. He was able to wrap his handkerchief around the break and keep the precious oxygen flowing.

The London Times *gave the Houston Expedition's triumph a two-column headline, rare for the understated London paper.*

The planes flew two complete circuits of the summit sometimes banking sharply to permit the photographers to get good pictures. The observers stood erect, their heads and shoulders thrust through the open overhead hatches, as they operated the oblique cameras. After fifteen minutes the little squadron banked toward the south and headed for home. As he lowered himself back into the compartment, Blacker found that his oxygen mask had become one large mass of ice plastered to his face.

Even before they completed the circuits of the peak, McIntyre noticed that Bonnett's upper body was no longer visible behind him above the open rear hatch. The observer had again felt faint and sank crumpled to the floor. The hastily mended oxygen tube supplied only a fraction of the normal flow of oxygen, and Bonnett completely lost consciousness. McIntyre realized something was dangerously wrong in the rear compartment, but he had his own problems.

> I suddenly had the sensation of freezing cold around the nose and mouth. I jumped immediately to the conclusion that the oxygen heating had failed. This was serious as it was only a matter of time until the water content would freeze in the valve and stop the flow. Actually, the complete metal nose-piece, carrying the microphone and oxygen feed, had dropped from the mask and was lying on my knee. In my anxiety for Bonnett, I had no doubt turned my head too far around and dragged the nose-piece away from the mask. I quickly tried to get it back in position and refix it, but found this impossible with heavy gloves. I was compelled to hold it in place. . . . Throughout that long half-hour, I was holding the oxygen feed against the mask with one hand and with the other flying the air-craft, regulating engine temperature, oxygen flow, and altitude boost control. I was worried about Bonnett lying unconscious or dead in the rear cockpit.

Only after they had descended to 8,000 feet over Forbesganj did McIntyre become aware of movement in the rear compartment. Bonnett struggled erect and tore off his goggles and mask. His face was "a nasty dark green shade," but he had survived.

The two planes arrived back at Lalbalu at 11 A.M. The entire flight had taken exactly three hours. The crewmembers were examined by doctors who found no ill effects, even to Bonnett. They discovered that the windows in the rear compartments of the Westlands had been cracked by the blowing ice crystals of the plume as they flew through it across the summit. They were mildly disappointed when they began to examine the developed pictures. The survey photos, which they had hoped to use to construct a map of the unknown southern approaches and south face of the mountain, had been affected by the dust haze. If they wanted to make the map, a second flight would have to be made. But they had obtained a wealth of other photographs, spectacular scenes the like of which no human being had ever before beheld. Their photographs of Everest confirmed that the topography of the summit posed no insuperable obstacles to prevent a climber from reaching it.

Ironically, on precisely the same day that the Houston Expedition was giving a dramatic demonstration to the world of the excellence of British aircraft and the daring of British pilots, American aviation was staggered by a major disaster. The U.S. Navy's huge dirigible, the *Akron*, crashed during an electrical storm in the Atlantic off the coast of New Jersey, killing most of the seventy-three officers and men aboard. American editors gave the tragedy the banner headlines that might otherwise have been devoted to the Houston Expedition's pioneering flight. The huge dirigible airships had been considered by many people to be the principal means for future passenger travel in the air, but they had already suffered several spectacular crashes. Four years later the fiery destruction of the huge German airship, the *Hindenburg*, as it was being moored in New Jersey, put a final end to hopes that dirigibles were the airships of the future.

The day after the Everest flight, the two Westlands, manned by different crews, attempted a flight over Kanchenjunga, at 28,200 feet the world's third-highest mountain. Unfortunately, the summit became completely encased in clouds, and they were unable to fly over it. Air Commodore Fellowes flew one of the planes which became separated as they circled the cloud-covered crest. On the return flight, Fellowes became confused and lost, due, he later decided, to a lack of oxygen caused by a poorly fitted mask which had caused problems throughout the flight.

As he emerged from the mountains to fly over the flat, brown Gangetic plain, he could find no landmarks to tell him where he was. His fuel was running low, and he decided to make an emergency landing on a flat piece of land abutting a railway line where he hoped he could find out his location. He made the landing, and the plane was instantly surrounded by a mob of villagers eager to touch the strange machine. He kept the engine turning over, and the observer located a man in the crowd who could speak English. He was able to show them on their map where they were located—a village some distance to the west of Lalbalu. They took off again and followed the railroad track, but with only 10 gallons of gas left, they could not reach Lalbalu. At the city of Dinajpur, with the gas gauge on empty, Fellowes looked

P

The New York Times *gave its front-page banner headline to the crash
of an American Navy dirigible on the same day which overshadowed
the British feat as a news item in the United States.*

frantically for another level, empty field on which to make a second
emergency landing.

The plain was punctuated with trees, and a crowd of people filled
what appeared to be the only possible landing site. There was no
gasoline left, so land I must somewhere. Selecting the best available
area, due to providence rather than my own good piloting, I alighted
safely, managing only by inches to clear a schoolhouse surrounded
by railings and a couple of large trees. It being the first time I had
flown this airplane, with two forced landings, the second an ex-

209

traordinarily difficult one, I felt that the inscrutable influence some call luck, and others providence, was with me, notwithstanding that I had been unfortunate enough to lose myself.

They were received by the Collector, the local British official, and sent a telegram to Lalbalu. Clydesdale soon arrived in his Gypsy Moth with gasoline, and the next day the lost crew returned to its headquarters.

On April 19, i.e., sixteen days after the Everest flight, the two Westlands, manned by the same crews, made a second flight over the mountain to obtain the survey photos they had missed on the first flight. They circled the peak several times and returned to Lalbalu after a flight marred by only one minor mishap. On the return flight, Blacker, after using his screwdriver to reload his movie camera, fumbled and dropped the tool through the open hatchway in the floor:

> In a moment, I saw it flashing through the open floor hatch with a glint of sun on its shaft as it sped on its way to Nepal.

The second flight brought the expedition to its conclusion, and the group broke up. Some remained for a while to travel in India. All eventually returned to heroes' welcomes in Britain.

The mountaineering expedition that had been forming in Britain for an attempt on Everest was moving north from Darjeeling toward the mountain just when the Houston expedition was making its flights. They made their assault in mid-May, but they were thwarted by blizzards and deep snow at the top elevations. The climbers succeeded in getting above 28,000 feet but, once again, the result was failure to reach the absolute summit.

When the climbers were near the maximum height they would reach, they experienced a shock when one of them came upon an ice axe, in perfect condition and looking like new, lying on a rocky slab. Never before had anyone set foot on that spot—except perhaps Leigh-Mallory and Irvine. It was later established with fair certainty that the axe had belonged to one of them, but how it came to lie for nine years on that particular gale-swept rock has never been determined.

Nine years after the flights by the Houston Expedition, during the dark months of World War II, a lone pilot in a single-seat plane duplicated their flight over Everest's crest. Colonel Robert Scott had flown as a Flying Tiger to duel Japanese fighters in dog fights over China and Burma. He had gained a reputation as a daredevil and "one-man airforce." One day in 1942 he took off from an airfield in Assam in a new fighter plane on what was described as a "routine test flight." On a whim, he decided to fly over the snow peaks of the Himalayas, although he had no authorization to do so and had made no preparations for such a flight. The higher he flew, the more exhilarated he became by the incredible panorama spread out below him, and he decided to fly directly over the highest mountain of all.

> Above Everest now, I withstood my temptation to fly close to the big peak on the down-wind side—there were bound to be terrible downdrafts there, and I had respected lesser down-drafts of lesser peaks in lower parts of the world. Passing directly over the South Peak, Lhotse, I photographed Everest against the sky, and as I opened the glass canopy of the plane, I felt the chilling blast of the wind. I noted then that my thermometer registered 22 degrees below zero.

Scott continued to climb until his altimeter measured 37,000 feet, although he estimated his actual altitude was probably closer to 44,000 feet, calibrated from temperature and pressure corrections. He tried, just for fun, to fire his machine guns, but they were frozen. He went into a power dive directly over the mountain and got caught in "the most violent downdraft I have ever experienced." He flew through the plume, as Clydesdale and McIntyre had done, and retained control of his plane only with difficulty.

> Fuel, oxygen, and film about gone, I turned now through the saddle of Everest's main peaks . . . and saluted with reverence the highest point on the Earth's surface. I tried to salute by firing the two 50-calibre guns into the glacier, but once more they failed to discharge. So I just waggled my wings and dove for my refueling base to the south.

A Calcutta newspaper published a report of his flight and took a swipe at British aviation by saying that while the Houston Expedition (which the report said had occurred in 1927) "required . . . many months of planning and the expenditure of some hundred thousands of pounds," Scott had needed only "about five hours of his morning on a routine test flight and the consumption of a few gallons of aviation gasoline." In his own published account of the flight Scott pointed out the basic error of the comparison:

> Of course, I blush when I think that my gallant newspaperman did not consider the difference in the advancement of aviation between the years [of the Houston Expedition] and 1942.

The two old soldiers, Etherton and Blacker, were too well along in years to go on active service in World War II. Etherton served as chief staff officer to the officer in charge of civil defense in London. He died in 1963. Blacker served as a lieutenant colonel in the Territorial Army during the war. He continued to tinker with armament design and succeeded in inventing a "bombard" that was modified into the "hedgehog," used so effectively against submarines. Another of his designs became the standard British antitank weapon. Blacker died in 1964.

Clydesdale succeeded to his father's title and became the 14th Duke of Hamilton and Brandon in 1940. The following year he was an involuntary participant in one of the more bizarre episodes of World War II. Rudolph Hess, Hitler's deputy, parachuted onto the Duke of Hamilton's estate in Scotland in a quixotic attempt to arrange peace between Germany and Britain. Hess was immediately arrested, but he insisted on seeing the Duke personally to explain his mission. The two men had never before met, but Hamilton acceded to Hess' request and heard his message. The Duke then immediately flew south in a Hurricane fighter plane to report to the Prime Minister. When Winston Churchill heard Hamilton's brief, preliminary account of what had happened, he found it all so improbable that he reportedly responded by saying, "Well, Hess or no Hess, I am going to see the Marx brothers." After the movie, however, he was given a full report.

After the failure of the 1933 mountaineering expedition, two more attempts to reach the summit were made before World War II (in 1936 and 1938), but both failed. Both expeditions encountered adverse weather that was unprecedented. Heavy snows, brought on by an early onset of the monsoon, choked the upper parts of the mountain with deep snow that could not be crossed, and produced constant avalanches.

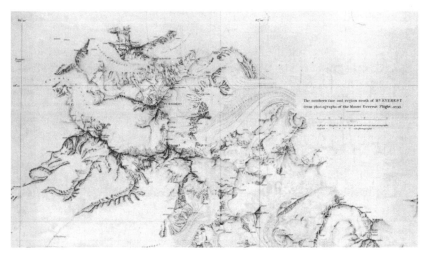

Map of Everest and its environs derived from the photographs taken by the Houston Expedition. For the first time geographers were able to map the south approach to the mountain, the approach taken by the successful mountaineering expedition of 1953, the first to reach the summit.

Neither expedition was able even to reach the altitudes attained by the earlier expeditions.

The Everesters had to wait until after War World II to renew the siege. Political changes in India and China after the war, however, caused further delay as newly formed governments, suspicious or hostile to the West, refused to grant permission to make ascents. Only in 1953, the year of the coronation of Queen Elizabeth II, did an expedition under the command of Sir John Hunt finally conquer the mountain. They approached from the south through Nepal rather than the northern approach through Tibet, used by all the previous expeditions, which had been closed to Western expeditions by the communist government of China. Edmund Hillary and Tenzing Norgay achieved the summit to become the first humans known for certain to stand on the spot that Stewart Blacker, almost exactly twenty years earlier, had feared was about to be scraped by his plane's tail skid.

Bibliography

The leading members of the Houston Expedition collaborated in writing an account of the undertaking that was published the following year. The two pilots, Clydesdale and McIntyre, jointly wrote their own separate account which was published two years later. Those are the only two books published about the expedition. By contrast, there have been numerous books published about the mountaineering attempts on Everest during the 1920s and 1930s.

Clydesdale, A.A.D. *The Pilots' Book of Everest*. London: William and D.F. McIntyre, Hodge & Company, 1936. The two pilots' firsthand account. A better book than the next one listed below.

Fellowes, P.F.M. et al. *First over Everest!* New York: Robert M. McBride & Co., 1934. The jointly written account of the expedition. The writing is often pedestrian and dwells excessively on arcane and technological details, but it is fascinating nevertheless for the sense of excitement it conveys and the ring of authenticity.

Hunt, Sir John. *The Ascent of Everest*. London: Hodder and Stoughton, 1953. The carefully documented account of the first successful climb to the summit by the expedition's leader.

Scott, Robert L. *God Is My Co-Pilot*. New York: Charles Scribner's Sons, 1944. An exciting, readable wartime memoir by the "one-man airforce" of the Flying Tigers.

Ullman, James Ramsey, ed. *Kingdom of Adventure: Everest*. London: Collins, 1948. An engrossing account of all the prewar attempts on Everest, comprised of long passages taken from various accounts by the mountaineers themselves. One feels the cold and the exhaustion and the challenge posed by the massive mountain. Especially interesting, because it was published before Everest was finally conquered.

Ella Maillart and Peter Fleming

"More an Escapade Than an Expedition"

As a friend to the children commend me the Yak.
You will find it exactly the thing:
It will carry and fetch, you can ride on its back,
Or lead it about with a string.

HILAIRE BELLOC

They first met in 1934 in London where they drank beer together in a nightclub. It was not love at first sight. He later remembered her as "tall, rather good looking, with a brown face and fair hair." But when they parted, he felt certain that she had developed a "strong dislike" of him. Of the meeting, she later recorded only that she was seeking information about China in preparation for a trip she planned to make there. She remembered that he, who had recently returned from China, advised her to take "hundreds of visiting cards and also notepaper with showy lettering"—it would impress officials in small villages. She recorded no recollections of him personally. When she asked him how to go into the areas in the south controlled by the communists, he replied, "you don't." When they parted, they exchanged off-hand assurances that they would probably meet again in China.

He was Peter Fleming, she was Ella Maillart. He was a correspondent for the London *Times*, she wrote for *Petit Parisien*, a leading Paris daily newspaper. They were both avid travelers and both had written bestselling books about trips they had made. They preferred to travel alone: his book had been entitled *One's Company*, while hers was called *Turkestan Solo*. But they were about to embark together on the most famous journey either of them would ever make.

Robert Peter Fleming (he is never identified by his first name) was born in London on May 31, 1907. His father, Valentine Fleming, was later elected a Conservative Member of Parliament. He was killed in action in France in 1917. Peter was the eldest of four brothers. One of his brothers was Ian who later created the fictional superspy, James Bond. Peter was educated at Eton and at Christ Church, Oxford, where he received a first-class honours degree in English in 1929.

As the eldest male heir, Peter was expected to go into the family business. But after a brief stint in the branch office in New York, he decided banking was not for him, perhaps in part because his brief excursion into banking occurred during the first years of the Great Depression. "The air was black with investors jumping off skyscrapers," he later said. In 1931, he joined the staff of *The Spectator* as assistant literary editor. He would maintain his connection with that publication for most of his life. During the same year he attended a conference of the Institute of Pacific Relations in Shanghai and thus made his first visit to China and to Russia, crossing the Soviet Union on the Trans-Siberian Railroad.

In 1932, as an unpaid correspondent for the *Times*, he accompanied an expedition to Brazil to search for a missing explorer, Colonel P.H. Fawcett. It was, in the words of one biographer, a "crack-brained and amateurish" undertaking, but it provided the material for his first book, *Brazilian Adventure*, published in 1933. This was a new kind of travel book, witty and literate in mocking the dangers—which were certainly present—as well as the author himself. It was a huge success. In 1933 he returned to China, again as a *Times* correspondent. He traveled from Manchuria in the north to the communist-held areas of the south. He was able to get an interview with Chiang Kai-shek. He returned to England via Japan and the United States, but he was already planning still another trip to Asia.

Ella Katherine Maillart was born in Geneva on February 20, 1903, the daughter of a furrier. She was given the nickname Kini, the name by which Fleming always referred to her. She was educated in Geneva. After graduation from school, she undertook an amazing variety of activities. She taught school in several places, including a brief time as a teacher of French in Wales. Early in life she learned sailing on Lake Geneva, and it became the passion of her life. At age twenty she served as deck hand on the yacht of a wealthy Englishman in the English Channel and the Irish Sea. She joined with three other girls to voyage from Marseille to Greece aboard an engineless sailboat. In 1924 she had (in Peter's words) "the abstruse distinction of sailing for Switzerland in the Olympic Games." Her life-long dream, which she was never able to realize, was to sail to the islands of the South Seas to "seek paradise." A world-class skier, she was a member of the Swiss Alpine team four times in world championship competition. She acted in a skiing film and spent a year in Berlin studying film production and playing small parts in films.

In 1930 she spent five months in Moscow studying film production. But as her youthful life had already demonstrated, she was not content to remain in one place long:

> The nomad's life enthralls me. Its restlessness pursues me; it is as much part of me as of the sailor. All ports and none are home to him, and all arrivings only a new setting forth.

She joined a group of Russians traveling to Russian Turkestan. They traveled as far as the eastern border of the Central Asian province.

> I climbed a mountain nearly 17,000 feet high on foot. . . . There, at last, from the heights of the Celestial Mountains I could descry, on a plain far away and further still to the east, the yellow dust of the Takla Makan Desert. It was China, the fabulous country of which, since my childhood, I had dreamed.

But the Soviet border guards would allow no one to cross the border. She said goodby to the group with whom she had been traveling and, alone, turned back to Samarkand, Bokhara, and Tashkent in Soviet Central Asia. Her trip became the material for her first book, *Turkestan Solo*. Two years later, she was sent to China by the *Petit Parisien* to cover events in northern China and Manchuria. But she had another idea in mind.

*Kini, as Ella Maillart was also known, relaxing with her pipe
in the Tsaidam. She says that smoking a pipe "keeps me awake."*

As the two correspondents had anticipated in London, they met
again six months later in Harbin, Manchuria. They traveled around
Manchuria together, reporting on developments in the recently created Japanese puppet state of Manchukuo. They found they had both
come to China with the same purpose in mind: to travel from Peking
to India across Central Asia, thereby transiting the western province of
Chinese Turkestan [or Sinkiang (New Dominion) as it was being called].
They both knew that under the conditions that existed in China such
a trip was probably impossible, and if it proved to be possible, could be
very dangerous. But such conditions only made the prospect all the
more alluring to such as Kini and Peter.

By 1935 the armies of the Kuomintang (National People's Party) under Chiang Kai-shek had victoriously completed their Northern Expedition from their base in Canton to the capital at Peking and had established a new central government in Nanking (the old capital's name had been changed to Peiping). After having made common cause with the communists in the early 1920s, they had turned on their erstwhile allies in 1927, and by 1935 had mounted four "Campaigns of Annihilation" against the communists' bases in the south. But the communists remained strong and cohesive.

The writ of the Nanking government by no means ran throughout China. Eight of the seventeen provinces of China proper remained autonomous under the control of local warlords. The treaty ports under various foreign powers continued to enjoy the status of extraterritoriality that had been established under various treaties concluded with the now-defunct Manchu dynasty. They therefore lay beyond the jurisdiction of the Nanking government. Tibet had attained independence more or less since the 1911 revolution and remained independent and isolated. Sinkiang was nominally under the control of Nanking. But Soviet influence had penetrated into the western areas of the province, and civil war had been raging for several years. No news of events or conditions there had been received in Europe for three or four years. Finally, the communists in the south had begun their epic Long March in October 1934, and were moving in a wide swing through western Szechwan Province north and west toward their eventual base in Yenan.

Peter and Kini were aware of all this, but they wanted to investigate for themselves what was happening in the mysterious, remote province of Sinkiang. The likelihood of success was remote. Peter:

> We should be lucky if we got into the province at all and luckier, perhaps, if we got out.

Neither of them knew anything about the country they proposed to cross, but they decided to try anyway, and they took the train to Peking to prepare for the trip. There, they had a stroke of luck. Kini met a geologist who had been with Sven Hedin's latest expedition to Sinkiang which had been undertaken under the auspices of the Nanking government. While on the Tsaidam plateau, he had met a White Russian couple named Smigunov who were living among the Mongols on the Tsaidam. They had been forced to move to Tientsin but wanted to move back to their home in Central Asia, and Kini's new acquaintance thought they would be willing to act as guides and travel with Peter and Kini as far as the Tsaidam. But from there on, the two correspondents would be on their own. Contacted in Tientsin, the Smigunovs agreed enthusiastically to the plan, and joined Peter and Kini in Peking.

The Tsaidam Plateau lies at 10,000 feet altitude in northeastern Tibet, between the Kunlun mountains to the south and the Altyn Tagh chain, a spur of the Kunlun range to the north. It is one of the most isolated areas geographically in the world, and its isolation from the chaos reigning in the rest of China is what made it attractive as a route to reach Sinkiang. More than forty-five years before Kini and Peter contemplated plunging into the Tsaidam—in April 1889, to be exact—an American explorer, William Woodville Rockhill, crossed the Tsaidam on the first of two expeditions he made from China deep into eastern Tibet. In his account of that journey Rockhill wrote:

> The name Ts'aidam appears to be Tibetan, ts'ai ("salty"), dam ("plain"), a very appropriate name, as salt is the chief if not sole product of this forsaken land. I am mistaken; it is not the sole product, for the Ts'aidam breeds mosquitoes so numerous and bloodthirsty that Mongols and cattle have to flee before them every year, and seek shelter in the adjacent mountains. Again, the name Ts'aidam is explained by a Mongol word tsavidam, meaning "broad, wide expanse of country"—also a fit appellation for this plain, some 600 miles from east to west, and 100 to 150 miles from north to south.

Peter and Kini knew they could legally enter Sinkiang only with a special permit from the Nanking government, but they also knew they would almost certainly never be able to obtain one. So they decided to travel as far as western Kansu Province, for which their passports were valid, and hope to be able to go forward from there. Their little expedition must have been one of the most sketchily supplied such undertakings on record. Aside from basic clothing, sleeping bags, a small medicine chest and toilet articles, they carried little baggage. Among their meager articles—all to be ultimately useful one way or another—

were a .22 caliber rifle; six bottles of brandy; a bottle of Worcestershire sauce; and Macauley's *History of England* (Kini kept their matches dry by carrying the packets between the volumes). To cook their meals, they carried a single frying pan which doubled as a washbasin.

On February 15, 1935, the four travelers set out from Peking. Their route was south by train to Chengchow, then west to the western rail terminus at Sian. However, they missed their connection with the Sian Express at Chengchow and had to travel third class from there. This meant being wedged into a wooden carriage much like a cattle car, with two wooden benches down the middle. It was stuffed with unwashed humanity including a great many soldiers recently drafted to fight against the communists.

Sian was the ancient capital of China during the Han and Tang dynasties, then called Chang-an. For centuries, it was one of the greatest cities of the world. In 1971 a farmer plowing his field near the city uncovered one of the greatest archeological discoveries of the century: a terra cotta army of hundreds of life-size figures buried to guard the tomb of Chin-Shr Huang-ti, the unifier of ancient China and builder of the Great Wall during the third century B.C. But that discovery was still twenty-five years in the future when Peter and Kini arrived. They were able to visit an ancient Confucian temple and the oldest mosque in China.

They called on the governor and received permits for onward travel. From some German missionaries they learned that Sven Hedin had passed through only a few days before on his return from Sinkiang. He was to depart China for the last time later in the year. He had told of very chaotic conditions to the west.

Their main concern was obtaining onward transportation by road. Peter and Smigunov were finally able to find space in a truck convoy bound for Lanchow, the capital of Kansu province. They traveled for a week on overloaded trucks. In Lanchow their passports were taken away by the authorities. They waited six days, each day receiving a promise that their documents would be returned momentarily.

Finally, the suspense ended: the passports of Kini and Peter were returned with permission to proceed, but the Smigunovs were ordered to return to Tientsin. No one of Russian origin was allowed in the northwestern regions, because of communist activity and Soviet influence. A group of White Russians had recently been turned back and returned to the coast. The news was a blow to all four of them. The Smigunovs would return to what fate, they knew not. For Peter and Kini, Peter summed up the import of it:

> Without the Smigunovs we could hardly hope to get much further. Three languages at least were needed to get us to Sinkiang—Chinese, Mongol and Turki (Tibetan would also have been useful); of these, I spoke only a few words of Chinese. We did not know the road or the people or the customs. . . . We were heading for a fiasco.

But Kini was more optimistic:

> It was true we were going to miss the services of the Smigs, even to miss them cruelly, but carrying it out alone added some suggestion of bravura to our exploit. Our conquest of Tartary would seem all the more fascinating if it were due entirely to our own efforts.

As they departed Lanchow, they tried to console the dejected and fearful Russians. It was only much later, after they completed their journey, that they learned what has befallen the Smigunovs. From Tientsin, they were able to gain passage by ship out of China to the West. They eventually landed in Uruguay where they settled down.

The two travelers were on the road to Sining, six days' journey to the west, the traditional departure point for camel caravans heading into the Tsaidam. Kini's spirits rose:

> It was a joy to be going forward, to be on the road again, to have left those poisonous bureaucrats behind us; a joy to be one's own master.

They traveled on three mules with a muleteer named Wang accompanying them. In Sining they looked up a friend of the Smigunovs who owned a photography shop and seemed to know all the influential people. Their passports were surrendered to the police with a request for permits to proceed onward. They waited several days. The familiar pattern set in: every day they were promised their passports, but at the end of each day nothing happened.

They decided to visit Kum Bum, the great Tibetan Buddhist mon-

Peter Fleming, in his comfortable American boots, playing patience somewhere in the Tsaidam. If the game played out, it was considered an auspicious omen for the next leg of the journey.

astery and temple complex which Sven Hedin had visited and where Alexandra David-Neel had spent more than two and a half years translating Buddhist manuscripts. It lay a half-day's journey to the south of Sining.

They toured the great religious center. Peter's reaction differed from that recorded by either Sven Hedin or Alexandra David-Neel:

> In the greatest temple, looking down from a high gallery upon the huddled chanting figures, I caught for a moment, and for the first time, something of that dark and powerful glamour with which western superstition endows the sacred places of the East. I had been, as every traveler has, in many kinds of temples; never before in one where I had that tight, chill, tingling feeling which I suppose is something between spiritual awe and physical fear.

In Kum Bum they were introduced to something with which they would become familiar in the coming months. The chief lama received them in his rooms and offered them tea. With the tea was served something else. Peter:

> Tea was brought in and with it, flanked by slabs of butter, a pyramid of some drab-coloured powdery substance. In the dim light we could only guess what this was. First we thought it was sugar, then we thought it was salt; finally we decided it was very fine ash . . . Then we tasted it and agreed it was sawdust.

Kini was equally mystified at first:

> Beside me was a bowl full of grey powder which looked like fine salt and on which rested two slabs of butter. . . . I ate a little of the unknown and unsavoury powder off the tip of my finger. Could it be ashes used in some religious rite? But when it came to his turn, our old man helped himself and with nimble fingers mixed the powder and butter in his tea, and kneaded them into a ball. Then I understood.

It was tsamba, toasted barley flour, the staple food of Tibet. They would eat a great deal of tsamba as they traveled across the desert. After he grew more familiar with it, Peter's opinion of it changed:

> Tsamba has much to recommend it, and if I were a poet, I would write an ode to the stuff. It is sustaining, digestible, and cheap. For nearly three months we had tsamba for breakfast and tsamba for lunch, and the diet was neither as unappetizing nor as monotonous as it sounds . . . I would not go so far as to say that you never get tired of tsamba, but you would get tired of anything else much quicker.

A half-hour's walk from Kum Bum, in a little village called Lusar, lived a rich Muslim merchant, Ma Shin-teh, who was a friend of Smigunov. They called on him to ask his help in locating a caravan from Sining to cross the Tsaidam. He was very friendly and helpful (Kini got the impression he owed Smigunov money and was helpful for that reason). He made arrangements for them to join a caravan he knew would soon be entering the Tsaidam, and he introduced them to a "timid sharp-eyed lad, half-Mongol and half-Chinese" whose name was Li (he is never identified by any other name) who would accompany them as far as Teijinar where lived Smigunov's old partner, a Russian named Borodishin. They hoped that Borodishin still lived in Teijinar and that he would help them go on from there. It was arranged they would meet Li and the caravan in a few days' time a little beyond Sining near the great salt lake of Koko Nor.

This important conversation with Ma Shin-teh was perforce carried on in Chinese, and Peter's command of the language was pushed to its limits, and beyond. Peter:

> By the end of the journey I spoke as much bad Chinese as was needed for the business of the road; but at this stage my vocabulary was exiguous and I still wonder how I managed this crucial conversation so successfully.

Kini spoke fluent Russian but knew no Chinese at all, so she was a silent, and somewhat amused, spectator:

> Peter tried to make himself understood, and I did not know which to admire more, Ma's patience or my companion's ingenuity. Peter made himself charming, apologized for his traveling clothes, smiled and protested his unworthiness of the compliments which he guessed were being paid him. Taking advantage of a respite to light his pipe, he remarked to me that he could make nothing whatever of the conversation.

One potentially serious misunderstanding occurred. Ma understood from Peter not that they needed four camels for the caravan, but that they possessed four camels, and he made no arrangements to obtain any. Fortunately, the mistake was discovered in time.

The two travelers departed Lusar relieved that their onward journey across the Tsaidam was arranged. But the long exchange in an unfamiliar language left Peter drained:

> After two hours' feverish guessing, I felt physically exhausted. Some of the guessing had been pretty wild; I learnt later, on a second visit to Lusar, that when Ma, looking at Kini and then back to me, had asked how old she was, I had replied without a moment's hesitation: 'No, only friends.' They must have thought us very odd indeed.

Back in Sining, they found their papers returned with the necessary permits to proceed. Peter was amazed that they were receiving permission to proceed so easily at each stop. He concluded that the local officials in each city, uncertain what to do with two foreigners traveling illegally, were really passing the buck to the officials at the next stop to decide what to do about them. They traveled twenty-five miles to a village called Tangar to await their rendezvous with the caravan. They stayed with missionaries—the man was from Austria, the woman from Scotland—who helped them prepare for their onward journey. Kini:

> Mrs. Urech was a witty Scotswoman who found it hard to take us seriously. How could we expect to cross Asia with so little luggage? It must be admitted that, having no scientific instruments, no cinematographic apparatus and no boxes of tinned food, we made a poor show.

They bought ponies and laid in supplies for the journey across the desert. Mrs. Urech even mended the torn seat of a pair of Peter's trousers that Kini had begun wearing.

On March 29 they departed Tangar and traveled to Koko Nor where they met Li and the caravan. The caravan belonged to the Prince of Dzun, a Mongol nobleman who was returning to his headquarters at Dzunchia in the Tsaidam. Soon after their arrival, Kini and Peter, accompanied by Li as interpreter, called on the prince. He turned out to be a taciturn young man dressed in a voluminous fur-trimmed scarlet robe. Following local custom, they brought a gift to present to their host, a second-hand telescope ("a gim-crack affair" according to Peter). Neither the prince nor any of his retinue had ever seen a telescope. They tried it out, squinting and contorting their faces trying to look through it, but without much success. The prince had difficulty keeping one eye shut while looking through the eyepiece with the other. Peter:

> We were a prey to those misgivings which assail you when you give a child a toy and the toy, in spite of all they told you at the shop, declines to work.

But the nomads finally adjusted the focus correctly, and there were murmurs of amazement as they looked at a distant camel brought magically close by the glass.

The caravan moved out from Koko Nor on April 1. Kini and Peter now entered into a life that must have been much like the life Marco Polo led when he crossed Central Asia, a way of life ancient even then: the life of a Silk Road caravan (although, technically, they were not yet on the Silk Road and would not join it for some weeks). Kini:

> Day after day our existence passed in accordance with the immutable rules of the centuries. Before dawn, without useless fuss or noise, 250 camels, 30 horses and about 80 human beings were ready to start.

Sven Hedin and Aurel Stein had crossed the deserts of Central Asia in caravans, but they traveled with their own caravans, much smaller than the Prince of Dzun's. Kini and Peter were traveling in a traditionally organized caravan. Again, Kini:

> While Li was saddling my horse and Peter taking down the tent, I packed our supplies in the kitchen box. . . . Then, the caravan gone, we would crouch over the still-warm ashes, putting off the moment when we must join the slow monotonous march. We swallowed a last bowl of tea. I hung the kettle on my saddle, pushed my mug into the saddle-bag—and there was no more to do but find a clump of earth from which to leap on to the saddle. . . . A gallop, and one overtook the long caterpillar crawling on its way westward.

They traveled from 6 A.M. to 2 P.M., then camped to allow the camels time to graze before dark. Breakfast and lunch were tsamba and buttered tea. Dinner was usually game shot by Peter with the .22 rifle during the day. He would leave the caravan's slow march and canter off into the desert. He brought back hares, partridges, ducks, occasionally even an antelope. It was cold. Kini often would alight from her pony, her teeth chattering despite the many layers of heavy clothes she wore, to walk for awhile to get her circulation going and warm up.

They traveled for seventeen days with the prince. The monotony of the travel across the featureless plateau brought out the differences in the personalities and temperaments of the two travelers. Kini:

Kini with a bored-looking marmot somewhere in the Tsaidam.

We did not see things from the same angle. Every night, Peter would repeat his refrain: "Sixty li's nearer to London" [li: Chinese mile, about seven hundred yards]. He did it to annoy me, and I would tell him to shut up, for I wanted to forget that we had, inevitably, to return home. I even lost the desire to return home. I should have liked the journey to continue for the rest of my life.

However, they did agree on one subject. Peter:

With the exception of perhaps an hour after the evening meal, there was no single moment in the day when we would not have eaten, and eaten with the greatest relish, anything that appeared remotely edible. Dog biscuits would have been welcome. A plate of cold tapioca pudding would have vanished in a flash. Your dustbins, had we come across them, would not have been inviolate.

The caravan broke up at Dzunchia, the prince's destination. They bought four camels of their own and a pony for Li and continued for three days alone to an oasis called Nomo Khantara where Li's brother lived. There Li announced he would go no further, despite his original agreement to accompany them to Teijinar. If he went on, he would have to return alone across the Tsaidam, and he was afraid to do that. But they finally prevailed on him to continue.

On April 23 they departed the desolate oasis for Teijinar where their hopes of continuing were pinned wholly upon finding Smigunov's old partner, Borodishin, and finding him willing and able to help them go on. On May 6 they arrived in Teijinar and were told the yurt of the Russian, the oross, was a bit further on. An old Mongol guided them to it. Outside the doorway covered by a felt curtain, they cried out a greeting, "Borodishin! Zdrastvuite!" An old man emerged. Peter:

> He looked at us with incredulity—a squat, stooping figure in a skull cap and an old Russian blouse. Slowly his sad eyes brightened, his bearded face broke into a grin. "Welcome," he said in Russian. "Where the devil have you come from?"

He was an old soldier who had been in Siberia when the revolution broke out. He had crossed into Mongolia with a White Russian army which later disintegrated. He had wandered in Central Asia until he found his way to this remote spot on the edge of the Tsaidam plateau. His wife and children were still in Siberia, and he continued to hope that they could join him some day. He was very friendly and helpful to the two travelers.

They found to their surprise they could still get no news of Sinkiang. Their next objective was the major oasis of Cherchen where they would join the Silk Road. It had been the scene of fighting by the Tungans against the Soviet-backed forces of the provincial government. The Buddhist Mongols of Teijinar were afraid to venture into areas controlled by the fierce Chinese Muslim Tungans, and no one had ventured to the west for several years. Li had fulfilled his agreement by guiding them as far as Teijinar, and he turned back eastward. They could find no guide among the Mongols around Teijinar willing to accompany them to Cherchen. Finally, Borodishin said he would go with them, but he dared not go to Cherchen among the rabidly anti-Russian Tungans. He would take them as far as Issik Pakte on the edge of the Tsaidam; that was as far as he dared to go.

After eight days in Teijinar, the three Europeans on three donkeys set out on the next stage of the journey. It was May 15, exactly three months since their departure from Peking. They climbed higher and traveled, according to their maps, at an altitude of 14,000 or 15,000 feet. They had to make at least one waterless camp where Peter experimented at dinner with a mixture of melted mutton fat, tsamba, and Worcestershire sauce washed down with brandy, and suffered as a result. Ten days' travel brought them to Issik Pakte. Peter:

> Half a dozen dilapidated yurts stood scattered on the shore of a small salt lake under the towering snows of Karyaghde; beyond them a cluster of domed mud tombs were surmounted by tall poles from each of which a yak's tail drooped like a dark plume.

They had passed from the land of the Mongols to the land of the Turkis. Borodishin was known in Issik Pakte and given a warm welcome. He was able to find two Turki guides and some camels. Peter's pony which he had obtained in Sining had given up exhausted and had to be left behind in Issik Pakte. Peter was able to buy another, a muddy and bedraggled mare that had been living in the swampy marshes near the settlement (Kini's pony, Slalom, was also weakening, and she was later forced, tearfully, to abandon him in the desert). They bid a sad farewell to Borodishin whom they had come to regard with great fondness. Peter:

> We had a great farewell feast with Borodishin, and he talked far into the night of Annenkov [a White Russian general who had terrorized Mongolia] and guerilla warfare with the Bolsheviks, and the ruses that the Whites had employed to secure admission into Chinese territory. . . . At dawn he left, hunched on his

*Kini and Peter aboard yaks in Hunza. The picture was posed;
they never actually traveled by yak.*

camel eternally sucking at his long pipe, his sad loyal eyes staring across the empty lands before him.

Kini and Peter, accompanied by the two Turkis, headed in the opposite direction. They were descending and drawing close to the Takla Makan Desert. They celebrated Peter's 28th birthday on May 31 with an extra ration of sugar in their breakfast tea and for dinner, a great feast cooked by Kini of rice and curried antelope meat.

Their animals were in bad shape. One camel collapsed and refused to go on, and they had to abandon him in the desert. This was a not uncommon occurrence in Central Asian caravans. Abandoning a dying animal in the desert was called "throwing him on the gobi." The superstitious nomads feared that if a dying animal were killed to put it out of its misery, its restless or angry spirit would wander abroad to haunt other caravans. Moreover, the animal, if left without a load to carry and able to rest, might conceivably recover. So animals unable to continue were simply abandoned, and the two European travelers did not dare flout the local custom. They shifted his load to the other animals and moved on. Peter:

> It was horrible to leave him there, hunched, apathetic, and somehow shrunken, with the snow plastering his inexpressive face: horrible, as we rode away, to watch him dwindle to a small dark speck in a great naked sweep of desert.

A few days later Kini's pony, Slalom, collapsed and had to be abandoned. Then, another camel. Half of their camels had succumbed to the desert, but the two Turki guides had two camels to which they could shift baggage. Even so, it was becoming a melancholy trek. Kini:

> If things continued like this, we would be on all fours before we arrived at the next inhabited point. Truth to tell, we were feeling conscience stricken. Why, on our account, should these camels die?

They were forced to walk for hours on end, trudging mechanically like "jaded automata" across the arid landscape. At one camp, Peter had to abandon the "horrid skeletons" of his last pair of socks. He wondered if he could continue the miles of walking with nothing to protect his bare feet against the rubbing of his boots, but he found that he need not worry:

> They were a pair of American field boots, stricken in years and seamed with outlandish scars, but they fitted me so well that, although one sole was almost and the other quite worn through, I was never inconvenienced by the lack of socks.

They began to descend through a gorge in the Altyn Tagh chain, the western spur of the Kunlun Mountains that formed the northern barrier of the Tibetan tableland. They followed the valley of the Cherchen River, flanked by rich grass. On the fourth day of the descent, they suddenly emerged in brilliant sunshine onto a desert of gravel stretching away from the foot of the mountains. It was the Takla Makan.

On June 15, exactly four months after leaving Peking, they arrived in Cherchen. Peter:

Wonder and joy fell on us. I suppose that the Earth offers no greater contrast—except that between land and sea—than the contrast between desert and oasis. We stepped clean out of one world into another. There was no phase of transition; we slipped into coolness and delight as smoothly and abruptly as a diver does.

The friendly, inviting face of the oasis soon turned hostile. They were taken into custody by a detachment of soldiers of the rebel Tungan forces that controlled the southern portion of Sinkiang. They were taken to the military headquarters. Their passports were taken away. They were placed under arrest. They were suspected of being Russians, or at least spies for Russia. But the long arm of His Britannic Majesty's Government reached even into Cherchen in the form of the British aksakal, a sort of local vice consul under the supervision of the British Consul General in Kashgar. The aksakal arrived, and their passports were soon returned. Peter:

> He was a tall, venerable Afghan with a dignified carriage and a shrewd eye, who saluted us respectfully and seemed genuinely pleased to see us. He talked through his nose in Turki, Hindustani, and Afghan, but unfortunately not in Chinese (nor, unfortunately, in English).

They accompanied him to his house to stay as his guests. Above the gateway to his house hung—"home-made, unorthodox in design, but infinitely reassuring"—a large Union Jack.

They learned that the aksakal had represented the British government in Cherchen for many years but had never actually met any of the British Consuls General in Kashgar under whom he served. He was obviously loyal to the Empire he served. He had actually met very few Europeans, but there was one about whom he spoke at length with great admiration, a superhuman figure, as the old Afghan described him. The aksakal called him Ishtin Sahib. They finally figured out that he was speaking of Aurel Stein.

They departed Cherchen on June 20 with five donkeys and their two camels, and two Turki animal herders. They were now on the southern branch of the Silk Road, and their route ahead was certain: through the oases of Niya, Keriya, Khotan, and Yarkand to Kashgar.

They traveled along the southern edge of the Tarim Basin, the Kunlun Mountains shielding Tibet on their left, the towering dunes of the Takla Makan Desert on their right.

In Keriya, they again stayed with the British aksakal. In his house were things to make their eyes open wide in surprise: an umbrella, an electric torch, clocks on the wall, a sewing machine humming in the corner. They were approaching civilization.

They arrived at Khotan on July 6, but even before entering the town, they were met by the secretary of the aksakal who escorted them to the aksakal's house. Kini was disappointed:

> I had expected [Khotan] to be a place of obvious archeological in-
> terest like Samarkand, and I was disappointed in it. Stagnant water
> stank in muddy alleys, the booths were black with flies and I no-
> ticed that most of the inhabitants, even the young girls, were af-
> flicted with enormous goitres. When, later, I went sightseeing, I
> found not the slightest vestige of the past, only some big modern
> mosques.

The aksakal's house was used as a storehouse by caravans coming from India, and they saw several Indian merchants. The day after their arrival, they saw a surprising sight: a donkey arrived carrying a man, apparently Indian, wearing a Union Jack and a gleaming metal plate which said British Indian Postman. He brought the monthly consular mail which, in a 45-day journey, traveled from Kashmir across the Karakorums to Kashgar, then southeast for two weeks to Khotan. Among the mail were copies, several weeks old, of the London *Times* addressed to an Armenian businessman in the town. Peter was able to borrow them, and he found one of his stories about Manchukuo in one issue. He showed it proudly to everyone.

Khotan was the capital of the Republic of Tungaria as it was called by its leaders. The two travelers called on the dignitaries of the town, including the commander of the Tungan rebel forces. He explained that the Tungans were opposed to the provincial forces of Urumchi, because they were really under the control of the Soviet Union. The staunchly Muslim Tungans considered themselves to be fighting the Bolsheviks. The commander said he considered himself a loyal servant of the Nanking government.

They departed Khotan on July 10. Just before arriving in Yarkand, they passed without incident from the area controlled by the Tungans to that controlled by the provincial government in Urumchi. Yarkand had been the scene of fighting, and the bazaar area was badly damaged. Houses throughout the city showed damage from bullets and shellfire. They now approached Kashgar where they would stay, not with a local aksakal but with the British Consul General. Peter:

> The Consulate's uninvited guests were determined to do their poor
> best not to disgrace it on their first appearance. Kini put on a clean
> shirt, and I got out my last razor blade.

Peter also pulled down his suitcase from the donkey to unpack a white tropical suit, meticulously pressed and packed in Peking in the bottom of the suitcase, and carried the whole journey just for their appearance in Kashgar. Peter opened the suitcase to find that, only a few days earlier, the donkey's load had been submerged while crossing the river and the suitcase filled with water (the boy herding the donkey had been afraid to tell his employer). The beautiful suit was not only soaked, but had been turned green by dye that ran from a scarf Peter had bought in Khotan and packed away in the suitcase. He regretfully concluded he must make his entry clad in his travel-worn shorts.

They were met at the edge of the city by an immaculately turned-out young Englishman who introduced himself as the Vice Consul and apologized for the absence of the Consul General who was away in the hills on vacation. He escorted them to the Consulate. Kini:

> The garden was a riot of flowers. Young ducks waddled about on
> the English lawn. And then, the house! It was a long house with a
> verandah, a cool hall, and well-polished furniture; armchairs cov-
> ered with chintz, books and newspapers everywhere.

This was Chini Bagh, the official British residence so familiar to Sven Hedin and Aurel Stein. Kini and Peter learned that they had been reported lost, and the consulate had received an inquiry about them from the Secretary of State in London.

They stayed two weeks in Kashgar. The Consul General, Colonel Thomson-Glover, and his wife returned from their holiday and es-corted them on calls on various dignitaries in the city, including the

Russian Consul General. Relations between the two consulates were officially cordial but personally distant. During their stay, two Soviet airplanes arrived carrying antiplague serum to combat an outbreak of pneumonic plague in the city. The British were also sending serum, but in the absence of a landing permit for an airplane, which the Chinese refused to grant, they were forced to send it by the land route from India over the Karakorums. The Soviets, to steal a propaganda march, had sent serum by plane, ignoring the absence of the required landing permit.

On their last night in Kashgar, they were given a huge farewell banquet cohosted by the Turki general in command in Kashgar, Mahmud Hsing Chang; the Chinese general in command of regional Chinese forces, Liu Pin; and the recently installed mayor, Mr. Hsu. The guests included Russians, Chinese, Turkis, English, Indians, and one lone Swiss. Benedictine, cognac, and vodka flowed freely as toasts were drunk to every conceivable subject. After the meal, there were numerous speeches. General Liu Pin delivered a long, rambling farewell in Chinese which was simultaneously translated into English, Russian, and Turki in different parts of the room (Peter: "Very soon, four speeches were being made in four languages, simultaneously, and at a feverish rate.") The General ended by saying he did not know what he was saying and was therefore probably repeating himself. He then began to dance to the music of a Turki dance orchestra that had been playing in the hallway, his holstered revolver slapping against his leg. Peter announced that Kini was an expert dancer in the Turkish style, and the evening ended with her being swung about by the General.

The next day, August 8, they departed Kashgar for India with splitting headaches, accompanied by a group of Turkis who proved during the journey to be lazy, stupid, and incredibly inefficient. They had still to cross the Pamirs, but they would follow an ancient and well-traveled caravan track, and this last leg of their journey did not seem in the least forbidding. Kini:

> Kashgar really represented our true return to civilization, the forty days that lay between us and Srinigar being no more than a final stage.

They crossed the Chichiklik Pass and passed close under Muztagh

Ata, "The Father of Ice Mountains," that Sven Hedin had four times tried and failed to climb in 1893. On August 18 they crossed the border into India and continued to Gilgit where they were welcomed by the British Political Agent and the ruler of the tiny Himalayan kingdom, the Mir of Gilgit.

They arrived in Srinagar, the capital of Kashmir, on September 12, three days short of seven months after their departure from Peking. They spruced themselves up as best they could for their grand entry, but it did little good when they entered the hotel to register. Peter:

> People were gathering in the lounge for dinner. . . . Everyone was in evening dress. Anglo-India, starched and glossy, stared at us with horror and disgust. A stage clergyman with an Oxford voice started as though he had seen the devil. A hush . . . descended on the assembled guests. We were back in Civilization.

Both travelers went on to other adventures in their lives, but they never again traveled together. Peter returned to China in 1938, again as a *Times* correspondent, and traveled the Burma Road to Lashio. When World War II began in 1939, he joined the Grenadier Guards and served in Norway, Greece, Cairo, and London until called to India by Field Marshall Wavell to head an Office of Deception in the intelligence branch to insinuate false and misleading intelligence among the Japanese. It was exactly the kind of assignment suited to Peter's impishly humorous personality. He shuttled between Delhi and Chungking and made an almost disastrous glider landing in Burma with Orde Wingate's Chindits.

After the war he returned to journalism with the London *Times*, but did no more traveling. He turned to history, and wrote well-received books on the Boxer Rebellion, the Younghusband expedition to Tibet, and White Russian forces in Siberia during the Civil War. He continued to write occasional pieces for *The Spectator* which were collected into several books.

In December 1935, soon after returning from Central Asia, Peter married Celia Johnson, the actress. They had a son and two daughters. Peter was an avid hunter and crack shot as he had demonstrated throughout the trip across Central Asia, and he continued to enjoy hours in the field with his dog throughout his life. On August 18,

1971, he died of a sudden heart attack while hunting grouse in Scotland. He was sixty-seven years old.

Ella Maillart returned to Asia in 1939, on the eve of World War II, traveling overland by automobile from Europe in the company of another woman. The trip became the subject of one of her most popular books, *The Cruel Way*. She spent the years of World War II in southern India, part of the time in an ashram writing a book about her sailing experiences in the 1920s. After the war she made many trips to India, sometimes guiding groups of visitors. She became acquainted with Edwina Mountbatten, the wife of the last viceroy, Lord Mountbatten of Burma, and with Jawaharlal Nehru. She visited Tibet as recently as the late 1980s and India in December 1993. At this writing, she lives in Geneva.

Why did they make the trip? They were journalists, but their newspapers did not send them to Central Asia. They both wrote news reports about the tangled political situation in Sinkiang as it unfolded to them, and sent them whenever they were able to send messages by wire or mail. After her return to Europe, Kini found, without surprise, that none of her dispatches to Paris had ever been published. A few of Peter's reports appeared in various publications. But in 1935 political developments in Sinkiang did not rank high as items of political or news interest in Europe or the United States. Subtle Soviet incursions into places few people had ever heard of were not causes for alarm when Imperial Japan was acting with increasing aggression in China proper, and Nazi Germany was rearming and threatening recovery of the Rhineland from Allied occupation. Editors and readers of the newspapers for which Peter and Kini wrote were focused on subjects of more immediate importance to them than a place few of them could locate on a map.

Nor were the two travelers explorers in any sense. Kini is quick to point out that they covered ground already traversed and mapped by Sven Hedin, Aurel Stein, and others. Peter:

> The world's stock of knowledge—geographical, ethnological, meteorological, what you will—gained nothing from our journey. Nor did we mean that it should. . . . We measured no skulls, we took no readings, we would not have known how. . . . Ours was more an escapade than an expedition . . . .

The two travelers on the last leg of their journey in Hunza.

They traveled because the journey was an exciting, even danger-ous trip to a remote, apparently inaccessible, exotic place. If successful, they both knew it would provide the material for interesting and en-tertaining books, and it did. The books Peter and Kini wrote about their trip have been reissued several times and are now called classics of travel literature. Peter's is the more witty, more idiosyncratic; Kini's is a more straightforward narrative. They complement each other. Both writers included detailed explanations of the complicated political situ-ation they found in Sinkiang, but if the books' principal subject was political analysis, they would have been forgotten long ago.

They are read and reread more than half-a-century after their ini-tial publication precisely because they are not primarily political discussions. They are reread because they are gracefully written, entertaining accounts of the daily encounters made on a journey few readers will ever make, but many would like to make—or like to think they would like to make.

As between Peter and Kini, Peter has the last word:

> The trouble about journeys nowadays is that they are easy to make but difficult to justify. The Earth, which once danced and spun before us as alluringly as a celluloid ball on top of a fountain in a rifle-range, is now a dull and vulnerable target. . . . All along the line we have been forestalled, and forestalled by better men than we. Only the born tourist—happy, goggling ruminant—can follow in their tracks with the conviction that he is not wasting his time.

Exploration has given way to travel which is giving way increasingly to tourism. We should be grateful that we have not only the Sven Hedins and the Aurel Steins, but also the Ella Maillarts and the Peter Flemings to tell us about how it used to be out there.

Bibliography

Peter Fleming and Ella Maillart each wrote a book about their trip from Peking to Srinigar. They each wrote several other books, including other travel books. Ella Maillart wrote in both French and English (the books cited below were written in French). No biography of Maillart has ever been published.

Fleming, Peter. *News From Tartary*. London: Jonathan Cape, 1936. Peter's hilarious, idiosyncratic account of the journey.

>   *One's Company*. New York: Charles Scribner's Sons, 1934. Peter's account of his first trip to China.

Hart-David, D. *Peter Fleming: A Biography*. New York: Oxford University Press, 1974. An excellent biography.

Hogg, Gary. *With Peter Fleming in Tartary*. London: F. Muller, 1960. Written for juvenile readers about the journey.

Maillart, Ella. *Forbidden Journey*. London: William Heinemann, 1937. Kini's account of the journey. It nicely complements Peter's book.

>   *Turkestan Solo*. New York: G.P. Putnam's Sons, 1935. Kini's account of her earlier journey to Soviet Central Asia.

Postscript

As they crossed and recrossed the deserts of Central Asia, none of those early explorers or travelers had the slightest inkling that under their feet, undreamed-of by them, lay the region's greatest secret of all. A vast pool of oil lies beneath the Takla Makan and Marco Polo's Desert of Lop. No one yet knows its full extent, because exploration has only just begun. According to Chinese estimates, the Takla Makan may hold seventy-four billion barrels of oil, three times the proven reserves of the United States.

The face of Xinjiang is being transformed as fleets of trucks and heavy equipment, and an army of some five thousand oil workers, fan out across the Takla Makan. An Oil Road 324 miles long has been constructed completely across the desert from north to south to connect drilling sights. More than 360 wells have been drilled, and in the summer of 1995, the Chinese government solicited bids for licenses to explore in eight additional blocks. If the Takla Makan's hidden riches prove to be as great as some geologists believe, the people and cultures of Xinjiang may soon experience a collision with the modern industrial world similar to that felt in recent decades in Iran and the oil sheikdoms of the Middle East. China's entire economy could be transformed.

Xinjiang, Tibet and Mongolia are already experiencing profound social changes in the wake of the collapse of communism and the end of the cold war. Cut off for decades since before World War II, Central Asia is joining the rest of the world as its borders are opened to travelers and traders, although the Chinese government still keeps vast swatches of territory in Xinjiang off-limits to outsiders for reasons of national security. Kashgar, now known as Kashi, boasts banks and office towers, and its streets are thronged with women still veiled but wearing knee-length skirts and high-heels. Urga, now called Ulan Bator, sports a skyline of high-rise apartment buildings. People living in village huts now enjoy electric lights and television. But the new openness also has caused political tension to grip Xinjiang and Tibet. Uigurs and Tibetans, in touch with the outside world after decades of isolation, chafe under Chinese rule.

Trade, the raison d'être of the Silk Road, has begun to flow again centuries after its demise in the 15th century. The people of Xinjiang are exchanging goods with the newly independent republics of former Soviet Central Asia. Western manufactures, not silk, are the most sought-after products.

The opening of Central Asia has permitted archeologists, paleontologists and other scholars to build upon the discoveries of Sven Hedin, Aurel Stein, Roy Chapman Andrews and other explorers. The American Museum of Natural History is resuming the quest that Andrews was forced to abandon in the early 1930s and again sponsoring exploration in Mongolia. Since 1989, its expeditions have uncovered the remains of more hitherto unknown dinosaurs and other Mesozoic animals. New finds continue to turn up in the Flaming Cliffs valley. Despite the benefits of modern technology, the rigors of desert exploration have not diminished since Roy Chapman Andrews' heyday. " It's just as hard to get into the desert from Beijing today as it was seventy years ago," the leader of the Museum's expedition in the summer of 1995 was quoted as saying.

At two sites along the northern Silk Road, man-made caves containing spectacular Buddhist frescoes similar to those of Tun-huang have been discovered. More than 360 caves have been explored, some situated 650 feet up a rock face. They apparently date from A.D. 400 to 700. Unfortunately, many of the paintings have been damaged, similar to the damage at Tun-huang, although photographs taken recently at the sites show dazzlingly colorful bodhisattvas that are still spectacular. A similar network of frescoed Buddhist caves has been discovered even more recently in western Tibet.

In the buried oases of the Silk Road, archeologists have recently uncovered tombs containing ancient mummies in a startling state of preservation. The discoveries tell us more about the unique ancient Central Asian civilization first revealed by Aurel Stein, and they push back its historical frontier by centuries.

In Zaghunluq, a village 150 miles east of Aurel Stein's Niya, an archeologist recently discovered a tomb containing an incredibly well-preserved mummy of a man who died around 1000 B.C. His unmistakably Indo-European features confirm that people from the west settled the Tarim Basin long before the Chinese ventured into it. At a site on the northern Silk Road, a Chinese archeologist has excavated 113 graves holding similar well-preserved mummies dating from about 1200 B.C. At Lou-Lan in 1980, a Chinese archeologist discovered the mummified remains of a woman with long brown-blond hair and wearing a woolen cape and leather shoes. Dubbed "the Lou-Lan Beauty" for her remarkably regular Indo-European features that are clearly defined even in mummified death, the woman lived 3,800 years ago. Carbon-14 testing of wood from the tomb of another mummy found nearby indicates that it could be six thousand years old. These discoveries suggest that China's civilization may not have originated so completely isolated from the West as previously thought. That such a hitherto unsuspected Indo-European culture extended across Central Asia to the very borders of China so long ago may force fundamental revisions in scholarship about the origins of Chinese civilization.

As Ella Maillart tells her correspondents, her journey with Peter Fleming cannot be recreated today because too much has changed in Central Asia since 1935. The modern world is impinging with accelerating speed and increasing impact upon a part of the world that until recently was kept in almost total isolation. But all these new discoveries suggest that Central Asia still holds intriguing secrets waiting to be revealed.

The author with Ella Maillart at her home in Geneva, Switzerland,
in November 1994.

About the Author

Kenneth Wimmel is well-qualified to profile the adventurers in *The Alluring Target*. He retired from the U.S. Foreign Service in 1991 after working abroad for twenty-five years, mostly in Asia. He has served as Cultural Attaché in American embassies in Taiwan, the Philippines, and Egypt, and in other senior diplomatic positions in New Delhi, Dhaka, Calcutta, and Kuala Lumpur.

Wimmel completed the two-year Chinese and one-year Vietnamese language courses at the Department of State's Foreign Service Institute. In 1976, as a Foreign Service Officer, he graduated from the U.S. Naval War College "with highest distinction," ranked number one in his class and awarded the Admiral Richard Colbert Memorial Prize. He holds a B.A. in English literature and a M.A. in International Relations.

Wimmel lives with his wife and daughter in Bethesda, Maryland, where he devotes his time to writing on historical subjects.

Index